Tourism in Ireland

Tourism in Ireland:
A Critical Analysis

Edited by

Barbara O'Connor
Michael Cronin

CORK UNIVERSITY PRESS

First Published in 1993 by
Cork University Press
University College
Cork
Ireland

British Library Cataloguing in Publication Data
A CIP catalogue record for this book is available from
the British Library.

ISBN 1 85918 006 X Paperback

Typeset in Ireland by Tower Books of Ballincollig, Co. Cork
Printed in Ireland by Colour Books of Baldoyle, Dublin

Contents

List of illustrations   vii
List of contributors   ix
Introduction   1

PART I THE HISTORICAL EMERGENCE OF TOURISM

1   Kilkee — The Origins and Development of a
    West Coast Resort   13
    John Heuston
2   For Health and Pleasure in the British Fashion:
    Bray, Co. Wicklow, as a Tourist Resort, 1750–
    1914   29
    K.M. Davies

PART II TOURIST IMAGES AND REPRESENTATIONS

3   Fellow Travellers: Contemporary Travel Writing
    and Ireland   51
    Michael Cronin
4   Myths and Mirrors: Tourist Images and
    National Identity   68
    Barbara O'Connor
5   'Embodying the Nation': The West of Ireland
    Landscape and Irish Identity   86
    Catherine Nash

PART III TOURIST POLICY

6   Irish Tourism Policy: Targets, Outcomes and
    Environmental Considerations   115
    James Deegan and Donal Dineen
7   Tourism, Public Policy and the Image of
    Northern Ireland since the Troubles   138
    David Wilson
8   Gifts of Tongues: Foreign Languages and
    Tourism Policy in Ireland   162
    Juliette Péchenart and Anne Tangy

PART IV THE HERITAGE INDUSTRY

9   The Construction of Heritage   183
    David Brett

10   City of Culture: Dublin and the Discovery of
     Urban Heritage   203
     Colm Lincoln

PART V   TOURIST SERVICES AND PRACTICES

11   Rural Tourism and Cultural Identity in the
     West of Ireland   233
     *Anne Byrne, Ricca Edmondson
     and Kathleen Fahy*
12   The Irish on Holidays: Practice and
     Symbolism   258
     Michel Peillon

     Index   273

List of Illustrations

Figure 2.1	Bray in 1838 (Ordnance Survey)	34
Figure 2.2	The Esplanade, Bray in the 1860s (Gaskin)	37
Figure 2.3	Marine Station Hotel and Esplanade, Bray, circa 1910 (Lawrence Collection, NLI)	40
Figure 2.4	Bray in 1909 (Ordnance Survey)	44
Figure 4.1	Turf Cutting Near Achill, Co. Mayo (Bord Fáilte)	73
Figure 4.2	Donegal Bay from Kildoney Point (Bord Fáilte)	75
Figure 4.3	Bewildherin' the Tourists (Lawrence)	80
Figure 6.1	Performance measures in the tourism sector	119
Figure 6.2	Relationship between environmental quality and tourism development	133
Figure 7.1	Tourism and violence in Northern Ireland, 1969–1987	143
Figure 8.1	The Irish School system	166
Figure 9.1	Simplified plan of directive and non-directive circulation in the Kings in Conflict exhibition	188
Figure 9.2	Simplified plan of directive and non-directive circulation in the Northern Ireland Folk Park, Cultra	188
Figure 9.3	Simplified plan of directive and non-directive circulation in the Ulster-American Folk Park, Omagh	188
Figures 9.4a-9.4l	Story-board: Ulster-American Folk Park, Omagh	191–196
Figure 9.5	In 'Pennsylvania'	197

List of Contributors

Barbara O'Connor is a lecturer in the School of Communications, Dublin City University. Her research interests include feminist studies and issues in popular culture and communication. She is co-editor of *Gender in Irish Society* and has published a number of articles on the representation of women in television drama and on television audiences.

Michael Cronin has taught in Tours and Paris and is currently lecturer in French and translation studies at Dublin City University. He is co-editor of the cultural journal *Graph* and Chairperson of The Irish Translators' Association and has written widely on translation, questions of language and identity and aspects of contemporary Irish literature in Irish and English.

John Heuston studied modern history and politics at University College, Dublin where he developed a strong interest in Irish social history. He has researched the settlement of Ulster linen weavers in west Tipperary during the middle of the eighteenth century, and is currently studying the social structure of Tipperary Town during the second half of the last century. He is a press officer for a third world agency.

K.M. Davies is a cartographic editor and general administrator of the Irish Historic Towns Atlas Project, Royal Irish Academy, Dublin. She is co-author with J.H. Andrews on *Mullingar: Irish Historic Towns Atlas* no. 5 published in 1992 and is researching the topographical history of Bray for a forthcoming fascicle in the series.

Catherine Nash is currently completing a Ph.D. at the University of Nottingham on issues of landscape imagery, gender and identity in Ireland in the twentieth century. Her research interests include visual and literary representations of place, feminist and post-colonial studies, and philosophical and methodological issues in contemporary theory.

James Deegan is Director of the National Centre for Tourism Policy Studies at the University of Limerick. His major research areas are in international and public sector economics and he has recently published in the area of tourism policy and associated environmental issues. His published works include *Tourism and the Environment: Some Policy Issues* (1992); *Environmental Problems Associated with Tourism: Is Alternative Tourism the Answer?* and *Employment Effects of Irish Tourism Projects: A Microeconomic Approach* (1992).

Donal Dineen is Associate Dean (Business Studies) and Head of the Department of Business at the University of Limerick. His research interests include employment and unemployment analysis, small business policy, tourism economics and local economic and employment development. Among his recent publications are *Atypical Work Patterns in Ireland —*

Short Run Adjustments or Fundamental Changes (1992); *Employment Effects of Irish Tourism Projects: A Microeconomic Approach* (1992) and *Financial Engineering and Regional Development* (1992).

David Wilson is a lecturer in social anthropology at The Queen's University of Belfast, and has carried out research in the Seychelles Islands and Cumbria, as well as in Northern Ireland. He is the author of a number of articles on tourism.

Juliette Péchenart is currently lecturing in French in Dublin City University where she specialises in French for business. She is a founder member and past president of the Applied French Association. She has worked for a number of years as a consultant on CERT language programmes.

Anne Tangy has taught French in Dublin City University and is currently a training adviser on language development for CERT. She is a member of the LINGUA National Committee for Ireland and external examiner in French for the College of Catering, Dublin.

David Brett is a lecturer in the History of Art at the University of Ulster at Jordanstown. He is an editorial member and a regular contributor to the Irish arts journal, *CIRCA*.

Colm Lincoln is a graduate of University College, Dublin where he was awarded an MA in modern Irish history. He has also studied at the University of Nice and the École Nationale d'Administration. He has a longtime interest in heritage both as actuality and concept. Previous publications are *Steps and Steeples: Cork at the Turn of the Century* (Dublin, 1980) and *Dublin as a Work of Art* (Dublin, 1992).

Anne Byrne has written and published on the concerns of rural women in Irish society and is a member of the Women's Studies Centre in University College, Galway. She lectures in the Department of Political Science and Sociology.

Ricca Edmondson was educated at Lancaster and Oxford Universities, and taught at the Free University, Berlin where she also was a researcher at the Max Planck Institute for Human Development. She is a lecturer in the Department of Political Science and Sociology at University College, Galway.

Kathleen Fahy works with Connemara West, a local community based development company involved in education and training programmes. She has an MA in community development from University College, Galway and her interests include rural development and distance education.

Michel Peillon is Senior Lecturer in Sociology at St Patrick's College, Maynooth. He is mainly involved in the comparative study of state and society but has retained a keen interest in the sociology of festivities, leisure and holidays and has published several articles on this theme.

Introduction

Tourism is a major feature of contemporary life and influences the economic, social and cultural fabric of almost every country worldwide. The democratisation of travel which began in the 1960s due to the introduction of paid holidays for industrial workers, increases in leisure time, disposable income for greater numbers of the population and improvements in transportation led to a phenomenal increase in tourist activity in the western world. This activity has continued apace and currently international tourism is growing at the rate of 5–6 per cent per annum and may well be the largest source of employment by the year 2000.

Tourism has had a major influence on the economic and cultural fortunes of Ireland for over a century. It has been the subject of White Papers, consultants' reports, and political manifestos: yet, to date, no single publication has offered a critical overview of the impact of tourism on Ireland. *Tourism in Ireland* aims to provide the reader with an insight into the many areas that constitute and are affected by the practice of tourism . The contributors consider the historical emergence of tourism in Ireland, the formation of tourist imagery and representations, policy directions in the Irish tourist sector, the question of heritage and the changing nature of tourist services and practices. The volume emphasises the complex, multi-faceted nature of tourism where social, cultural, economic, and political factors do not operate in isolation from each other. In an area as central to the future development of Ireland as tourism it is essential that critical literature is made available to policymakers and tourism researchers so that fully-informed decisions can be made concerning the future direction of Irish tourism.

Ireland is not the only country whose economic and cultural fortunes are intimately bound up with the success or failure of the tourist sector.

The representation of heritage in areas of conflict, the effects of tourist imagery and travel writing on the construction of identity, the economic consequences of mass tourism and the role of rural tourism in rural development, to name but some of the questions addressed in the present volume, have obvious parallels in the experiences of countries in both the developed and developing world. Ireland has much to learn from the response of other nations to tourism and it is arguable that a critical analysis of the Irish experience can provide other countries with fresh insights into a complex and changing phenomenon.

While the academic study of tourism does not have a long history, and there are still substantial gaps in research, the increasing importance of tourism in recent years has given an impetus to critical analysis at both a theoretical and empirical level. Urry's *The Tourist Gaze* (1990), for instance, addresses many pertinent questions about leisure and travel in contemporary societies, while other research, particularly empirical studies, has continued to be documented in journals such as *The Annals of Tourism Research*. The increasing importance of tourism in Ireland has not spawned such scholarly work. Indeed, there has been a remarkable absence of critical discussion of the subject either in the public sphere generally or within academic debate. This book hopes to initiate that debate by aiming to analyse critically the major social, economic and cultural dimensions of tourism in Ireland. It does not purport to be a comprehensive volume — since there is not a thriving body of tourism research there are inevitable gaps — but we see it as an agenda-setting volume by pinpointing the lacunae in knowledge and suggesting areas for further research and analysis.

Tourism studies is not so much a discipline as a constellation of disciplines. There is no room for what Malcolm Crick calls 'disciplinary imperialism'. [1] The complexity of the phenomenon of tourism in contemporary societies necessitates a multidisciplinary approach which can do justice to many facets of an activity which eludes simple definitions. In this volume, the disciplines of economic science, sociology, social history, architecture, ethnography, literary criticism, modern languages' pedagogy and cultural criticism, to name but a few, are brought to bear on the complicated and fragmented nature of travel and tourism in Ireland. To privilege the economic or the linguistic or the ethnographic in a reductive definition of tourism studies is to ignore the myriad ways in which travel and tourism affect a people's livelihood, environment and culture. The very paucity of published research on a key area of Irish life makes the case for multidisciplinary investigation of tourism all the more compelling.

The book is arranged in five sections corresponding to five major areas in tourism studies: 'The Historical Emergence of Tourism', 'Tourist Images and Representations', 'Tourist Policy', 'The Heritage Industry', and 'Tourist Services and Practices'.

The first section, 'The Historical Emergence of Tourism', opens with

Heuston's historical case study of the holiday resort of Kilkee in which he explores the changing fortunes of a seaside town over two centuries. He concentrates on the social class origins and activities of the holiday makers and examines the ways in which social and political changes, including changes in modes of transportation, affected the class base of visitors to the resort.

With the emergence of the fashion of sea-bathing combined with a romantic interest in scenery, Kilkee began to attract visitors during the last decades of the eighteenth century. The dominant social classes of Irish society used the resort both for medicinal/health purposes and also, importantly, for providing opportunities for social contact for a dispersed rural élite. The fall in numbers of the Anglo-Irish gentry and the Protestant merchant families after the First World War was compensated for by the growth of the Catholic commercial and farming classes in the post-independence Free State. The introduction of paid holiday leave in the 1920s and the growth of bus transport helped to broaden the social base of visitors and led to an increase in the numbers of lower-middle-class and working-class holidaymakers. The far-reaching economic changes of the 1960s were a mixed blessing to the resort. Higher standards of living resulted in more families being able to afford seaside holidays, and caravan sites became popular but concurrently young single people were taking advantage of the newly introduced and relatively inexpensive holiday packages to travel abroad.

Davies's account of the emergence, development and decline of the east coast town of Bray as a resort provides a useful comparison to Heuston's study of Kilkee. While they are both historical accounts, Davies's article is anchored in a social geographical framework and focuses on changes in the built environment and spatial dimensions of the town following tourist development.

Davies outlines the conscious decisions which were made to develop the town along the lines of comparable seaside resorts in Britain, particularly Brighton; Bray was successful to the extent that for a while it basked in the soubriquet of 'the Brighton of Ireland'. The author details the increase in the number of dwellings (doubling from 879 in 1851 to 1,726 in 1901) and in population size, the building of hotels, Turkish baths, an esplanade and the initiation of a railway service from Dublin to Bray in 1854. Many of these changes in the built environment added substantially to the appearance and status of the town and attracted a 'desirable' type of resident and visitor alike. The authorities expressed concern for cleanliness and order embodied in such actions as the introduction of by-laws to control the activities of net fishermen on the seafront. However, the gradual increase in visitor numbers raised a number of problems for the town commissioners in the form of pressure on sewerage services, water and gas supplies, and maintenance of certain amenities. The period of expansion of the resort had halted by the end of the First World War and Davies links Bray's decline to a number of factors, chief amongst them its failure to attract a sufficiently high-spending clientèle when its more affluent visitors had moved further down the coast.

The section, 'Tourist Images and Representations', begins with an article by Cronin in which he examines a number of post-1945 travel accounts of Ireland. By treating these accounts as part of a genre with its own conventions and rhetorical devices rather than merely as a form of journalism or simplistically reflective ethnography, Cronin shows how strategies of writing are related to the writers' experiences of Ireland. Amongst the topics he explores are the varying responses to the political, visual, spatial, temporal and linguistic dimensions of travel.

Cronin observes a number of constants in many of these areas. In relation to language, for example, he notes the air of 'comic condescension' in writers' responses to the use of vernacular forms of speech and accent. He also draws attention to the way in which the loquaciousness of the Irish is seen to parallel a penchant of women for gossip, both groups being regarded in language terms as illogical, intuitive and somewhat lacking in the ability to tell the truth.

In the political sphere, Cronin examines the response to travel as a form of political commentary, specifically as it relates to the conflict in Northern Ireland. With several notable exceptions, writers have tended to ignore the causes, and have failed to offer explanations, of the conflict. In other cases Cronin observes how writers have 'naturalised' the political or transformed it into myth.

Because of the Irish orientation to time, which is commonly perceived as non-linear and anarchic, the author suggests that Ireland is a country particularly suitable to the 'itinerant gaze' of the travel writer. The disrespect for time in Irish culture is parallelled in the non-linear structure and rhythms of travel writing itself which contains constant digressions between the outward and the homeward journey.

Tourism has had important, if largely unanalysed, consequences for the construction of Irish national identity. O'Connor examines the tourist images that are used to market Ireland and asks what the consequences are in terms of Irish ethnic self-perception. Ireland is said to hold the promise of escape from the pressures of modernity to a pre-industrial society where leisure is paramount and the work ethic a foreign notion. Landscapes tend to be empty and the constraints of time another absence. O'Connor suggests parallels between tourism and colonialism in the economic imbalance of tourist/local relationships, the romanticisation of the peasant as a kindly, noble savage and the dehumanisation of landscape.

Visitors to Ireland often comment on the friendliness of the Irish which is, indeed, one of the major selling points of Ireland as a tourist destination. O'Connor, while recognising the genuine basis of this perception, points out that part of this desire to please may be rooted in anxiety, whether about collective identity or the advantages of a rural lifestyle. Noting that many initiatives such as the Tidy Towns Competition were articulated in terms of how the country was perceived by tourists rather than what the obvious benefits would be to the local population, the author claims that it will be increasingly difficult to formulate self-determining national tourist policies in the face of the pressures of commercialisation and commodification.

From colonial travellers in search of a romantic *frisson* to the apostles of the Irish-Ireland movement and Dubliners on bank holiday weekends, the West of Ireland has always had a powerful fascination for visitors. Nash analyses the development of the West of Ireland myth in colonial and nationalist discourses as it emerges from travel writing into the novel form. The West was the wild, vigorous, anarchic opposite to the trim, organised, verdant richness of the Home Counties. For nationalist thinkers, the West stood in opposition to English urban industrial materialism and provided access to the Real Ireland (a notion still consecrated in postcards).

Nash examines two novels, *Grania — the Story of an Island* (1892) and *Children of Earth* (1918). *Grania* was written by Emily Lawless whose political sympathies were unionist and the author of *Children of Earth* was Darrell Figgis who was active in the movement for Irish independence. Both novels use the West of Ireland as a setting for the narrative and through them Nash contrasts the manner in which the West is seen as an important imaginary locus for both Anglo-Irish and Irish-Ireland writers and thinkers. She situates representations of the West in the larger context of European romantic primitivism and the incorporation of landscape and climate into nineteenth-century evolutionary theory. As a means of stemming emigration and countering the simianisation of the Irish peasant in the English popular press, the virtues of Western landscape and weather were praised for their role in promoting health, moral strength and physical beauty. The West would also become the site of gender conflicts, the feminine West of Celticism challenged by the masculine West of Gaelicism. Nash demonstrates that tourist destinations are not arbitrary choices and that the frequent depiction of Western landscapes in promotional literature is as much to do with the region's cultural and political significance as with any intrinsic physical beauty.

Deegan and Dineen's article in the 'Tourist Policy' section advocates a more structured approach to Irish tourism policy if the tourist sector is not to be subject to the caprices of international demand. In particular, tourism policy, they suggest, should be linked to broader national objectives such as the protection of the environment. By considering tourism in quantitative rather than qualitative terms — more tourists means more money — the potential for generating revenue may not, in fact, be maximised and the environmental costs may be ignored. A major attraction of Ireland as a tourist destination is its 'green' image so that mass tourism with its concomitant problems of pollution, traffic congestion, and bottlenecks would ultimately undermine the country's attractiveness to foreign visitors. Deegan and Dineen contend that the long-term interests of the Irish tourist sector would be better served by concentrating on high-spending, long-stay visitors and by building the cost of environmental protection into the cost of doing business in that sector.

Wilson investigates the ways in which the conflict in Northern Ireland has affected tourism and how tourist agencies there have been attempting to reverse the negative image of 'the North' as a 'war zone'. He utilises a number of data sources to examine both tourism trends and the promotion policies of the Northern Ireland Tourist Board including the images it wishes to project. In examining tourism trends over a twenty-year period from the late 1960s, Wilson shows that there was a substantial decline in the numbers of 'independent holidaymakers'. Since 1987, however, he notes that tourist numbers are on the increase despite a rise in levels of violence indicating a growth in what could be termed the 'tourism of turmoil'. The increase in numbers may also be attributed to the promotion of special interest holidays which has been a feature of NITB policy since the late 1980s and there has also been increased funding for tourism development projects from the European Regional Development Fund. He points to the fact that changing tourism patterns in 'the South' have a direct influence on tourism in 'the North' and notes that the sole category showing an overall increase is the actual number of tourists crossing the border from 'the South'.

Wilson traces the changes in NITB's promotion policy over the same period from a less than optimistic approach in the early 1970s manifested in cutbacks in overseas promotion (with the exception of Britain) to a more confident approach during the 1980s marked by an expansion of the marketing 'net' and an increased co-operation with Bord Fáilte and Aer Lingus. In terms of the images which NITB wishes to project, he suggests that the desire is to convey a sanitised picture and to pretend that 'the troubles' do not exist.

One of the most significant developments in Irish tourism in recent years has been the exponential growth in the number of visitors from continental Europe. Péchenart and Tangy consider the implications of this development for the tourist industry in one crucial area, language learning. They point to the lack of any coherent language policy at national level and the poor provision of foreign languages in Irish second-level education as factors which have seriously restricted the availability of tourist services and information in languages other than English. When tourism is considered as a service, the perception of the quality of the service for the non-anglophone tourist is crucially linked to the language in which it is provided. For the French, Italian or German tourist, having access to information and services in their mother tongue greatly enhances the quality of the tourist experience.

Péchenart and Tangy describe the strategy adopted by CERT, the state agency for tourism, to remedy this situation. The stress on an analysis of actual as opposed to imagined needs and a move to practical, communicative, task-based courses are two features of the strategy that are highlighted. Indeed, the attempt to systematically address the question of languages and the tourism industry has brought Ireland from the linguistic rearguard to the frontline in anticipating future developments in the area, such as, for example, the linguistic consequences of the growth in Japanese tourism in Ireland.

Heritage management and policy have emerged as key growth areas in tourism over the last two decades. Brett examines the concept of heritage and lays the basis for a method of critical analysis that draws on a theory of heritage. He takes issue with the notion of heritage as merely nostalgic, a response to political or cultural decline, and argues that concentration on heritage can often be didactic and celebratory. In the context of heritage policy, objects and places are mediated in order to give them meaning, they are situated in a narrative which allows us to make sense of them. The effect of the historical theme park is all the more powerful because it gives the visitor the impression of an immediate confrontation with the past — 'as if you were there'.

Brett demonstrates that the immediacy is not innocent but highly structured. Taking the example of the Ulster-American Folk Park, he shows that the park is structured in a way that reflects a partial reading of the history of emigration from Northern Ireland and that facts presented as givens are, in fact, highly debatable. The danger in the heritage industry is that it will promote unproblematic pseudo-histories, in a country where there is no agreed national history, and that Irish people will become spectators of their own history, existing for the entertainment of others rather than their own enlightenment. Brett argues that the concept of heritage must be subjected to the scrutiny of critical theory if it is to make a constructive rather than disabling contribution to people's knowledge of themselves and their origins.

Dublin has only recently become the focus of tourism policy, particularly in the area of cultural tourism. Lincoln studies the fortunes of Dublin in Irish life in this century and underlines its uneasy status in a post-Independence Ireland wedded to the virtues of (imaginary) rural life. Against a background of economic decline in the Dublin area in the 1970s and 1980s and the pursuance of car-centred and non-residential planning policies by national and local authorities, the task of presenting Dublin as a desirable tourist location has not been easy.

Lincoln claims that what makes Dublin distinctive as a physical entity may not survive into the next century. He cites the destruction of the city quays and the neglect of many of the city's remarkable domestic interiors as evidence of trends that are doing irreparable damage to the physical fabric of the city. Memories are bound up with this fabric as are names. To demolish a building or change the name of a bridge is to obliterate a part of what people remember of their city. Lincoln stresses the importance of linking heritage to the continuing life and active memory of an urban community. This means relating architectural heritage, for example, not to what tourists are expected to want but rather to what city-dwellers actually need. The living, not the themed city, is the essential basis of any genuine claim by Dublin to distinctiveness.

The final section of the book opens with an article by Byrne, Edmondson and Fahy which explores the implications of the development of rural tourism in economically disadvantaged areas. The authors are critical of the simplistic view of tourism as a 'development panacea' and, while they would support a cautious development of rural tourism, they argue that its provision is a complex matter with profound consequences for the communities which engage in it.

Drawing on the findings of a survey of households which are involved in tourism in North-West Connemara the authors show that it is the economically more advantaged sections of the community which benefit most from tourism to the exclusion of the weaker sections. They go on to claim that low-income households, and in particular women, are unlikely to benefit from tourism which is based on market demands alone and that, if they are to benefit, they need assistance in acquiring the prerequisite skills and facilities.

The authors also draw attention to some of the costs of tourism for cultural identity. Contemporary tourists expect, as indicated by survey findings, to see Connemara maintained as a locale of romantic 'authenticity': as a place of unspoilt scenery and way of life. Ostensibly, this entails minimal interference with the status quo of the area. However, the authors suggest that subtle, but profound, changes in cultural identity will take place, nonetheless. One of the likely threats to local culture is the vulnerability of local identities contained in their special 'thought worlds' to the weight of the 'tourist gaze'. It is suggested that locals will be tempted to adapt to visitors' expectations because the latter come from economically and politically more powerful cultures. The authors call, finally, for a holistic approach to the development of rural tourism, one in which individual economic gain is not the objective but which includes every aspect of the social and cultural development of the community.

The habits and attitudes of Irish tourists are the subject of the final article by Peillon, who argues that holidays reveal one of the main tensions within Irish society: the tension between modernism and anti-modernism. He uses survey material to point to the gap which exists between the practice and the imagery of holidaying. The survey data reveal that Irish people do, in fact, engage in typical tourist activity and behaviour. The data also highlight the reluctance to acknowledge this fact. It shows a discrepancy between general statements about holidays and statements about holidays which respondents had taken in the previous year. While there are perceived differences in a holiday orientation between different groups with farmers being the least involved, other groups, even the middle-class and urban groups, underestimate their participation in holidays.

So what is the source of this reluctance to acknowledge the level of participation? Since holidays represent a break in the routines of everyday life and allow people to indulge in excess (eating, drinking etc.) this reluctance, according to Peillon, has its source in a culture which has retained puritan elements as part of a strong anti-modernist tendency.

The articles in this volume demonstrate that it would be facile to adopt an *a priori* uncritical optimism or pessimism with respect to tourism. The impact of tourism is not standardised or uniform. Tourist infrastructure and activities vary from country to country. But even within national boundaries there may well be tensions and contradictions between different levels and strands since it is both a multi-layered and multi-faceted phenomenon having an effect at local, regional and national level in addition to having impacts in the social, cultural and economic domains. Before we can begin to assess the impact of tourism in Ireland, then, we need to engage in empirical research in all aspects of tourism. It would be invidious, if not impossible, at this point to draw up an exhaustive list of areas for further research but one that comes to mind is an investigation of the levels of vertical integration in the industry. In the past the levels of such integration have been comparatively low which meant that profits were more widely distributed amongst the population. Does the increasing commodification of the leisure industries internationally mean that there will be increasing levels of vertical integration — more foreign investment or indigenous corporate investment? Further research into the 'heritage industry' would also be timely. Who owns and controls it? What is the ratio of public to private funding? To what extent is funding from the European Regional Development Fund dictating the shape of the 'heritage industry' here? Another question which might usefully be addressed is the impact of internal tourism on local communities, in particular the creation of the Gaeltacht as 'other', the growth of Irish colleges and so on.

The future for Ireland as a tourist destination depends partly on the future of tourism itself which has always been shaped by the kind of society which produces tourists and tourist needs. While the latter are multiple and varied, each kind of society generates dominant tourist desires and expectations which offer a temporary release from the constraints of everyday life.

The general collapse of structural differentiation in post-modern tourism is certain to have a decisive effect on the lives of everybody living on the island. As Urry points out, the distinction between tourism and other social and cultural practices is breaking down so that post-modern tourists are ironic observers of their own transformation.[2] The distinction between education, the media and tourism is blurred in the world of theme parks so that Celtworld is simultaneously classroom, spectacle and site. If the ironic distancing of the post-modern tourist is largely a response to middle-class concern over the advent of mass tourism and likely only to affect a small section of any population, the collapse of clear distinctions between tourism and other areas of human activity is more far-reaching in its consequences.

If the future of tourism promises change what is the outlook for tourism studies? Crick notes the absence of what he calls the 'local voice' on the effects of international tourism. By this, he means the voices of those whose countries as tourist destinations often provide the raw material for cultural analysis but who rarely do the interpreting themselves. He claims that 'without close attention to the local voice [voices, for tourism produces a range of local reactions], our social scientific work risks being descriptively poor and ethnocentric.'[3] The present volume is part of that strategy of re-appropriation and should contribute to an understanding of the fall-out of tourism development both in terms of policy choices and socio-cultural responses. Ireland's historical and political experience and the nature of its economic development have resulted in a nation that is partly Third World and partly First World. It is this somewhat ambiguous state that makes the Irish case both difficult and instructive. Instructive because the local voice becomes a global one and moves centre-stage. The shifts and transformations in tourism in both the First and Third Worlds co-exist in Ireland reflecting an ambiguity that is both a theoretical and empirical challenge. It is the hope of the editors of the present volume that many other researchers will take up that challenge.

NOTES AND REFERENCES

1   Crick, M. (1989), 'Representations of International Tourism in the Social Sciences: Sun, Sex, Sights, Savings and Servility', *Annual Review of Anthropology*, **18**: 314.

2   Urry, J. (1990), *The Tourist Gaze: Leisure and Travel in Contemporary Societies*, Sage, London, p. 100.

3   Crick, op. cit., p. 338.

PART I

The Historical Emergence of Tourism

1

Kilkee — the Origins and Development of a West Coast Resort

John Heuston

Today, taking a holiday is a central characteristic of modern societies. Every year millions of people travel away from home for the purposes of pleasure and recreation. Underlying modern mass tourism is the widespread assumption that people need to 'get away from it all' for the sake of their physical and mental health, to rest and recuperate from the pressures and demands of everyday life.

The idea goes back to the eighteenth century when only a tiny minority of the population could enjoy a period of time away from home for reasons unconnected with work. The grand tour, the spas and the popular fashion for gazing on the wonders of nature were all the preserve of the aristocracy. The onset of the industrial revolution in Britain and in other European countries in the course of the last century made holidays possible for the middle class and, somewhat later, for the working class.

In Ireland, however, holidaymaking was confined to a relatively small minority of the population until the middle of this century. Irish coastal resorts were to be the preserve of the Anglo-Irish rural and urban élite up to the First World War. After independence, the Anglo-Irish were replaced at the resorts by growing numbers of middle-class holidaymakers. It was only with the upturn in the economy in the late 1950s and early 1960s that holidays became possible for lower-income Irish families.

This study charts the fortunes of one of Ireland's oldest seaside resorts — Kilkee on the west coast of Co. Clare. The story of Kilkee is largely the story of Irish holidaymaking over two centuries. The resort and its hinterland have long been perceived to possess suberb natural attractions — a safe, clean beach, unpolluted waters, spectacular coastal scenery, interesting marine life. Initially no more than a tiny fishing community, it progressed to being a fashionable 'watering-hole' for the dominant social class in Irish society during the Victorian and Edwardian era; it gradually became accessible to middle-class visitors during the interwar period, but only relatively recently became accessible to lower-income holidaymakers.

Kilkee today reflects the decline in popularity of Irish seaside resorts which began with greater prosperity and the growth of foreign 'package holidays' in the 1960s. It continues to be dependent on Limerick, its nearest large urban centre, for the majority of its holidaymakers but there are indications that it may now be faced with increasing competition from other Irish resorts, as well as from those in Britain and on the continent. Kilkee is now at a crossroads, needing considerable investment in all-weather recreational facilities if it is to retain its traditional holidaymaker from the region *and* attract tourists from further afield.

Early Tourism in West Clare

Much early tourism was based on the supposedly health-giving properties of the sea or of the mineral waters to be found at spas. Bathing in the sea, 'taking the waters' or 'taking the cure', was recommended by the medical profession of the time as a remedy for a range of physical disorders.[1]

In Ireland during the 1700s, spas had developed at Lucan, Mallow and Castleconnell, among other places. Although limited in comparison with continental and English spa centres, the Irish spas were, in effect, the first Irish holiday resorts. Towards the end of the eighteenth century, sea-bathing became popular among the Anglo-Irish social élite. Visitors began to frequent coastal villages such as Malahide, Skerries and Tramore for the purpose of taking 'a dip'. Dorothea Herbert, then living near Carrick-on-Suir, recounted how she and her family had suffered 'a Variety of personal Inconveniences' in a miserable cabin at Bonmahon, Co. Waterford 'because we had never been to any Sea bathing place and the girls were all mad to go'.[2]

Furthermore, the intellectual climate of the time led to the development of scenic tourism among the upper class, stimulating an appreciation of mountains, rivers and lakes, the sea and magnificent stretches of coastline.

Given the emergence of such trends, it is not surprising that the wild and isolated west coast of Clare should attract visitors during the later decades of the eighteenth century. Travellers and writers of the period lauded the superb scenery and fresh air of the Clare coast. Lloyd wrote in 1780, 'multitudes repair to various parts of this coast for the benefits of the northern waters and numbers of different ranks from far and near resort hither to see the amazing appearance and curiosity of nature.'[3]

As early as 1795 the *Ennis Chronicle* was running advertisements for the renting of houses on the coast of Clare 'for the Saltwater season'.[4] The Napoleonic Wars stimulated tourism in the area, as local tourism entrepreneur Henry Morony of Miltown Malbay noted in his diary in 1829:

> In the year 1809, and preceding years, the Continent being closed against travellers and tourists and money plentiful, the country was not found to afford sufficient accommodation for the greater influx of company. . . . with the view of benefitting this place I endeavoured to draw the gentry to this, then deserted country, and for that purpose, gave every encouragement to the building of houses etc.[5]

Many seaside resorts in Ireland and in Britain were originally no more than small fishing villages. On the rugged west coast of Co. Clare, Kilkee, or Douagh as it was then called, was one of a number of villages on the coast whose population in the early 1800s relied almost totally on fishing. Certainly, by the 1820s visitors were travelling to the village for the sea-bathing afforded by its sheltered, shallow bay and its safe strand. Its added attraction of spectacular coastal scenery ensured that by the 1830s the humble fishing village was well on its way to becoming a fashionable seaside resort attracting as it did considerable numbers of the gentry of Counties Limerick, Clare, Tipperary and Offaly, as well as the prosperous merchant and professional families of Limerick City.

Ease of access is a crucial factor in the development of any tourist centre. Kilkee's progression from isolated fishing village to fashionable Victorian seaside resort was largely due to the fact that visitors could reach it relatively easily by travelling by boat from Limerick to Kilrush and completing the journey by carriage or open car. In the last century, the River Shannon was very much a major communications artery, linking West Clare and North Kerry with the city of Limerick.[6]

In this respect, Kilkee differed considerably from other Irish seaside resorts which developed during the 1800s. Bray, Bangor, Tramore, Youghal and Salthill, were all very much closer to the major population centres from which they drew their visitors (see article by Davies in this volume). Kilkee is some sixty miles by road from Limerick, but despite the distance, ease of access by river guaranteed its development as Limerick's seaside resort. This occurred at a time when roads in Co. Clare were all but non-existent, and long before railways were constructed in the county in the latter decades of the last century.

By the 1830s, the summer months saw large numbers of visitors making their way to and from Kilkee. Some even brought with them horses, carriages, servants and supplies of food.[7] In 1842 W.M. Thackeray noted: 'on board a capital steamer (from Foynes to Limerick) there was a piper and a bugler, a hundred of genteel persons coming back from donkey-riding and bathing at Kilkee.'[8]

Most of those who visited the resort in the last century travelled in family groups and generally stayed for at least a month. The town's prosperity depended greatly on those families who came year after year. The families stayed in lodges — houses let by local inhabitants for the duration of the season. It is likely that most of those who let lodges used them as their own dwellings during the off-season, moving to other accommodation in the locality during the summer months. As local curate Fr Sylvester Malone noted in 1867, 'what was realised by the lodge went to the payment of rents, to (the lodge's) further adornment, and to the purchase of the most necessary articles of dress.'[9] Large lodges, described as 'fit for noblemen and their families', were rented for £15–20 per month. Average size lodges cost £6–8 per month, while smaller ones were £3–4. The prices included milk, potatoes and turf. There were also three hotels in the town in the mid-1830s, each of which charged 25 shillings per week.[10]

Social Origins of Visitors

During the 1800s, and until well into the present century, the majority of the Irish population would not have even contemplated a period of time away from home for the purpose of rest and recreation. For the ordinary people, a 'holiday' was an outing to a fair, a 'patron', perhaps a race meeting or a football or hurling match.

In a regional and localised sense, Kilkee's patrons were representative of the very few people in Victorian Ireland who could afford a holiday away from home. They reflected the dominant social grouping of the time — the families of gentry or gentlemen farmers, prominent merchants of Limerick or the major towns of Counties Limerick, Clare, Tipperary and Offaly, doctors, lawyers, clergymen, bank managers, army officers and the like.

Newspaper reports in the *Limerick Chronicle* during the 1850s give some indication of the social tone of Kilkee's visitors during the middle decades of the last century. In September 1855 the *Chronicle* reported:

> On each Monday a large assemblage of the rank, beauty and fashion of the neighbourhood attended in Merton Square to take part in the new and popular game of Croquet and to enjoy the delightful strains of a band hired for the occasion.

In August 1858 the same paper observed that

> several noblemen and others of the élite with their families have already come and gone, and many highly fashionable people are staying at

present in Kilkee. . . . Kilkee is evidently rising to importance as a fashionable maritime resort and unquestionably to the residents of the west of Ireland, it is an agreeable place of resort.[11]

Charlotte Brontë is believed to have spent part of her Irish honeymoon at Kilkee in 1854; Alfred Lord Tennyson visited Kilkee in the company of his friend Sir Aubrey de Vere; and William Smith O'Brien of Dromoland was also a frequent visitor.

Socially Constrictive

Life at nineteenth-century seaside resorts has been described as resembling life on a modern cruise liner or in a small winter sports hotel where the company is small and self-contained.[12] Many of the families at Kilkee would have been related by kinship and religious affiliation or would have been known to each other through meeting at the resort during successive seasons. In this respect, Kilkee catered for a dispersed rural élite of Irish society — the Anglo-Irish families of the mid-western counties and their merchant and professional kinsfolk of Limerick and the major towns.

By far the largest proportion of holidaymakers at Kilkee for most of the last century was Protestant. The records of the local Church of Ireland parish in the 1880s and 1890s show that the normally small Anglican congregation of about sixty during the off-season steadily grew to ten times that number from April onwards, reaching a peak in August and early September.[13] In addition to the Anglican church, a Methodist chapel was built in 1900. Kilkee's image in the last century was that of being a unionist island in a sea of nationalism. At the height of the land war, Kilkee was bitterly referred to by one local nationalist as 'the millstone on the National Cause in West Clare and its sour porter'.

Local anecdotal evidence suggests that Kilkee was a popular meeting place for the sons and daughters of Protestant farmers, professionals and business people during the Victorian and Edwardian periods. Even as late as 1944, a holiday centre was established at the resort as a place where Protestants from the region could come together with a view to meeting prospective marriage partners.[14]

Local people also recollect that seafront evangelists frequented Kilkee up to the 1930s. Nicknamed 'the Sankey-Moodys' by the locals after the famous Victorian revivalists, it is understandable that evangelists would have been active in a resort where such a relatively large number of Protestants congregated during the summer months. There is a recollection that at the end of the last century, a temporary gospel hall was erected at the start of every holiday season and removed for storage in late September when the visitors had departed.[15]

Resort Life

Life at Kilkee in the middle of the last century was in many ways similar to life at spas in an earlier period. Spas had two basic functions. One was medicinal, providing access to mineral waters for drinking and bathing. The other was social, with the whole apparatus of spa life designed to provide 'a concentrated urban experience of socialising for a dispersed rural elite'.[16]

Kilkee fulfilled these functions admirably. In addition to the excellent strand for sea-bathing, visitors could avail of the same basic medicinal facilities to be found at spas — including chalybeate springs and baths erected by the enterprising local entrepreneur, Mr Hogan. In an age when respiratory and other illnesses were widespread, Kilkee became famous as a place 'to take the air'. In 1831 Mrs Shannon's boarding house was advertised 'for people seeking the benefit of their health . . . [where] the most perfect order and quietness may be depended on being observed.'[17] In fine weather the invalids were brought on couches to the strand. Some were dipped in the sea while lying on a broad board which was carried by two or more persons. Visitors could walk on the spectacular cliffs, gazing on the impressive coastal scenery of the area or they could take excursions by open cars to local scenic attractions.

In addition to the resort's natural attractions, Kilkee provided many social activities for its 'genteel' clientèle. Horse races were regularly held on the strand attracting large crowds 'of every class'. There were balls and concerts by visiting artists and artistes. The town must have been quite a lively place to judge by a letter written to a Limerick newspaper in August 1840: 'At night the real divarshin' comes on. Everything imaginable gattin forward. Lashins o'punch, cards, pitch an'toss — dice or a divilment. God help the bathing boxes about two in the mornin'.'[18]

In common with English spas and seaside resorts, Kilkee provided its visitors with an urban pattern of socialising — balls, dances, concerts, races, and other activities — all transplanted from the city to the resort for the duration of the sea-bathing season. In late September, after the visitors returned to their estates or to their homes in Limerick's fashionable Georgian squares, the resort reverted to being an isolated, coastal fishing community until the following April or May when tourists again began to arrive for the season.

Visitors and Locals

Perkins contends that a central factor in determining the development of seaside resorts in England in Victorian times was the interaction between three fractions of capital: local large capital, local small capital, and highly capitalised enterprises.[19]

There is clear evidence of each of the three fractions of capital in Kilkee during the last century. There was the local large capital of the enterprising Mr Hogan who opened a shop for the sale of 'Provisions in General', built seaweed baths and who published his own guidebooks to Kilkee in 1844 and again in the early 1860s.[20] There was the local small capital of hotel owners, those who offered lodges for rent, shopkeepers, publicans etc. Finally there was the large, externally owned capital of the Limerick businessmen who operated in Kilkee for the season, including a Mr Ely who set up a fancy bazaar selling clocks, musical boxes, Dresden china, London jewellery etc. The capitalists who actually owned the town — the Marquis of Conyngham and Major MacDonnell — no doubt well appreciated the value of their Kilkee properties at a time when large numbers of landlords were facing bankruptcy in Ireland. Furthermore, the important railway developments in Co. Clare in the later decades of the last century were made possible by the injection of significant amounts of external capital.

It is difficult to assess how much the ordinary residents of Kilkee benefitted from the influx of well-heeled vistors during the season. Local businesses such as those owned by Hogan, the proprietors of shops, the employees of hotels, were all obvious beneficiaries of the tourist influx. But there were other beneficiaries, including the local fishermen and their families who brought fish to the lodges, those who supplied milk, turf and other needs, as well as local people who carried out a variety of services for the visitors.[21] The proportion of locals who gained directly from the tourist influx every year is not easily assessed. However, the presence of relatively large numbers of prosperous people in such a poor part of the country would have benefitted the town significantly. The influx of cash into the local economy arguably had a trickle-down effect, in that poorer sections of Kilkee's population benefitted from the relative prosperity of those above them in the social hierarchy.

Landlord and Tenants

A major setback to the resort's fortunes occurred in the 1860s with a bitter feud between the tenants of the eastern end of the town and the Marquis of Conyngham, one of the two local landlords. In complete contrast, the other landlord, MacDonnell, was a humane and enlightened man who did everything in his power to promote the development of his portion of the town.

In common with tenants throughout Ireland at the time, those on the Conyngham Estate learned that their rights as tenants were virtually non-existent, even on property which they had made more valuable by building lodges and by draining and manuring land. By 1869, after evictions, destruction of dwellings by the 'crow-bar brigade', and what at the time

was an extraordinary degree of co-operation between Catholic and Protestant clergy in defence of tenants' rights, the struggle ended with almost
total unconditional victory for the marquis.

The dispute was to have serious implications for the longterm development of the resort. The number of inhabited dwellings dropped from 466
in 1861 to 322 in 1871, with the population dropping from 1,856 to 1,605.

None of the large-scale developments promised by the Marquis of
Conyngham ever materialised and even though new hotels and other
buildings were erected during the following twenty years, the momentum
of the half-century before 1860 was almost completely halted.[22]

The Coming of the Railway

In Britain and on the continent the development of railways in the last
century contributed greatly to the popularity of seaside resorts. The potential benefits of linking Kilkee by rail to the point near Kilrush where the
steamer tied up was not lost on the tourist interests at the resort. As early
as 1840, when there was as yet only one railway in Ireland (the Dublin-
Kingstown, built in 1834), local tourist interests began a campaign for a
rail link. The famine of 1845–49, and later shortage of capital, ensured
that it would be another half-century before a train would pull into the
town. The South Clare Railway opened in May 1892, linking the resort
with Cappa Pier, outside Kilrush, where the steamer from Limerick tied
up. Between Kilkee and Kilrush the South Clare Railway joined the West
Clare Railway at Moyasta Junction.[23]

The coming of the railway to Kilkee was a major stimulus to the resort.
From 1892 there was a significant increase in the numbers of worshippers
at the Church of Ireland church during the peak months of July, August
and September.[24] A new golf links was opened at the west end of the town
in September 1892.

The railway companies of the time promoted travel by providing
through-tickets from major cities in Ireland, England and Scotland through
Holyhead and Dublin and onwards by train to Connemara, the West Clare
resorts, or Killarney.[25] This made Kilkee accessible to visitors from further afield than the traditional hinterland of Limerick, Clare and the
midland counties. By the turn of the century there were ten hotels in the
resort and the hoteliers had founded a tourist development association
which published a well-produced guidebook to the area.

Up to the First World War there was little perceptible change in the
social makeup of the holidaymakers who stayed at the resort. They came
from the same upper-class Limerick and rural backgrounds — the families
of the Limerick professionals and merchants, and of some of the bigger
farmers in the region, with a sprinkling of gentry.

A Kilkee visitors' list in a locally produced newsletter of 1908 mentions a number of prominent gentry, the Anglican Bishop of Limerick, military personages, well-known professional families, merchants and others. Even though it is by no means a complete list, of the 140 names listed, over 100 can be identified as being of Anglo-Irish origin. The holidaymakers are listed as having come from Dublin, Cork, Derry, Limerick, Tipperary, Athenry, Naples, Chicago and New Zealand.[26]

Significantly, the newsletter hoped that 'the proposed improvements to the Kilkee links will bring back to West Clare a great many former visitors who now go elsewhere.' This would seem to indicate that, as early as 1908, the resort was losing its traditional clientèle to other Irish resorts. They may have opted to holiday elsewhere simply to avail of better golfing facilities but it is tempting to speculate whether the resort's traditional clientèle was attracted to other resorts because people from lower down the social scale were beginning to holiday at Kilkee.

Another reason may have been that the railway itself was at this time being criticised for the length of time it took to travel from Limerick to Kilkee, with some Limerick families deciding to travel to Bray, south of Dublin, because it took three-quarters of an hour less to get there than to the West Clare resort.

Over a period, the coming of the railway inevitably led to a broadening of the social base of the resort's visitors. The growing popularity of day excursions in the decades before the First World War allowed middle-class Limerick people an opportunity to experience the fresh air, bathing and scenery at Kilkee for one day in the year, at least.

The cost of a trip to Kilkee would have been expensive, with a single day's excursion for a family of five or six amounting to £1 or more. This would have been the equivalent of about £50 in present-day values, a significant sum of money for an outing even today. Given that the wages of an unskilled labourer at the time could be as low as fifteen shillings a week, it is not surprising that the holidaymaker at Kilkee before the First World War could sleep soundly in the knowledge that the resort would not be invaded by the 'improper classes' of Limerick, in the way that the North of England seaside towns were frequented by the mill-workers of Lancashire and elsewhere.

A feature of summers in Kilkee before the First World War (and indeed later) was the practice of wives and children spending up to two months at the resort, with the 'heads of families' arriving for the weekend and 'returning to business' in Limerick on Sunday or Monday.[27]

In Ireland, seaside resorts were to be socially exclusive until well into this century, reflecting the gulf between the small minority of the population who could afford a holiday, and the vast majority of rural and urban poor for whom a holiday was totally out of the question. Unlike England, where the coming of railways had democratised travel, enabling thousands of working class people to visit seaside resorts, the general level of poverty in Ireland before the First World War and the absence of paid holiday leave, meant that taking a holiday was totally beyond the expectations of the vast majority of the population.

Kilkee Between the Wars

The First World War and the Troubles which followed led to a significant reduction in the Anglo-Irish population of the southern and midland counties. Large numbers of those who would have inherited estates, professions and businesses in the region never returned after the war. Added to this were the tensions of living in Ireland during the War of Independence and the subsequent civil war, tensions which spurred many of those who holidayed at Irish resorts before the war to opt for fashionable English or continental resorts.

The Anglo-Irish gentry, the professional and merchant families who formed the backbone of Kilkee's pre-war clientèle, became ever scarcer at the resort during the 1920s and 30s. They were gradually replaced by the families of the newly dominant grouping in the post-Independence Free State, the Catholic commercial, professional and farming classes of the region.

Kilkee in the 1920s and 30s, like many resorts in Ireland, was struggling to attract visitors. Economic depression, emigration and the general shortage of cash during the Economic War, meant that it had to fight for its clientèle in the face of stiff competition from other Irish resorts, north and south. (In 1927, even the *Limerick Leader* carried advertisements for holidays at Portrush, a development which prompted a spirited advertising response from the West Clare resorts during the late 1920s.)

The brochures of the 1920s and 1930s advertised Kilkee rather grandiosely as 'the Biarritz of Ireland'. In addition to the natural attractions a guidebook listed

> vocal and instrumental concerts, a recital by a brass and reed band twice a week, three concert halls, two of which open nightly for cinema shows, dancing, cheap drives by motor and horse cars to places of interest, perfect sanitation and water supply, town lighted by electricity.[28]

Late in the season, after the wearying harvest months, farmers and their families came to Kilkee to benefit from Purtill's therapeutic seaweed baths which were widely acclaimed as cures for all kinds of aches and pains.

Inevitably a gulf remained between those who could afford to reside at the resort for one, two or more weeks and those who had to be content with a day-trip by excursion train or bus. Such excursions provided a much-needed boost to the economy of the resort at weekends.[29] The growth of bus transport in particular during the 1920s made Kilkee accessible to growing numbers of working-class day trippers who now had a cheap and faster form of transport than the notoriously slow and unpunctual West Clare Railway. The railway tried to counter the new bus excursions by providing an 'accelerated tourist train service' to the Clare resorts during the season.[30]

From the 1920s holidays at Irish seaside resorts became possible for people from what could be described as lower-middle-class backgrounds — clerks, shop assistants, nurses, teachers, gardaí, among others. The introduction of six days paid holiday leave in the mid–1930s encouraged the trend whereby young men and women could holiday at Irish resorts, away from the social control of families and communities. This clientèle became increasingly important to Irish resorts during the decades before the war, being catered for at less expensive hotels and boarding houses.

Not surprisingly, Kilkee reflected the subtle gradations of social class in the Ireland of the time. With dancing sweeping the country from the 1920s, the major social activity during the interwar period was centred on the dance-hall. Hotels at Kilkee, like hotels all over Ireland at the time, had their own dance facilities. These ranged from Moore's Hotel which is recalled as catering for the 'élite', to other hotels and halls for patrons from what were perceived to be less elevated rungs of the social ladder.

Bathing

The 1930s saw the growing dominance of Catholic social values and the emergence of a range of crusades aimed at resisting 'decadent' foreign influences. All kinds of activities were actively discouraged; campaigns were conducted against modern music and dancing, especially jazz, there were crusades against films and books which were considered 'dirty' and against 'immodest dress' on beaches and other public places.

With young single people increasingly frequenting Irish seaside resorts during the 1930s, controversy arose over what was considered the 'immodest behaviour' of the young at the seaside. The *Clare Champion* of 1 August 1935 carried the full text of a sermon entitled 'Seaside immodesty — modern laxity of morals' by a Fr Murphy. It warned those who frequented seaside resorts of

> the danger of being scandalised by the unbecoming and sometimes shocking conduct of young people who flock to the seaside. It would appear that many of these young people seem to think that holiday time is a time for general looseness nor do they refrain from exhibitions of the most flagrant immodesty in dress and in general conduct at the seaside. Sometimes even, they use the recesses of the seaside to scandalise respectable people and indeed many parents are in doubt as to whether it is advisable to bring their families to the seaside on holiday.[31]

Holidaymakers attending Mass were reminded every Sunday of the bathing rules at the resort whereby people were asked not to walk through the streets in bathing costumes. There were also separate rock-pools for males and females at Kilkee, which, like any other community in Ireland up to the early 1960s, reflected the values of a country preoccupied with maintaining high standards of sexual morality.

The Post-war Period

The Second World War brought problems of access to Irish resorts. Almost all private cars went off the road for the duration of the war, the number of buses was greatly reduced, and train travel became extremely difficult due to reliance on turf as the main source of fuel. For Kilkee, sixty miles from its major population centre, the travel difficulties were serious.[32]

In Britain in the decade after the war, more people than ever before took holidays at seaside resorts. The Irish resorts also saw an upsurge in popularity, with the increase in car ownership from the early 1950s resulting in growing numbers of day-trippers, particularly on Sundays. The newly established Bord Fáilte Eireann sought to attract British holidaymakers to Irish resorts in a promotion which was moderately successful. However, Kilkee's reliance on the domestic tourist market was to remain unchanged, with Bord Fáilte listing it in the second rank of Irish resorts likely to attract British holidaymakers.

By the early 1960s, Kilkee's future appeared promising. There was a general improvement in the economy of the the mid-west region. The setting up of major new industries at Shannon Airport and Limerick resulted in growing employment in the region, particularly of young, single people. The optimism at the resort is reflected in a building boom which occurred there in the early 1960s. In 1963, the then Dutch-owned Atlantic Hotel was built at the eastern end of the resort with the intention of attracting Dutch and other continental tourists on 'package holidays' through Shannon Airport. Modelled on resort development in southern Europe, the venture was a failure and today the building stands as an ugly eyesore, in total contrast to the attractive Victorian and Edwardian single-storey lodges with their distinctive bay windows. Another indicator of the increasing numbers at the resort is the fact that two new Catholic churches were opened in the parish in 1963.

The rise in the standard of living throughout the 1960s did result in an increase in the numbers of families taking holidays at the resort. Up to that time the preserve of middle-income holidaymakers, holidays at Kilkee now became possible for lower-income groups, particularly for families of skilled workers. In the early 1960s, three caravan sites were opened which broadened the social base of the resort's clientèle.

The 1960s, however, brought a mixed blessing to Irish holiday resorts as a whole. While growing numbers of families took holidays at the seaside, young single workers began to holiday outside the country in large numbers for the first time. 'Package holidays' (chartered inclusive tours) to continental beach resorts were introduced to the Irish market in 1960 and by the early 1970s over 110,000 Irish people a year were taking holidays abroad, attracted by well-marketed promotional campaigns by Irish tour operators.

Irish holiday resorts quickly lost their appeal for the young single worker who could have a Mediterranean sun-holiday for little more than he or she would spend at a resort in Ireland.[33]

Today, Kilkee remains heavily dependent on holidaymakers from Limerick — families who own holiday homes at the resort, mobile-home owners, or those who rent accommodation during the season. For the most part, the hotel sector is greatly reduced, with some larger hotels converted to holiday apartments. Availing of tax concessions, new holiday apartments have been built, aimed at both Irish second-home buyers and a growing number of continental holidaymakers. Recently, plans for a multi-million pound recreation centre have been announced.

Whether or not Kilkee can continue to attract its traditional Limerick holidaymaker remains to be seen. There is now stiff competition from Irish, British and even continental resorts. Irish middle-income families are increasingly attracted to holidays at camping or mobile-home sites in France, while lower-income families are taking 'all-in cost' holidays at revamped British holiday centres where there has been considerable investment in all-weather recreational facilities in recent years.

It would seem that Kilkee's future will largely depend on its ability to maintain the loyalty of its traditional holidaymaker from Limerick and the region generally, while at the same time attracting new holidaymakers from further afield.

It is possible that Kilkee could benefit from the current shift in holiday preferences. There are indications that the cancer scare connected with ozone depletion may be leading to a growing aversion to sun-holidays among Northern Europeans. Co. Clare has considerable attractions for ecologically-minded continental holidaymakers. It could well be that Kilkee's future will be assured by the very same attractions which brought the first tourists to the area two centuries ago — fresh air, unpolluted seas, interesting marine life, beautiful coastal scenery. The added attraction of the rich and unique cultural heritage of a community on the edge of Europe may also be a selling point in the coming years for Europeans in search of recreation, peace and tranquillity.

ACKNOWLEDGEMENTS   The author gratefully acknowledges the generous assistance of Fr Ignatius Murphy whose research into the early history of Kilkee was invaluable; Mr Patrick Barry NT for access to Church of Ireland documents relating to Kilkee and for many interesting recollections and

observations; Mr Timothy McInerney, Town Clerk, Kilkee for their recollections; and Mr Bill McInerney and Mr Chris O'Mahony, Archivist, Mid-
West Regional Archives, Limerick for access to documents relating to Kilkee
from the town clerk's office.

NOTES AND REFERENCES

1   Urry, J. (1990), *The Tourist Gaze: Leisure and Travel in Contemporary Societies,*
     Sage, London, p. 17.
2   Herbert, Dorothea (1988), *Retrospections of Dorothea Herbert, 1770–1806,*
     Town House, Dublin, pp. 396-7.
3   Lloyd, John (1780), *A Short Tour of the County Clare,* Ennis. See also Lewis,
     Samuel (1837), *Topographical Dictionary of Ireland,* London, and Mr and
     Mrs Hall (1841), *Halls' Ireland,* London.
4   *Ennis Chronicle,* 8, 15, 25 June, 1795.
5   Quoted in Ewan, Molly (1977), 'The Light of Other Days', *The Other Clare,*
     no. 3.
6   Wallace, P. (1972), 'The Organisation of Pre-Railway Public Transort in Co's
     Limerick and Clare', *North Munster Antiquarian Journal.*
     In 1812 the first regular boat service between Limerick and Kilrush was in-
     troduced by James Paterson, a Scottish merchant who had settled in Kilrush.
     In 1829, a 100-horsepower paddle steamer, the *Mona,* was introduced, to be
     replaced a year later by the *Kingstown.* In 1832 the *Garryowen* arrived, com-
     plete with iron bulkheads and a 90-horsepower engine, having cost £16,000
     to build.
7   Murphy, I. (1973), 'Pre-Famine Passenger Services on the Lower Shannon',
     North Munster Antiquarian Journal.
8   Thackeray, W.M. (1887), *An Irish Sketchbook,* London.
9   Quoted in Murphy, I. (1991), 'Kilkee — a Town for Sale — Landlord/Tenant
     Relations in Kilkee in the 1860s', *Dal gCais.*
10   Murphy, I. (1977), 'At the Seaside in Kilkee in the 1830s and 1840s', *The Other
     Clare,* no. 1.
11   Quoted in Murphy, I. (1991), op. cit.
12   Younger, G., 'Tourism: Blessing or Blight?', quoted in Urry, op. cit., p. 17.
13   Records of the Church of Ireland parish of Kilferagh (Kilkee), 1878-98.
14   Armitage, E. (1984), *The Story of Clar Ellagh, Christian Endeavour Guest
     House, Kilkee, 1944-84,* Dublin.
15   Information on seafront evangelism at Kilkee supplied by Mr Patrick Barry
     and Mr Timothy McInerney.
16   Urry (1990), op. cit.
17   Murphy (1977), op. cit.
18   *The Limerick Standard,* 24 August 1840.
19   Perkins, H., *The Social Tone of Victorian Seaside Resorts in the North-West.*
     Cited in Urry, op. cit.

20 Hogan, Hugh (1842), *A Directory of Kilkee in the County of Clare, on the Western Coast of Ireland, with a Map showing the Situation and Number of the Lodges,* Limerick.

21 The variety of services carried out by the locals is illustrated by an interesting recollection that the nick-name given to a visitor to Kilkee by the natives was *ruachach,* literally 'red turd'. One view on the origin of the nickname, meaning 'a stranger' or an 'uninitiated' person, is that it goes back to a time before proper sanitation when locals employed to remove night soil noticed that the visitors' waste was of a different colour to their own. This was due to the fact that the well-fed visitors had more protein in their diets than the natives, who rarely, if ever, ate meat.

22 Murphy, I. (1991), 'Kilkee — a Town for Sale', op. cit.

23 On Sunday 13 August 1892, a huge crowd left Limerick on the first excursion to Kilkee by steamer and train. Afterwards the *Munster News* commented: 'We are sure that large numbers will avail of the opportunity now afforded of seeing the Brighton of Ireland, especially considering that excursionists will not be left to the tender mercies of the local jehus [car drivers].' The journey from Limerick to Kilkee took a total of about 4½ hours; return fares cost between 3s 6d and 5s.

24 Kilferagh Parish records 1892-8. From 1892 to 1898, an average of 550 people attended Sunday morning service at Kilkee during August, an average increase of about 25 per cent on previous years.

25 O'Carroll, Cian (1988), 'Tourist Development in 19th. Century Co. Clare', *The Other Clare.*

26 *Cill Caoi,* no. 2, August 1908. (A locally published newsletter kindly provided by Mr Patrick Barry, Kilkee.)

27 Counihan to Doherty, Kilkee 11 July 1911, Kilkee documents, Mid-West Regional Archives, Limerick.

28 *Co. Clare Tourist Association Guidebook,* 1929, Mid-West Regional Archives, Limerick.

29 On 2 August 1927, 600 people from Limerick travelled to the 'Brighton of the West' on an excursion train specially organised by St Vincent de Paul. Three excursion trains were reported to be arriving at the resort on Sundays. On August 9th it was the turn of the excursion organised by the Athlunkard Boat Club, while the following Sunday saw the arrival of 200 people under the auspices of St Michael's Temperance Society of Limerick. (*Limerick Leader,* August 1927).

30 On 27 July 1935, the *Clare Champion* reported that

> over seventy employees of the Ennis Braid Mills on their first annual excursion to Kilkee . . . left Ennis on Saturday morning on two Great Southern Railway buses specially chartered for the occasion. On arrival at Kilkee the party, who were accompanied by the Managing Director, Mr. W. Chapman made their headquarters in the Royal Marine Hotel where they had tea and afterwards lunch. Sports were held on the strand and the winners of the various events were presented with prizes by Mr. Chapman. The party arrived back in Ennis at 11 p.m. on Saturday night after a thoroughly enjoyable day of glorious summer weather.

31   Interestingly, in the regional context, a national organisation known as the
     Crusade against Immodest Dress had its headquarters at Mary Immaculate
     College of Education, Limerick, during the 1930s.
32   Travel difficulties did not deter some people from making their annual
     pilgrimage to the resort. There were many who cycled from Limerick during
     the war. Residents recall long queues for the Limerick bus and there was even
     a system whereby Kilkee boys and girls made half-a-crown by holding a place
     in the bus queue from early morning on behalf of people who were returning
     to the city.
33   Gillmor, D. (1973), 'Irish Holidays Abroad: the Growth and Destination of
     Chartered Inclusive Tours', *Irish Geography*.

2

For Health and Pleasure in the British Fashion: Bray, Co. Wicklow, as a Tourist Resort, 1750-1914

K.M. Davies

The present-day traveller driving into Bray via Main Street enters the town through a mixture of shops, offices and dwelling houses no different from that of any other medium-sized town in Ireland. But if, instead, the traveller arrives by train and alights at the Victorian railway station next to the esplanade, he or she is transported into an altogether different environment: a seaside resort on the British pattern of the second half of the nineteenth century. Like the seventeenth-century plantation towns — Bandon, Coleraine, Londonderry — or eighteenth-century estate towns such as Maynooth and Westport, the seaward part of Bray was shaped not by chance, but by a vision of what form the town should take. The plantation towns and estate towns drew their inspiration from across the Irish Sea. So, in its late-nineteenth-century incarnation as 'the Brighton of Ireland', did Bray, even though in practice the role the town was to adopt was rather different from that envisaged for it by its creators.

At the same time, however, there is a mistaken tendency to look no further back than the 1850s and to regard Bray as purely a product of the railway age: the comment in the *Shell Guide to Ireland* is typical: 'The town is essentially the creation of the nineteenth-century railway entrepreneur, William Dargan ...' It is true that until the middle of the eighteenth-century Bray was little more than a village, but from then onwards the town had a respectable history of growth as a resort, extending over the best part of a hundred years before William Dargan and his associates entered the scene. Indeed, in the last two hundred and fifty years Bray as a tourist resort has undergone two separate periods of rapid growth, one unplanned and one planned, during each of which the town doubled in size; these were followed by a period of consolidation and, in the last two decades, a period of decline.

The physical evidence for the first period of growth has largely been subsumed into the later town; only a few dwellings once let as 'bathing lodges' still survive, unrecognised, as testimonials to Bray's early-nineteenth-century prominence as a resort. The fabric connected with the second, post-railway, period of resort growth still gives Bray its distinctive ambience, although in terms of extent it has now itself been swamped by the great expansion of late twentieth-century dormitory suburbs around the perimeter. Bray today, more than many Irish towns, would be quite alien to its eighteenth-century inhabitants, and yet it might also seem greatly diminished to those who frequented it for pleasure a generation or so ago.

The Bray of the mid-eighteenth century was in no sense a seaside town. Consisting of a church, barracks, mill and a cluster of houses. it lay close to Bray Bridge at the lowest crossing point of the Dargle River, ten miles south of Dublin on the main route to Wexford. The only road down to the sea, some half a mile away, was the forebear of the present Seapoint Road on the south bank of the river, and Bray's main street (with, as yet, houses only at the northern end) was otherwise separated from the coast by a largely unpopulated area of green fields. Standing on the seafront, the traveller looking towards Bray Head would have seen only a curving, pebbly, storm beach edging the bay and a rough, unfenced track with a scattering of fishermen's cottages aligned along it lying close to the high water mark.[1]

But from this period onwards Bray began to grow, not only as the small market town that might in any case have been expected to develop in the northern part of Co. Wicklow, but also as a fashionable watering-place and a centre for touring the scenic areas to the south and west. These twin functions were the consequence of two parallel movements that began after 1700: the Romantic Movement and its interest in beautiful scenery and the fashion for sea bathing, which grew out of the earlier fashion for 'taking the waters' at inland spas.

Ireland had several areas of outstanding natural beauty that appealed to the romantic sensibilities of the period. The lake region of Killarney was the most famous, but the north-eastern part of Co. Wicklow, notably the rocky wildernesses of the Glen of the Downs, the Scalp and the Dargle Glen, together with Powerscourt Waterfall, also quickly became popular with travellers, including many from outside Ireland. Co. Wicklow was being eulogised in print for its fine scenery by 1752, when Pococke described

the landscape as 'most exceedingly Romantick and beautiful' and mentioned Powerscourt Waterfall as a 'famous fall of water'.[2] Arthur Young
wrote of Wicklow's 'most magnificent scenery', and described Powerscourt
House as being in 'the most beautiful situation in the world'; he visited
the Glen of the Downs, the Dargle Glen and Powerscourt Waterfall in 1776,
and published a lengthy glowing description.[3]

Bray itself gradually came to feature prominently in the tour itineraries
of the time, particularly as the roads improved at the turn of the century
and the number of visitors increased. Some of these early tourists stopped
in Bray only briefly, others for one or more nights' accommodation. An
account of a lengthy day's touring from Dublin in 1823 may be regarded
as typical; it describes the party as arriving in Bray for breakfast at 9 a.m.
before spending the day in the Delgany area; on the way back through Bray
again the visitors stopped at an inn to refresh the horses and walked about
a little before heading home.[4] On a three-day excursion into north
Wicklow the journey was outward via The Scalp, with breakfast at Enniskerry followed by visits to the Dargle Glen and Powerscourt Waterfall and
a night at Newtown Mount Kennedy. On the second day the party visited
Delgany and the Glen of the Downs before spending the night in Bray,
and on the third they travelled back to Dublin.[5]

When travellers of this period mention Bray, they are unanimous in
their praise of one establishment — Quin's Hotel, which was by this time
one of the best-known hotels in Ireland. This hotel, still operating today
as the Royal Hotel, was opened in c. 1770 by William Quin and developed
over the better part of a century by his son and grandson, both named
John Quin. Even now, the hotel dominates the north end of Main Street;
in its heyday it was the most important commercial building in the town.
It stood on the mailcoach route to Wexford, and Bray's markets and fairs
took place outside its windows. A tour guide of 1827 describes it as: 'a
very capital hotel, kept by Quin, who gives good dinners, excellent wines,
furnishes the best post chaises, barouches, and other vehicles, for the use
of parties making the tour of these mountains'.[6] There were some sixty
bedrooms, more than twice as many as in the next largest hotel in east
Wicklow, and extensive livery stables; Quin is said to have kept stabling
for 170 horses, with twenty-two post chaises available for travellers.[7]

Without the Quin family's initiative, Bray would have been a less
desirable stopping point for travellers touring Co. Wicklow. Indeed as a
tour base the town might have found it difficult to compete with Enniskerry
three miles inland and much the same distance from Dublin. Enniskerry
had the advantage of being a picturesque estate village, approached from
Dublin through the spectacular gash of The Scalp and within easy reach
of Powerscourt demesne and the Dargle Glen. But it was Bray — not Enniskerry — that in the event came to describe itself as 'the gateway to the
garden of Ireland'. This came about at least partly because the town had

another factor in its favour, and this too was exploited by the enterprising owners of Quin's Hotel: the proximity of the Irish Sea allowed Bray to develop as a fashionable watering place.

The fashion for sea-bathing as a 'cure' originated early in the eighteenth century in Britain. Small fishing villages were the beneficiaries of this new restorative diversion of the leisured classes and before long the best-known of these was Brighthelmstone in Sussex, soon to figure prominently in this chapter under its later name of Brighton. These new resorts offered fresh air, at a time when the growing urban areas were becoming increasingly polluted, together with healthy exercise (attractive scenery in the vicinity was important) and, as they developed, an active social life with balls, concerts, circulating libraries and lectures.

Just as Brighton developed because of its proximity to London, so Bray was able to attract visitors from the Irish capital. At first, these visitors probably rented, or took lodgings in, existing houses and cottages, but before long good houses seem to have been built especially for summer use. Three substantial villas, Bay View (Novara, Novara Avenue), Eden View (Marino Clinic, Church Road) and Rich View (Killarney Road, demolished), were described in the Ordnance Survey's name books of 1838 as among the 'numerous bathing lodges' rented out for the season to 'casual tenants' by the Hon. Sidney Herbert (whose family, the Pembrokes, owned part of the town), while Arbutus Lodge, off the Dublin road in Little Bray, was also let 'to persons who come there for the purpose of receiving the salt water'. In addition, there was an increasing number of lodging houses — over 150 by 1841[8] — and, at the other end of the scale, there was, of course, Quin's Hotel. Here the visitor could have 'baths, fresh and salt, hot and cold, with shower, ditto, always ready'[9] and work up an appetite by walking along the 'broad gravel walk' laid out before 1835 through the private grounds of the hotel to reach the sea near the present railway station.[10] This route to the seafront was to be thronged in years to come by a far more socially-mixed gathering than could have been envisaged in the 1830s, but when 'Quin's Walk' was first constructed it must have been very genteel. Quin's Hotel charged 2s 6d a night in 1852, a price equalled elsewhere in Ireland only by a few Dublin hotels and Hunter's Hotel further south at Rathnew.[11] Its distinguished guests included the Lord Lieutenant, who stayed several times, including a visit for his 'flying gout' in 1842.[12]

A contemporary guide summarises the facilities offered by Bray in the early years of the nineteenth century:

> The town of Bray . . . has been for many years a place of summer resort
> to the gentry from all parts of Ireland. As might be presumed from this,
> it affords all the various accommodations necessary for the visitor, in
> the highest degree of perfection. Quin's hotel has long deservedly held
> a high place in public estimation: and in addition to the ordinary merits

of a first rate hotel, it is provided with excellent barouches for parties to all parts of this county. Cars are also to be had on reasonable terms for the same purposes. Lodgings, handsome cottages and boarding houses, on different scales of economy, are also in abundance in and about the town. There are also in general some places of greater pretension and extent among the gentlemen's seats in the vicinity, for those whose rank and fortune require accommodations on a more extensive scale.[13]

It was only the upper classes, of course, who had the means or the leisure to visit a resort such as Bray, whether briefly, as part of a tour in Wicklow, or for an extended stay to gain the benefit of sea-bathing and bracing air. Quin's Hotel was not the only place to stay that was expensive, renting a house could cost as much as £100 for the season.[14] The town expanded significantly, if in an unplanned fashion, however, as a result of the demand for services as well as for accommodation. The population increased rapidly (perhaps by a multiple of four between 1761 and 1821[15]), and by the 1820s there were houses on both sides of the main street as far as the present town hall, spilling over beyond the junction into the northern portions of what are now Killarney and Vevay Roads. By 1838 Bray had the appearance of a substantial one-street town, albeit one that still appeared largely to turn its back on the Irish Sea (see Fig. 2.1).[16]

But a greater impetus to change was imminent: on 10 July 1854 the Dublin and Wicklow Railway line was opened to link Dublin with Bray. If it had not been for various difficulties and disagreements, the railway might have reached Bray a decade or so earlier — in which case the town might, shaped by other hands, have developed very differently — but in the event it was only after William Dargan, already famous both as railway engineer and as organiser of the 1853 Industrial Exhibition, took a share in the Dublin and Wicklow Railway Company that the link with Dublin was completed.[17] Dargan's interest in Bray extended far beyond the provision of a fast and comfortable means of access; he became intimately involved in the development of the town.

In addition to Dargan, three other individuals stand out in this development: Dargan's associate, Edward Breslin, who was to have a long and distinguished connection with Bray as hotelier and as chairman of the town commissioners into the 1890s; local builder, John Brennan, still commemorated in his Brennan's Parade; and, not least, John Quin junior, who had inherited in 1852 not only Quin's Hotel but also his father's extensive landholdings, essential to any expansion in the area between the northern part of Main Street and the sea.[18] These businessmen, together with others in the town, set out to transform the existing resort. They would have been encouraged in their ambitions for Bray by developments elsewhere. Nearest to home, there was the growth that had already taken place on the south Dublin coast following the opening of the Dublin and

Figure 2.1   Bray in 1838 (Ordnance Survey)

Kingstown Railway in 1834. The population of Kingstown (Dún Laoghaire) had almost doubled between 1831 and 1851, as the borough became not only a place of residence for affluent Dubliners but also 'one of the most frequented seabathing places in Ireland'.[19] At the same time, across the Irish Sea, the opening of the Chester and Holyhead Railway was leading to the establishment of resorts along the North Wales coast in a mushrooming that one observer described as 'like a gold-rush'.[20]

By the time the railway company ran its inaugural train, a number of conscious decisions had been taken concerning the new form Bray was to take as a seaside holiday resort. The overall concept was ambitious; the new Bray was to be modelled on the new English south-coast resorts, specifically Brighton, by this time the largest resort in Great Britain with a population of over 50,000. Its pre-eminence as a watering place was originally derived from patronage by the Prince Regent in the last decades of the eighteenth and first decades of the nineteenth century, and the opening of the railway to London had encouraged wealthy Londoners to settle there within easy commuting distance of the capital. Bray was perceived as having a similar history and offering the same advantages. In fact, it was a comparatively recent happening in Brighton's history that was the real pointer to the future: the first excursion train from London had run in 1844. In the second half of the nineteenth century most British resorts — and, in the event, Bray — were to become dependent on 'modest middle-class holidaymaking', rather than on visits by the upper classes, and, eventually, with the arrival of bank holidays, weekly half-holidays and annual holidays with pay, on the patronage of the working classes as well.

It was convenient, if fortuitous, that identification with Britain's premier resort was to give Bray an impressive sobriquet: 'the Brighton of Ireland'. This was both suggestive of a high-class resort, implying the best of its kind in Ireland, and also easy to trip off the tongue. The railway companies in Britain were to foster the development of titles and catch-phrases, 'Sunny Rhyl', for instance, or (for the Torquay region) the 'Riviera of the south coast'. The 'Brighton of Ireland' was not the only title appended to the Irish resort — another was 'Bray the Splendid'[21] — but it was the one that soon passed into common usage, with its first appearance in print apparently dating from 1863.[22]

As far as the layout was concerned, the new seaside resort area of Bray had to be grafted onto the existing town, where the main shopping street ran parallel to the coast rather than towards it. There was the advantage that the railway line could be laid out without much difficulty through the fields close to the sea, with the station only a matter of yards from the shore itself (ideal for day trippers) rather than tucked away at the rear of the town as happened in many English and Welsh resorts.[23] The disadvantage with this, however, was that the station buildings and the railway embankment cut off the view of the sea from most of the town, leaving Bray with seaward-facing sites — greatly prized elsewhere — only along a narrow coastal strip. The actual position of the railway station and of the important new road link between it and the existing main street were determined by an agreement made between the Dublin and Wicklow Railway Company and John Quin.[24] Accordingly the railway station was sited close to the seaward end of 'Quin's Walk', and a wide roadway was constructed alongside the Walk at the expense of the railway company, leading to the seafront via a level-crossing adjacent to the station. This new thoroughfare, Quinsborough Road, became the main artery between the old Bray and the new, breaking into the main street just to the south of Quin's Hotel and offering an enticing vista towards the sea from the heart of the old town. William Dargan himself built one of several imposing terraces of houses that soon faced onto it.

Dargan also provided Bray with three major facilities: the esplanade, the Carlisle Grounds and the turkish baths. The first was, of course, an essential amenity. Dargan leased the old storm beach from the Earl of Meath (ground landlord of the greater part of Bray) and converted it into a wide grassed strip, vulnerable on the shore side to rough seas, with chain-link fencing suspended from granite posts marking it off from the road along the seafront (see Fig. 2.2).[25] The Carlisle Grounds, on Quinsborough Road across from the railway station, was opened by the Lord Lieutenant of that name in 1862 and served for many years as an open-air pleasure ground.[26] The most distinctive new edifice in Bray, the turkish baths, elaborately built of red and white brick with tall minarets at the corners, was also located on Quinsborough Road: it is perhaps not too fanciful to see the structure as Dargan's answer to the Prince Regent's exotically domed Brighton Pavilion.[27]

Two major new hotels were quickly built in prominent positions adjacent to the railway station, making this area the new focal point of activity in the town. Edward Breslin's Royal Marine Hotel, opened in 1855, had the advantage of sea views from its corner site on the seaward side of the level crossing: by 1860 it had ninety bedrooms and twelve sitting rooms.[28] The International Hotel, with 180 bedrooms, was built by John Brennan on a site acquired by Dargan from John Quin, and opened in time for the summer season in 1862 (the name was taken from that year's International Exhibition in London). It lay inland of the railway, facing onto Quinsborough Road; its imposing square bulk, grand entrance and elaborate window pediments according well with its status as the largest hotel in Ireland.[29] Among the smaller hotels which opened in the first flush of growth, Lacy's Bray Head Hotel, in business by 1860, formed a counter-attraction at the Bray Head end of the esplanade. In the 'old' town the Quin family built a large extension to their hotel, curving it elegantly round into Quinsborough Road; although rapidly dislodged from its position as Bray's premier hotel it did acquire a more dignified name — it

Figure 2.2   The Esplanade, Bray in the 1860s (Gaskin)

became the Royal Hotel. Bray thus had three or four hotels, at least, with names of the same order as Brighton's Grand Hotel or Hastings's Queen's Hotel: such titles would have been important in establishing the confidence of prospective English visitors and also in providing residents with addresses they would be pleased to flaunt on their letters home.

Meanwhile the picturesque thatched cottages and lodging houses of the 'old' Bray were swept away in a fever of building and re-building. New roads were laid out across the coastal fields in a relatively regular grid pattern, with Meath Road stretching for nearly half a mile parallel to the railway and shorter avenues at right-angles passing under the tracks to reach the seafront. New villas and terraces of houses in a mixture of styles sprang up along these roads and along the esplanade. The number of dwellings in Bray doubled from 879 in 1851 to 1,726 in 1901 (with the largest increase in the intercensal period 1861–71) and the population rose from 3,152 to 7,424 during the same period.[30] The physical extent of the town trebled between 1854 and 1870, with most of the area east of Main Street all the way from the Dargle River to the newly laid-out Putland Road incorporated into the built-up area.[31]

The 'old' town also benefited from the growth of the 'new'. The old bridge across the Dargle was replaced in 1856, and over a period of years Bray acquired new churches, chapels and schools, a handsome town hall and market house, and a public park, both the last the gift of the Meath family. There was a conscious strategy of maintaining the standards of the resort. The fairground was moved to a new peripheral site in Little Bray, and bylaws — some of them modelled on those of Brighton itself — were promulgated to control the activities of net fishermen on the seafront and generally to keep the town clean and orderly.[32]

Part of the intention in promoting Bray was to encourage the upper and professional classes to take up residence in and around the town, and substantial houses occupied by Dublin's lawyers, doctors, professors and businessmen were soon scattered around the neighbourhood. The situation was agreeable and access to the city was easy.[33] The presence of such residents was obviously of importance to Bray, not only for the trade they engendered but also because they helped to maintain the tone of the resort.

Once settled in Bray, the visitor, whether there for the whole summer season, or only for the day, required appropriate entertainment. Firstly, there was the salt-water bathing. The first permanent baths, still visible next to Martello Terrace, were erected at the north end of the esplanade in 1861, offering 'hot, cold and open sea baths'.[34] Ladies' bathing boxes, an indispensable amenity of the time, had already been erected on the strand by the railway company: they were to be superseded in 1878 by new ladies' baths built mid-way along the esplanade. There was also a men's bathing place at Naylor's Cove, close to Bray Head. In the early days there was still a strong emphasis on the curative aspects of the holiday, and infirm visitors could patronise Dr Haughton's hydropathic establishment in Galtrim House (formerly home of the Quin family). Rather briefly there was also the turkish baths, under the supervision of Dr Barter of Blarney, but this operated fully only from late 1859 until 1864 (subsequently the building became the Assembly Rooms, hired out for concerts and enter-tainments). Another diversion was to take a drive into rural Wicklow in one of the several hundred horse-drawn vehicles that plied for hire in the vicinity of the station, causing congestion there and in Dargan (now Dun-cairn) Terrace nearby. There were many events of an occasional nature, some open to all, some requiring an entrance fee: sports meetings and military band concerts on the promenade, boating regattas with firework displays; archery and athletics competitions, cricket and croquet matches, athletics and flower shows in the Carlisle Grounds.

Four thousand rail visitors were reported as having visited Bray at Easter 1861, while in the same year 930 trippers arrived at Whitsun on the 10 a.m. excursion train from Dublin. Presumably the number of day visitors in the height of the season was of the same order of magnitude, and com-bined with the holidaymakers actually staying in the town must have added up to a considerable total. The large numbers of visitors required more than entertainment, however, they needed basic services, and from 1857 these were the responsibility of the Bray township commissioners, who were frequently exercised with their provision and costs.[35] A letter to the *Freeman's Journal* in 1865 complained that although nearly £250,000 had been spent over the previous decade on building, the sewerage was defec-tive and the water supply was inefficient. The first water supply came from a small local reservoir, but from 1869 there was a link with Dublin Water-works' new Vartry reservoir. There were complaints about the high costs, however, and the quantity available remained unsatisfactory: in the sum-mer of 1875 the water supply was being cut off every evening from 5 p.m. to 11 p.m., in the following year the daily supply was estimated to be 30,000 gallons short and in 1877 the Bray township commissioners served Dublin Corporation with a writ for compensation for the inadequate supply. (The estimated requirements would have been modest by our standards — even in the mid-twentieth century holidaymakers in seaside boarding houses were not expected to take a bath during a week's stay.) Approval was given for a new sewerage system in 1866,[36] but the commissioners were still borrow-ing large sums to complete the system in the 1870s, and in 1874 85 per cent of the houses in Bray were said to be defective from a sanitary point of view. None of this can have been good for Bray's reputation as a healthy resort in an era when an outbreak of cholera was still a real possibility.

Provision of a satisfactory gas supply also took several decades, and again the Bray town commissioners found the high charges a problem; the town's street lights were said to have been switched off during the whole

Figure 2.3   Marine Station Hotel (formerly Breslin's Royal Marine Hotel) and Esplanade, Bray, circa 1910
(Lawrence Collection, NLI)

of the 1874 season. The gas supply was augmented by electricity from the mid-1880s, and a full electricity supply was generated from 1892 onwards. The town commissioners were also faced with substantial bills for new roads, and for paving and curbing the footpaths in the town, a process that continued at least into the 1880s.

The other ongoing problem for the town commissioners was the esplanade, which was exposed to the full blast of easterly gales. The state of Dargan's original esplanade was already the subject of complaints by the mid-1860s, and matters seemed to have reached such a pass that at the end of 1869 Lord Meath's solicitor wrote to the town commissioners on the subject of its 'bad order', threatening to resume possession.[37] After innumerable repairs and repeated incursions by the sea, a substantial concrete sea wall was built in the 1880s at a cost of some £25,000. This was in some ways a considerable embellishment to the seafront with its iron railings and raised promenade, but there were also disadvantages. Except at the Bray Head end, the wall forms a barrier between the resort and the beach area; access to the northern end of the shore is very limited and there is, today at least, a considerable drop. The crowds arriving by train and spilling out onto the esplanade were offered none of the easy access to beach and sea found in resorts elsewhere. (There must, indeed, have been a temptation to remain on the esplanade, exemplified by a Lawrence photograph of c. 1910 (see Fig. 2.3) which shows groups sitting primly on the grass with other visitors sunning themselves in a row on benches along the inner wall or leaning on the railings.[38]) The threat from the waves has not entirely receded, however, and the sea defences have continued to cause problems for the local authorities up to the present.

While the town authorities were struggling to maintain acceptable standards in the face of recurrent financial problems and complaints about high rates,[39] there are other indications, both large and small, that Bray's prosperity was shaky. Bray was unlike most other Irish towns in the second half of the nineteenth century in that it was expanding, and considerable sums of money were pouring into development, particularly in the first decade after 1854. But as a resort it could not compete with those across the Irish Sea, where both the money available for investment and the spending power of the multitude of visitors were far greater. The condition of the former turkish baths within some twenty years of its construction is perhaps symptomatic. Lying as it did in full view of everyone who passed from the seafront to the main street, the Assembly Rooms was bitterly criticised in 1877 as 'a perfect eyesore', dirty, with a dilapidated hedge in front, lines of 'household linens' suspended from stunted trees and fowl 'busy in obliterating all signs of regularity or order'.[40]

In one major respect, at least, Bray was successful in acting out its role as a resort. After complaints in the 1870s that there was not sufficient entertainment provided for visitors 'such as in England', the Bray Improvement

Committee (later the Bray Amusements Committee) was formed, an annual subscription was raised, and the various band performances, rowing regattas, polo matches, flower shows and other events were systematically and regularly organised.[41] Matters did not go so well, however, where one paramount seaside amenity of Victorian times was concerned: no entrepreneur ever considered it an economic proposition to invest in a pier. An act of parliament in 1867 authorised the Bray Promenade Pier Company to build an iron pier at a cost of £25,000; the civil engineer proposed for the scheme had already built a number of notable piers in England. Plans were again considered in 1876 for the construction of a substantial edifice, 'similar to that of Brighton', 1,000 yards long by 45 wide, with a bandstand and promenade ground at the end.[42] The idea was revived in 1884, and again in 1890 but was finally abandoned in 1906. Bray was thus left without the important entertainment and focal point found in most resorts in Great Britain, where some seventy seaside piers were built during the nineteenth century as the Victorian equivalent of the modern 'funland'.[43]

By the turn of the century, several other enterprising plans had also been abandoned. The Bray Aquarium Company's plans in 1877 to transform the Carlisle Grounds by spending £20,000 on a marine aquarium, concert hall, lecture and exhibition rooms, reading and refreshment rooms, with grounds laid out as rink, croquet, archery and promenade grounds, never progressed very far, although a skating rink did operate for a while. A proposal for a switchback railway was abandoned at an even earlier stage, when it was rejected by the town commissioners on the grounds that it would attract an undesirable class of people. Separate proposals to build an electric tramway along the seafront and six tramlines around the town both came to nothing, as did plans for the Bray Pavilion and Winter Gardens. The Bray-Enniskerry light railway was the only scheme actually to get under way, but it was never completed and the company was wound up in 1901.

Several contemporary sources make it possible to paint a picture of Bray as it was in the early years of the twentieth century.[44] According to Porter's directory, the same four hotels continued to dominate the resort, although by 1910, after the death of its eponymous owner, Breslin's Royal Marine Hotel had been renamed the Marine Station Hotel. There were also nine private hotels, seven of which were on the esplanade, and, scattered around the town, 147 houses offering accommodation. (Many other households, of course, also took visitors, without aspiring to appear in a directory.) Sixteen car proprietors were included, and some 150 'witty jarveys' were said to be employed in the summer. Presumably the sixteen boat owners, nine laundries and twelve tea rooms were also largely dependent on the summer trade. Boating, bathing, fishing, croquet, tennis and golf were available (the latter on the new 9-hole course in Little Bray) and the Bray Amusement Committee was still providing entertainment for the visitors. One hundred and twenty trains a day ran in and out of the railway station. There were three bandstands on the esplanade and several boat slips down to the beach. Relatively substantial houses lined the principal roads, although there were still many undeveloped sites, particularly along Florence Road and further south-east towards Bray Head (see Fig. 2.4).

Unlike the English and Welsh resorts, however, which underwent a new surge of development at the turn of the century, Bray's great period of expansion as a resort was now at an end, and the outbreak of the First World War can be regarded as a watershed. The Marine Station Hotel was burned in 1916 and not rebuilt, while the International Hotel was used as a military convalescent hospital during the war and seems never to have regained its former status,[45] it too was to be destroyed by fire in 1974. The amount of development or renewal of properties along the seafront after 1900 seems to have been small; the terraces of three-storey boarding houses along the esplanade have remained modest affairs compared with the impressive seaward-facing frontages found in other resorts around the Irish Sea. Apart from the addition of a few garish amusement arcades and the removal of a group of small cottages in the middle of the road at the north end of the esplanade, the view along the seafront houses does not appear to have changed greatly in this century. (There is no evidence, for instance, that there were ever large numbers of shops catering for visitors facing the esplanade, such as might still be found in an English or Welsh resort, although there were clusters of small outlets selling buckets and spades, postcards and other holiday items alongside the railway in Albert Walk, and also near Bray Head, until the late 1960s.) Between the seafront and the main street, twentieth century infill has consisted largely of small suburban houses; many of those of the 1930s and 40s being single-storey and apparently designed for retirement rather than for seaside letting. Although some good houses were built in the early twentieth century — along King Edward Road, for instance — the general failure of Bray to develop as an 'up-market' resort, at a time when it was still perceived as too far from Dublin to become a dormitory town, is reflected in the smallness of their number.

Some aspects of Bray's success or failure as a seaside resort can now be briefly evaluated. As far as the 'Brighton of Ireland' is concerned, it can be argued that the comparison with the English resort was never one to be taken seriously. Dublin, unlike the English capital, is itself adjacent to the sea and ten miles of attractive coastline stretch between it and Bray. Neither the day visitors seeking sea-bathing and fresh air nor the prosperous residents able to afford to commute into the city from scenic coastal locations needed to travel as far afield as Bray to satisfy their requirements. Ironically, the Bray of the 1830s and 40s, patronised by the Lord Lieutenant and the gentry, was perhaps more closely akin to the Prince Regent's

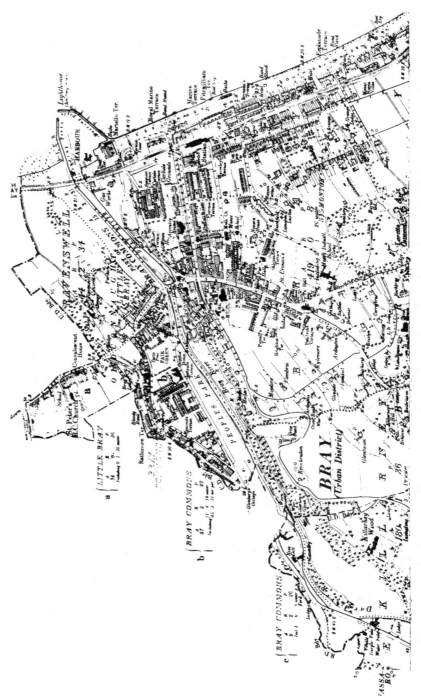

Figure 2.4   Bray in 1909 (Ordnance Survey)

favourite watering place than the town was ever to be again.

Valid comparisons can be made, however, with other Irish Sea resorts: Morecambe, Blackpool and Southport on the Lancashire coast; Rhyl, Colwyn Bay, Rhos-on-Sea and Llandudno in North Wales; and Douglas, Isle of Man. Like these, Bray was a product of the railway era, and of progressively cheaper rail travel and longer holidays with pay. The town had the same advantages of beautiful scenery nearby, ideal for touring, as does Morecambe in relation to the Lake District or the North Wales resorts in relation to the mountains of Snowdonia. Like the North Wales resorts, it lies in a rainshadow, and the number of sunshine hours is high. For the visitor from Britain,[46] a holiday in Bray would have offered the same excitements of a sea voyage and sense of being in a foreign yet familiar country offered by Douglas, Isle of Man.

On the debit side, one important ingredient that Bray lacked as the seaside holiday reached its peak of popularity in the early twentieth century was a good beach. An extensive sandy area was a great asset to a resort: Rhyl, Morecambe, Southport and Blackpool all eulogised their 'golden sands'. The condition of Bray's beach is said to have worsened after the construction of the harbour in the 1890s, but no nineteenth-century writer, however favourably inclined, ever suggested that it was sandy. Indeed the best that could be said for it was that it was 'decorated in profusion with an endless variety of rare and curious pebbles and shells'.[47] Apart from the lack of good sand, the beach at Bray is insufficiently wide to provide the right carefree ambience or, indeed, to accommodate a large number of people. When Dargan and his associates chose Bray as a suitable location for a resort town, a stay at the seaside was still closely associated with the idea of its medicinal benefits; if they had been able to anticipate the popularity of the light hearted bucket-and-spade holiday they might well have looked elsewhere — perhaps to nearby Killiney or Greystones, or, better still, to the extensive strands north of Dublin city at Portmarnock, Laytown and Bettystown.

Bray's greatest handicap, however, was that, almost from the first, it did not have enough visitors with enough money to spend. The town would appear to have gradually lost its pretensions to gentility. This was partly because by the end of the nineteenth century it had a new rival in Greystones, a few miles further south, which, although smaller and lacking in tourist amenities, attracted the 'better' class of Dubliner from the fashionable southside suburbs.[48] (In the twentieth century, with the arrival of the private motor car, prosperous Dubliners increasingly rented houses or caravans close to sandy beaches further south in Wicklow or Wexford, or acquired holiday homes of their own in the west of Ireland.) At the same time the factories, shops and offices of Dublin could not provide hordes of weekly holidaymakers for Bray in the way that the factories of Lancashire, Yorkshire and the English midlands decanted their workers

— often whole towns at a time — onto the beaches of northern English and Welsh resorts.

In the Irish context, however, Bray must count itself a success. Other than Kingstown, where from the first the holiday resort was intrinsically mixed with the affluent dormitory suburb, there was no other Irish seaside town to compare with it during the nineteenth century. In the twentieth century only a few northern resorts, particularly Bangor, Co. Down, drawing upon Belfast's factory workers, have had similar success. Bray has provided the Irish holidaymaker with the authentic flavour of a quintessential seaside holiday resort; a taste at least of the splendour common to Brighton, Bournemouth, Blackpool and the other resorts of Great Britain in their heyday.

ACKNOWLEDGEMENTS   The author's thanks go to Dr J.H. Andrews and Mr Richard Hawkins for helpful comments and discussion.

NOTES AND REFERENCES

1   Barker, Jonathan (1762), 'A Map of Great Bray in the County of Wicklow surveyed in 1762 by Jonathan Barker', MSS, Pembroke estate office, Dublin; Taylor, John (1816), *The Environs of Dublin,* scale 1:31,680; both maps reproduced in Davies, K.M. (1989), 'The Cartographic Record: Bray from Maps', in O'Sullivan, J., Dunne, T. and Cannon, S. (eds.), *The Book of Bray,* Blackrock Teachers' Centre, Blackrock, pp. 26-44. There is a myth that there was then only one cottage on the coast between the Dargle River and Bray Head, illuminating the contrast between the pre-railway town and the bustling late-nineteenth-century resort.

2   Stokes, G.T. (ed.) (1891), *Pococke's Tour in Ireland in 1751,* Hodges Figgis and Co., Dublin and Simpkin et al., London, p. 162.

3   Young, Arthur (1780), *A Tour in Ireland,* Messrs Whitestone et al., Dublin, 1: pp. 132-7.

4   A.B. [1823], *Observations Made During a Short Excursion to Dublin, Delganny, &c in 1823,* R. Smith and Co., Liverpool and R. Grace, Dublin, pp. 4-7.

5   [John Gough], n.d., *A Tour in Ireland, in 1813 & 1814,* M. Gough & Co., Dublin, pp. 181-8.

6   Anon (1827), *The Pleasure Tours in Ireland,* Edinburgh, p. 9.

7   Cosby, Major (1835), *Kevin's Bed,* Dublin, p. 60; A.B., op. cit., p. 4; Gough, op. cit., p. 186.

8   Moylan, Isolde (1989), 'The Development of Modern Bray, 1750-1900', in O'Sullivan et al., op. cit., p. 52.

9   *Freeman's Journal,* 30 April 1832.

10   Cosby, op. cit., pp. 61-2; Ordnance Survey (1838), Co. Wicklow sheet 4, scale 1:10,560.
11   Anon (1852), *The Irish Tourists's Illustrated Handbook,* National Illustrated Library, London and M'Glashan, Dublin, pp. xi-xiii.
12   *Freeman's Journal,* 6 May 1839, 15 March 1842.
13. (1835), *A Guide to the County of Wicklow,* William Curry, jun. and Co., Dublin, pp. 6-7.
14   Moylan, op. cit., p. 52.
15   Moylan, Isolde (1972), 'The Development and Growth of Bray, *c.* 1750-1900', B.A. Mod. dissertation, Department of History, Trinity College, Dublin.
16   Taylor, op. cit.; Ordnance Survey (1838), op. cit.
17   For a history of the completion of the railway line, see Murray, K.A. (1989), 'The Coming of the Railway', in O'Sullivan et al., op. cit., pp. 78-85.
18   See O'Sullivan, John (1989), 'The Quin family of Bray', in O'Sullivan et al., op. cit., pp. 71-7, based on the collection of Quin papers in the possession of Peter Pearson, Dublin.
19   Knox, Alexander (1845), *The Irish Water Places,* William Curry, jun., and Co., Dublin, p. 147.
20   Pimlott, J.A.R. (1947), *The Englishman's Holiday,* London, p. 123.
21   Rodenberg, Julius (1861), *The Island of the Saints,* Chapman and Hall, London, p. 41.
22   Moylan (1989), op. cit., p. 54. The term is now almost forgotten.
23   Comparisons made with British resorts are partly based upon the author's acquaintance with the North Wales and Lancashire seaside towns in the last, post-1945, decades of their heyday.
24   O'Sullivan, op. cit., pp. 53-4.
25   See Gaskin, J.J. (1869), *Varieties of Irish History,* William Kelly, Dublin, illustration facing p. 313.
26   Except where otherwise stated, facts for the period 1854-1914 are taken from Charles J. Coghlan's MS compilation of items referring to north-east Co. Wicklow in the *Freeman's Journal* (1774-1884), the *Wicklow Newsletter* (1885-1910) and the *Wicklow People* (1910-1914), Bray Public Library.
27   Even so, it was not as impressive as the pavilion in Kingstown/Dún Laoghaire; see, for instance, photograph of Kingstown 689 W.L., Lawrence Collection, National Library of Ireland (NLI).
28   *Freeman's Journal,* 30 May 1855; Powell, G.R. (1860), *The Official Railway Handbook to Bray,* M'Glashan & Gill, Dublin, pp. 13-14; see also Ordnance Survey (1870), Bray town plan, scale 1:500.
29   *Freeman's Journal,* 1 Jan. 1863; see 'International Hotel, Bray', 457 W.L. Lawrence Collection, NLI, reproduced in O'Sullivan et al., op. cit., p. 125.
30   Census of Ireland.
31   Ordnance Survey (1870), op. cit.
32   Moylan (1989), op. cit., p. 56.
33   So easy, in fact, that there was nothing remarkable in making the journey four times a day. According to his unpublished diaries (1839-83), Phineas Riall of Old Connaught frequently returned to his home, two kilometres from the nearest railway station, for lunch. There were twenty-eight trains a day in the winter of 1867, and the journey by express took half an hour; see *Freeman's Journal,* 13 Nov. 1867.

34 *Freeman's Journal,* 8 April 1861.
35 Bray adopted the Towns Improvement Act (Ireland) 1854, in 1867. The re-
    lationship between the township commissioners and private sector interests
    was complex; William Dargan was a commissioner until his death in 1867 and
    Edward Breslin remained active until 1897. For a preliminary study see Moylan
    (1972), op. cit., pp. 60-91.
36 *Dublin Builder,* **viii** (1 Nov. 1866): 268.
37 Certainly the wooden palisade shown on an 1860s postcard as the only defence
    at the north end of the beach (O'Sullivan et al., op. cit., p. 126) cannot have
    been effective.
38 Marine Station Hotel, Bray, 468 W.L. Lawrence Collection, NLI.
39 Moylan (1989), op. cit., p. 57.
40 *Freeman's Journal,* 16 February 1877.
41 *Freeman's Journal,* 21 May 1875; see also Mary Davies, 'Flower Shows in Bray,
    County Wicklow, 1863-1888', *Moorea,* **v** (1986): 7-9.
42 *Freeman's Journal,* 8 March 1876.
43 See Adamson, S.M. (1977, reprinted 1983), *Seaside Piers,* Batsford, London,
    in association with the Victorian Society. Even minor resorts in Great Britain
    aspired to a pier and major ones such as Blackpool and Brighton built two
    or three. Seaside piers were and are commercial propositions, with an entrance
    fee, providing 'all the advantages of going to sea with none of the attendant
    dangers or discomfort' (ibid., p. 22). The stone-built harbour piers at
    Kingstown/Dún Laoghaire, although different in many respects, offer the
    nearest equivalent experience.
44 Doran, A.L. (1903, facsimile reprint 1985), *Bray and Environs,* A.L. Doran,
    Bray; Frank Porter (1910), *Porter's Post Office Guide and Directory of the
    County of Wicklow 1910,* Cahill & Co., Dublin, pp. 1-72; Ordnance Survey
    (1909), Co. Wicklow sheet 4 xiii & xiv, scale 1:2500.
45 For an entertaining account of a visit to Bray and a sojourn in the International
    Hotel in August 1947, see S.P.B. Mais (1984), *I Return to Ireland,* Christopher
    Johnson, London.
46 It would be interesting to know the proportion of non-Irish to Irish visitors
    at different periods; certainly it was a tradition up to the late 1960s for many
    holidaymakers from Scotland to visit Bray.
47 Gaskin, op. cit., p. 313.
48 A satirical article in *The Leader* of 17 Aug. 1901 (p. 396) called Greystones
    'Rathmines-super-Mare', and snobbishly castigated the throngs on Bray's
    seafront as shop girls and housemaids putting on airs in an atmosphere of
    'real waves and imitation quality'.

PART II
Tourist Images and Representations

3

Fellow Travellers: Contemporary Travel Writing and Ireland

Michael Cronin

> Amer savoir, celui qu'on tire du voyage!
> Charles Baudelaire, *Le Voyage*
>
> No one can write about Ireland without getting into trouble.
> Halliday Sutherland, *Irish Journey*

Introduction

'I am assuming that travel is now impossible and that tourism is all we have left. Travel implies variety of means and independence of arrangements.'[1] The magisterial pessimism of Paul Fussell in *Abroad: British Literary Travelling between the Wars* is more affecting than accurate. The American critic's work first appeared in 1980 at the beginning of a decade that would witness the dramatic disproof of his gloomy diagnosis. Bruce Chatwin, Paul Theroux, Jonathan Raban, Lisa St Aubin de Terán, Dervla Murphy, Jan Morris demonstrated that epitaphs make for poor criticism in works that retained the formless unpredictability of exploration alongside the ironic self-awareness of contemporary tourism. The mediation between tourism and exploration that Fussell believed characterised the golden age of travel[2] did not end with chartered air travel but has on the contrary renewed itself in a latter-day revival of travel writing.[2] Ireland as a destination for modern travel writers has been an interesting beneficiary of the attentions of those whom Fussell had consigned to the oblivion of the prosaic.

For centuries Ireland has been a point of departure and a point of arrival. From the *iomramh* to the *navigatio* to the Tour, travellers in search of salvation, instruction or the godsend of novelty have either left the island or landed on it, tracking the signs of specificity. However, movement in the eyes of a settled community is rarely innocent. If Henry Mayhew believed that the London poor bore all the traits of uncivilised nomads even down to the anatomical detail of larger jawbones,[3] it is significant that the generally agreed term for Ireland's most despised minority is 'Travellers'. Travel writers who come to Ireland are therefore regarded with a mixture of awe and suspicion, an ambivalence which is often reciprocated by the writers themselves in their accounts of journeying through modern Ireland. What is surprising, however, is not the ambivalence but the initiative.

Strategies of Renewal

Ireland, it could be argued, has lost that sense of remoteness which drew Carlyle, Thackeray, Latocnaye, Nicholson and Young to the island in previous centuries. Jonathan Swift's eighteenth-century fictional traveller was already sensitive to the writer's difficulty in investing the *déjà-vu* with the appeal of the new and avoiding the dangers of unintentional plagiarism. Gulliver observes, 'I thought this account of the *Struldbruggs* might be some entertainment to the Reader, because it seems to be a little out of the Common Way; at least I do not remember to have met the like in any Book of Travels that hath come to my Hands: And if I am deceived, my excuse must be, that it is necessary for Travellers, who describe the same Country, very often to agree in dwelling on the same Particulars, without deserving the Censure of having borrowed or transcribed from those that wrote before them.'[4]

In the period since 1945 the books of travels on Ireland have continued to come out in ever increasing frequency and the strategies of renewal of the Irish theme in travel are as various as the books themselves. These strategies might be loosely grouped into the thematic, the exotic and the existential, though they rarely appear in pure form in travel accounts. To the category of the thematic belong Dervla Murphy's *A Place Apart* (1978), Colm Tóibín's *Walking Along the Border* (1987) and Peter Somerville-Large's *The Grand Irish Tour* (1982).[5] By choosing a particular theme, the North, the Border, Anglo-Irish Ireland, it is possible to enliven political or historical abstractions with geographical and human realities which in their turn are seen differently through the viewfinder of the chosen theme. A subset of the thematic is the modal. Here, it is primarily the mode of transport which defines the account as different. Examples are Eric Newby on a bicycle in *Around Ireland in Low Gear* (1987), Rosita Boland hitch-hiking in *Sea-Legs, Hitching the Coast of Ireland Alone* (1992) and John M. Feehan sailing in *The Magic of the Kerry Coast* (1979).[6] The category of the exotic is more inclusive and difficult to define but it is principally centred on difference, how the Irish or Ireland differ from other people and places. Gary Hogg's *Turf Beneath My Feet* (1950), Charles Graves's *Ireland Revisited* (1949), Halliday Sutherland's *Irish Journey* (1956) and Heinrich Böll's *Irisches Tagebuch* (1957) could be said to belong to this category.[7] However, as we shall see throughout this essay, the 'exotic' is an element present in all travel accounts.

The third category, the existential, is what Jean-Claude Guillebaud calls the 'soliloquy-voyage'. Guillebaud argues, 'This time, the literary subject-matter, the subject that is celebrated is no longer really travel but the various torments, desires and heartaches of the traveller.'[8] Travel is less an exploration of the other country than an investigation of the self. The text exploits the metaphorical appropriateness of travel with the notion of life as a journey from cradle to tomb to examine the traveller's own inner wanderings. A number of contemporary foreign-language travel accounts tend towards this existential form, accounts such as Louis Gauthier's *Voyage en Irlande avec un parapluie* (1984) or Giuseppe Conte's *Terre del Mito* (1991).[9] It is interesting to note that whereas in English-language accounts the existential element does appear it is far less obviously present than in foreign-language travel writing. This may be due in part to questions of language which can be considered alongside the relationship of the visual to writing in Irish travel accounts.

The Spectacle of Travel: Responses to the Visual

John Urry in *The Tourist Gaze: Leisure and Travel in Contemporary Societies* proposes a number of minimal characteristics to describe the set of social practices that are commonly referred to as tourism. Among these characteristics he lists the manner in which the tourist gaze is directed to landscapes or townscapes that are set off from ordinary experience and defined in some way as out of the ordinary. He goes on to say, 'The viewing of such tourist sights often involves different forms of social patterning, with a much greater sensitivity to visual elements of landscape or townscape than is normally found in everyday life. People linger over such a gaze which is then normally objectified or captured through photographs, postcards, films, models and so on.'[10] Perception is also a form of control and implicit in the notion of 'gaze' is the Foucauldian sense of seeing as culturally determined and politically coercive (see article by Nash in the present volume). Sara Mills in *Discourses of Difference: An Analysis of Women's Travel Writing and Colonialism* notes that 'in travel writing the narrator gazes at the "natives" — and is irritated if they have the temerity to gaze back'.[11] It has indeed become customary to think of travel writing in terms of the primacy of the visual, the spectacular exoticism of the unfamiliar (and misunderstood), the 'sensitivity to visual elements' a founding article of Orientalist faith as exemplified in the writings of Gautier, Fromentin, Loti and Nerval in the last century.

The relationship to the visual, however, is a lot more problematic than many post-colonial analyses suggest. In the case of Ireland, the objects of the travellers' gaze in contemporary travel writing are constantly being redefined. The Italian writer Giuseppe Conte opens his account of his Irish travels by declaring, 'Galway could not be called a beautiful city, if in a city we are accustomed to giving pride of place to works of art, buildings, streets'.[12] Eric and Wanda Newby are not impressed by the interior decoration of Malachy's Bar in Quin, Co. Clare but Newby reflects, 'Its occupants were kind and welcoming and I realized that if we were going to equate aesthetics with happiness while travelling through Ireland we might just as well give up and be miserable in the comfort of our own lovely home.'[13] An attention to the material fabric of Irish life invites aesthetic disappointment so the focus shifts to the landscape but here too travellers encounter difficulties. Garry Hogg finds that Ireland takes him in thrall but his problem is locating a vocabulary for the magic. He declares wistfully, 'The day of the purple passage in prose (as in verse) has passed; though amid so much aridity of expression some of us would be prepared to welcome its return.'[14] He imagines describing Irish landscapes in different coloured inks, soft blues, greens and reds. The Irish writer Peter Somerville-Large uses a much more sombre palate to describe a landscape scarred by the flotsam of modernity, 'I went back to Carrick by the tannery where effluvia from the slaughterhouse stank, pieces of torn plastic were scattered by the wind and rusty cans showed brown among the weeds.'[15]

These differing responses to the visual highlight a number of constants in contemporary travel writing on Ireland. Firstly, cities and particularly Dublin are largely either ignored or condemned on account of what is perceived as their visual poverty. One has to go back to Charles Graves's *Ireland Revisited* to find an unashamedly benign view of the capital (another exception is Jan Morris's essay on Dublin in *Among the Cities* (1985)).[16] This visual deficit has interesting consequences. Conte's view of Galway city is utterly transformed by his readings in Celtic mythology so that swans gathering or salmon leaping invest the city with sacred significance. In Dublin, he mourns his inability to respond to a dull, maritime city of the North and remarks, 'I thought how everything would have been different if I had been a Joycean. I wouldn't have found the city of Leopold Bloom, Stephen Dedalus and Molly Bloom so insignificant.'[17] Therefore, Ireland does not invite passivity. If the outer eye is to find satisfaction in urban surroundings or indeed in the scatterings of stones described as national monuments, then the inner eye must be invoked to supply the missing dimension of fiction, myth, history that transforms a reality that disappoints. Paul Fussell sees this act of restitution as at the heart of serious travel writing, 'Supplying the missing dimension is exactly what real travel used to require.'[18]

The second point concerning the visual is the appropriate response to landscape. There is the practical problem of the rain which falls steadily throughout most post-war Irish travel accounts and veils the promised beauty of hill and lake. The French-Canadian writer Louis Gauthier's plaintive comment, 'It's raining, it's raining, it's raining, it's interminable' is a common refrain. [19] However, even when the sun breaks through there is a threat of the picture postcard, the tourism advertisement, the promotion video which makes the travel writer in Ireland nervous. In a review of Rosita Boland's travel account, Mary Russell takes the writer to task for her occasional lapses into a 'tourist-brochure style', a criticism that is often anticipated by the ironic evasiveness of descriptions of scenery.[20] Newby describes Poulnaclough Bay in Co. Clare with 'water in it like steel, with the mountains black above it and above that cobalt clouds against an otherwise pale sky in which Venus was suspended'. He immediately qualifies this passage with a distancing comment, 'When it comes to thoroughly unnatural effects it is possible to equal Ireland, difficult to surpass it.' This comment is in turn further qualified by a footnote where Newby wonders what Evelyn Waugh would have made of the scene. He quotes Waugh on a sunset over Mount Etna, 'Nothing I have seen in Art or Nature was quite so revolting.'[21] The distancing irony of what John Urry refers to as the 'post-tourist' aligns itself here with the humorous scepticism of inter-war English travel writing to protect the writer from the uncritical hyperbole of advertising copy.[22]

Another possible response to scenery is a determined anti-romanticism. This is a bleaker form of post-romantic disillusion where the reality of the foreign land is always at variance with the traveller's imaginative anticipation.[23] Louis Gauthier details the December rain falling and declares, 'The Emerald Isle ... poets who are stuck for symbols. Ireland is grey, black and brown. Existence is not symbolic, it's dull and cold, damp and demoralising.'[24] Somerville-Large describes his approach to Killala in Co. Mayo, 'The first sight of Killala was the Asahi complex, a lot of big grey sheds spreadeagled across a hill, chimneys that rivalled Killala's round tower, a vast parking area crammed with cars and a golf course.'[25] Ireland's very popularity as a destination for travel writers means that it must of necessity generate an anti-romantic tradition that subverts what are imagined to be stock responses to 'natural' beauty, itself a construct of the romantic gaze.

The third point that emerges in an examination of the place of the visual in travel accounts of Ireland is that description increasingly gives way to dialogue. A striking difference between Hogg's account published in 1950 and Newby's which appeared in 1987 or Roy Kerridge's *Jaunting through Ireland* (1991)[26] is the increasing reluctance to detail the scenic backdrop to their Irish journeys. This reticence is in part due to competing claims of postcards, television, cinema and coffee-table picture books to cater for the visual presentation of Ireland and its people (or often preferably the landscape without its people). Thus, travel writing on Ireland is in fact less about post-modern spectacle and more to do with a highly developed sense of theatricality that has long been a feature of what is defined above as the exotic travel account. Margaret Sabin writing on D.H. Lawrence's use of dramatic narratives in *Sea and Sardinia* alludes to Henry James's remarks on the drama of travel, 'Henry James, in *Italian Hours*, suggests that to travel anywhere is, "as it were, to go to the play, to attend a spectacle", especially among the Italians who show, at least to the foreign spectator, such an "enviable ability not to be depressed by circumstances"'.[27] James acknowledges, however, in Sabin's words that 'it is the privilege and presumption of the tourist to take in the human misadventures of a foreign scene with the indifferent frivolity of a play-goer.'[28] The Irish are in fact described by Charles Graves as the 'Spaniards of the north' and like James's Italians are seen to be possessed of an innate theatricality which is, however, more verbal than gestural.[29] One of Graves's set-pieces is a four-page transcript of what his driver Mackey assures him is a typical piece of haggling at an Irish cattle fair. The purpose of dramatic dialogue appears to be two-fold. On the one hand, it confers authenticity on the account and on the other, it is obviously intended to provide comic relief. For English visitors such as Graves, Kerridge and Newby, Irish playacting is comic rather than tragic. Furthermore, the intrinsic burlesque of encounters with the natives is intimately bound up with the nature of Hiberno-English and the pitfalls of translation.

Language Games, Translation and Feminisation

The Irish, like Oscar Wilde's Americans, would seem to have everything in common with the English except language. Eric Newby is told by a Miss Boylan to watch the traffic on Sarsfield Bridge on the way out of Limerick, 'Be careful, now, on the Sarsfield Bridge, for there are a whole lot of people blown off their cycles on it every year by the wind of the lorries and *kilt*!'.[30]

Newby italicises the last word and defends his reproduction of Irish speech in a footnote, 'For those who find my attempts at reproducing fragments of Irish English unacceptable, I can only plead that this is what they sound like to me. What my own fruity accent sounded like to them can only be a matter of conjecture.'[31] Newby finds a somewhat unlikely defender of this practice in Dervla Murphy. Travelling through Tipperary on her way to Northern Ireland she stops in a pub where one man discusses the cost of going to Lourdes, 'You'd want a fierce amounta cash goin'out to them places these times. Th'oul pound's worth nathin' no more.' Murphy comments, 'English writers who report such turns of speech are sometimes wrongly accused of stage Irishry.'[32] It is interesting to note, however, that in the rest of the book, except in isolated instances, Murphy does not reproduce accents. Peter Somerville-Large similarly refrains from reporting real or imagined pronunciation in reported speech.

Newby's defence is plausible and Hiberno-English accents in all probability sounded to Graves and Newby as they transcribe them on the page. On the other hand, language and varieties of speech exist in contexts that are rarely innocent. Thus, when the Newbys meet two Dublin students in a Galway bed-and-breakfast Newby observes that 'the air fairly rang with the "I tinks" and "I tought" of these hopes for the future of Ireland.'[33] The juxtaposition of these Irish students and highlighted examples of incorrect pronunciation creates an effect of comic condescension. It also gives succour to enduring stereotypes of the Irish as genial but stupid. Language is a much neglected area of travel writing criticism which often emphasises the biographical or the socio-political elements through visual metaphors but speech and its contexts, as we saw in the examples above, are also powerful carriers of implied meanings.

All travel can be seen as an act of translation. In the geometrical sense, the traveller is 'translated' or moved from one point to another. In the linguistic sense, travel can involve inter-lingual translation, speaking a foreign language in another country, or intra-lingual translation, speaking the same language but in a different country. In addition, there are intellectual and emotional acts of translation, converting the experiences of the other place and people into the traveller's own native currency. If English travellers are sensitive to lexical differences that call for intra-lingual translation, words such as 'yoke', 'ass-cart', 'butt'(of a hill), non-anglophone travellers are faced by the more daunting task of inter-lingual translation. Giuseppe Conte appears to have abandoned any attempt at communicating with the Irish which must explain the more intensely private and 'existential' nature of his account. In the absence of dramatic narrative, he favours mythico-historical speculation on selected sites. Heinrich Böll appears less disadvantaged linguistically and positively delights in Irish expressions referring to time. Louis Gauthier is a willing interpreter but finds himself defeated by the rate of the source-language output. He encounters an Irishman on the ferry to Ireland who buys him a drink, 'I don't really understand what he's saying but that doesn't seem to matter very much.'[34] In Cork he meets a woman who gives him directions and tells him about her husband in Canada, 'She tells me the whole story at breakneck speed, something about her husband over there. I can't get a word in edgeways to stop this verbal outpouring and explain to her there are bits I can't follow. She is not even looking at me.' [35]

The last example is significant for two reasons. Firstly, it suggests that travel accounts differ less for cultural than linguistic reasons. That is, the ability to understand or not understand a language will, more than social, political, philosophical prejudices, determine the form of travel account produced. Secondly, it raises the question of the feminisation of host cultures. Contemporary travel writers to Ireland are almost all agreed that the Irish talk a great deal and indeed Newby dedicates his book to the Irish whom he describes as the 'Eighth Walking (and Talking) Wonders of the World'. This garrulousness accounts for the much-quoted humour and verbal inventiveness of their Irish hosts. Women have also been characterised in patriarchal mythology as being typically loquacious, gossiping endlessly about trivia. In Gauthier's example, the two images fuse; interestingly, academic critics such as David Cairns and Shaun Richards make much of the identification between Ireland and women in colonialist and national thinking. [36] The incessant chatter of the female was seen as proof of her profound duplicity. Sara Mills argues that this deceitfulness was one of the traits women shared in common with Africans in imperialist travel accounts of the last century: 'It is true that the way women and Africans were discussed is similar: simple, childlike, deceitful, passive, not capable of intellectual thought, and more closely allied to nature.' [37]

Charles Graves declares that 'the Irish are more illogical than the men and more intuitive than the women of any other nation in the world.' [38] More feminine than females, they are consequently more unreliable. Gary Hogg, looking for a logan stone near the Gap of Dunloe, asks some pony drivers if they knew of its whereabouts but notes balefully, 'The pony drivers like most Irishmen I met, had told me what they did because they knew it was what I wanted to hear.' [39] Eric Newby, almost forty years later, finds the advice of locals maddingly misleading in his search for Ballyline House in Co. Clare, 'I felt my reason going. Perhaps, it had, already. Was I already one with the great Gaels of Ireland, the men that made God mad, as most of the other Gaels I had met on this, my first day in Ireland, appeared to be.' [40] Hence, the very loquacity of the Irish makes them suspect. Illogical, intuitive and possibly crazy, they have a characteristically female attitude to language and truth, spendthrift with the former and economical with the latter. The Irish as the objects of the contemporary travel writer's gaze find themselves in something of a double bind. If they say nothing, they are regarded as surly, distant and unwelcoming whereas if they start talking, anything they say is to be treated with due scepticism. Jonathan Culler sees tourism as a branch of the semiotics, the science of signs, claiming, 'All over the world the unsung armies of semioticians, the tourists, are fanning out in search of the signs of Frenchness, typical Italian behaviour, exemplary oriental scenes, typical American thruways, traditional English pubs.' [41] The travelling semioticians in Ireland might indeed redefine their discipline as the science of signposts as these embody for many travel writers the archetypal female treachery of their effusive hosts. Joyce, as they discover, is not the only Irishman to play with signs.

The Rare Ould Times

Discourse theory sees all texts as the products of multiple constraints, influenced by the various discourses in circulation at the time of their production. Mills sees the intertextuality of travel accounts as exemplary proof of the appropriateness of discourse theory in any study of travel literature, 'Most travel writers portray members of the other nation through the conceptual and textual grid constituted by travel books.'[42] The evidence of post-war travel accounts on Ireland would suggest, however, that the specific intertextuality of travel writing varies greatly from its almost total absence in the accounts of Gauthier, Hogg and Sutherland to its overwhelming presence in the work of the Irish travel writer, Peter Somerville-Large. The degree of intertextuality has interesting consequences for the general thrust or perspective of a travel account.

Somerville-Large, inspired by eighteenth and nineteenth-century travel accounts of Ireland, sets out on a grand tour of Anglo-Irish Ireland. Quoting copiously from the accounts, he journeys from Big House to Big House or to what remains of them. Everywhere he travels he find evidence of the persistent decay of post-Independence Ireland which compares unfavourably with the bright industriousness of the nineteenth-century Big House. Tourism, native neglect and modernity blight the present so that when he arrives in Cork city he notes wistfully, 'My absorption in nineteenth-century travellers coated my impressions with the varnish of the past. I found that the traffic snarl-ups, the acres of new suburbs, the new glass County Hall, the new hospital, the hamburger heavens and chain stores could not disperse the shadows lingering among shabby terraces of Montenotte or the narrow climbing streets of Shandon.'[43] Many of the houses mentioned in the accounts of the last century are in ruins. Somerville-Large's reaction is not one of romantic reverence but of dismay. In this he is akin to Waugh whom Martin Stannard sees as in thrall to illustrious pasts, 'One senses that even in *Labels* he is writing not so much about the exciting possibilities of the future as the relentless decay of what was valuable in the past.'[44] The presence of ruins is less an occasion for romantic reverie than an indictment of native fecklessness, illustrated for Somerville-Large by the Land Commission's treatment of Bleach House in Villierstown. Mills, along with Edward Said and Mary Louise Pratt, claims that the Western convention for writing about ruins was to reduce present-day societies to remains of a once glorious past.[45] Obviously, the greater the intertextual pressure, the greater the temptation to see the present as the degraded remnant of an irretrievably magnificent past. It is to this extent that travel writing which is often thought of as the literature of escape, risk, adventure can in fact be a deeply conservative genre, a literature of entropy. Here, earlier travel accounts are invoked as markers against which the paltry pretensions of the present are judged.

Ruins are not givens. Like sites or views they are constructs, selected for observation on the basis of political, social or cultural criteria that change with circumstances.[46] Conte and Hogg choose the ruins of Ireland's Celtic and pre-Celtic past, Graves and Somerville-Large are drawn to the remnants of the country's Anglo-Irish heritage. The ruins that Dervla Murphy observes in Belfast and Derry are more recent but already they are historicised by the duration of the conflict, the sense of no return. If travel involves deciphering people and landscapes, ruins are part of the code but the writer's selection of one type of ruin rather than another involves a retroactive commentary on contemporary Ireland, implicit in the decision to apply one grid rather than another to break the code of the present. Eric Newby, cycling near Rosscarbery Bay, spots a dilapidated building, 'a gimcrack motel with forty rooms and with broken windows for sale, already an Irish ruin.'[47] Fortunately for Newby and other travel writers Irish ruins are plentiful and in constant supply for the exegetical exploits of travellers.

Distance, Time and Digression

Space and time are two fundamental dimensions of movement. The journey over land can be a movement forwards or backwards in time, a speculative glimpse of the future (Baudrillard in America) or a vision of times past. As if obeying an unstated law of relativity for travel, the actual position of the observer determines how s/he will situate the host culture on the axis of time (see article by O'Connor in the present volume). Johannes Fabian sees the co-ordinates of the observer's position as inherently political, he 'states that travel writers and anthropologists consign the other nation to a time which is distant from their own, through the use of words with temporal aspects such as "primitive", "backward" or "developing".'[48] It would be incorrect, however, to see this phenomenon in travel writing on Ireland as a strict corollary of a colonial or post-colonial relationship. The French-Canadian writer Louis Gauthier notes people in Dublin who make the sign of the cross when they pass by churches and comments, 'You'd think you were back in Quebec in 1954.'[49] When he meets a British businessman who claims that the pace of life in the city had been much slower fifteen years previously, Gauthier exclaims, 'Slower? What must it have been like back then. I already have the impression that I am travelling back into the past.'[50] Charles Graves finds etymology revealing. When a young man in Enniscorthy compliments Graves's chauffeur on his car saying, "'Tis a fine yoke ye have', the writer responds by linking language and time, 'That single word shows how slowly time passes in County Wexford, dating straight back to the days of the oxen.'[51] The method of distancing through time can be internalised as becomes apparent in Dervla Murphy's comment on a part of Co. Cavan, 'Near here cows were being milked into buckets in the fields. My own part of Ireland was like this forty years ago.'[52] Thus, an Irish, British and Canadian travel writer all experience this temporal disjuncture in different forms. There is a sense in which the presentness of the past is less to do with the imperialist convictions of narrators who judge other cultures by the triumphant progress of the colonist's culture than with the very nature of travel writing itself as illustrated by the case of Ireland.

Fussell states that the space/time metaphor is central to the appeal of travel writing as a genre, 'Like no other kind of writing, travel books exercise and exploit the fundamental intellectual and emotional figure of thought by which the past is conceived as back and the future as forward. They manipulate the whole alliance between the temporal and the spatial that we use to orient ourselves in time by invoking the dimension of space.'[53] Hogg's marvelling at a primitive wheel in Co. Kerry or Newby's interest in the antiquity of agricultural implements used by farm labourers should not be seen solely as examples of amused condescension. Temporal distancing is part of a much larger preoccupation with time and its configurations in Ireland. Heinrich Böll's fascination with the Irish notion that when God made time he made plenty of it endures in countless postwar travel accounts as a strong belief that time is ordered differently in Ireland. Whether this belief has any basis in reality is almost irrelevant insofar as its popularity is addressing other needs.

Travel in Ireland is an 'extra-ordinary' experience. This experience is represented spatially by descriptions of landscape, Hogg's purple prose and Newby's 'unnatural effects', and temporally by repeated references to the Irish indifference to punctuality. Charles Graves claims that 'you are "within your rights" if you arrive a quarter of an hour early or a quarter of an hour late for the most important business interview. The Irish, in fact, do not believe in saving time or wasting time. Both phrases are entirely outside their philosophy. They believe in using time and refuse to be the slaves of time.'[54] Ireland's specificity is not simply spatial (landscape) but temporal. The edge of Europe is seen as a refuge from the tyranny of timepieces (though the downside is exasperation with the disorganisation that can result from a cavalier attitude to arrangements). In this sense, Irish travel runs counter to the linear time and the chronological order of the medieval pilgrimage which Christoph Wulf sees as prefiguring the rise of 'la chronocratie'.[55] This 'chronocracy', the hegemony of linear, unidirectional time in the post-Renaissance West, is subverted by the digressive, anarchic disrespect for its imperatives in daily life in Ireland. In this respect, the very nature of Irish life as perceived by contemporary travellers matches the rhetorical strategies of travel writing itself. If guidebooks describe, travel books digress. It is in the nature of the comment, digressing endlessly to take in history, economics, politics, art, literature, personal anecdote, that travel accounts reveal their art. The adventures and misadventures that befall travellers before their return home are themselves a series of digressions from the stated objective of the journey, to travel as directly as possible from one point to another and back again. Thus, the peripeteia of incident are paralleled by the wanderings of narrative, shifting between description, comment and speculation. Hence, the Irish failure to espouse the linear logic of Newtonian time makes the country eminently suitable for the itinerant gaze of the travel writer.

Political Journeys

A traditional function of travel literature from Mandeville's *Travels* to Gide's *Voyage au Congo* has been to look critically at the writer's country or culture. Writers in the eighteenth century use real or imagined travel accounts to highlight the damaging ethnocentrism of Western beliefs and introduce the subversive scepticism of cultural relativism.[56] Internal travel, Orwell on his way to Wigan Pier and external travel, Paul Nizan and André Gide in Africa of the 1930s, in this century have often been a vehicle for savage indictments of political abuses and colonial brutality originating within Western Europe.

    Post-war travel writers on Ireland vary greatly in their response to travel as a form of political commentary. In more recent accounts, any references to political questions are dominated by the Northern crisis. Indeed, two accounts, Colm Tóibín's *Walking Along The Border* and Dervla Murphy's *A Place Apart* are born out of a desire to arrive at an understanding of the conflict through travel. Mills argues that women travel writers in the nineteenth century differed from their male counterparts in their attitude to the objects of the colonial gaze, 'Because of their oppressive socialisation and marginal position in relation to imperialism, despite their generally privileged class position, women writers tended to concentrate on descriptions of people as individuals, rather than on statements about the race as a whole.'[57] Murphy, in the foreword to her Northern travel account, appears to situate herself in this gender-specific tradition by distancing herself from the investigative empiricism of previous writing on the North, 'It is not a study of history, politics, theology, geography, sociology, economics or guerilla warfare. It is simply an honest portrayal of emotions — my own and other people's — and an attempt to find the sources of these emotions.'[58] Twentieth-century Ireland is not nineteenth-century India or Africa, however, and the combination of individual description and general statement is equally present in the accounts of both Tóibín and Murphy. If anything, indeed, Dervla Murphy's account is more concerned with attempting to draw a number of broad conclusions about the origins and nature of the Northern conflict based, of course, on personal encounters but also on the books of history, sociology and politics listed in the bibliography. It is in this respect that her writing is closer to Helena Sheehan's vision of a new rationality where emotion and reason are not seen as mutually exclusive antitheses with women as custodians/prisoners of the former, 'It is a definition of rational of which the opposite is not emotional but irrational. It is rationality transcending the existing division of labour. It is reason, which is no longer specifically masculine, organically connected to emotion, which is no longer specifically feminine.'[59] Travel accounts may, in fact prefigure the feminist renegotiation with reason that would bring alive the intelligence of emotions and make apparent the emotional drama of the intellect.

Murphy's eagerness to understand the causes of political violence in the North is not shared by many other contemporary travel writers on Ireland. Eric Newby, after issuing a disclaimer similar to Murphy's then refers to political events in Ireland as a kind of comic misadventure, 'We were not going to travel in the guise of sociologists, journalists or contemporary historians. I was unlikely to write a book called *Whither Ireland?* or *Ireland Now.* We were not going there, we hoped, to be shot at.'[60] The North, he feels, can wait. Gary Hogg displays a similar reluctance to get involved in political analysis and is proud of the fact that he resisted attempts in Co. Sligo to make him pay more than he should for eggs and get embroiled in a discussion about partition. He ultimately prefers geology to history but as an English traveller is acutely sensitive to any demonstration of hostility. Grafitti seen on a wall outside Galway, 'Boycott the British', sours his whole experience of the city and seems to emphasise further the alien character of Connemara. Charles Graves meets the then Taoiseach of Ireland, John A. Costello, but rather than detailing Costello's political background or beliefs, he reports that the principal subject of discussion was the tragedy of the 1948 alterations to the Portmarnock golf course. The denial of political contexts has curious consequences. Travel writers repeatedly comment on the emptiness of the Irish countryside which is presented as a geological given. When emigration is occasionally mentioned, it too has the character of a natural Irish phenomenon like strong wind and rain and there are few attempts to explain the historical or political origins of the desertion of the Irish countryside. The naturalisation of politics is by no means only a feature of English travel writing. Somerville-Large meets a group of fishermen from Lancashire and declares, 'They had travelled all the way over in a bus from Rochdale to Belturbet and now sat in great contentment ignoring rain and border politics.'[61] The problems of Ireland are as natural as rain falling and as dispiriting. Meteorology and history mingle and the result is that discord and dissent become part of a landscape that is as immutable and ancient as stone.

The view from beyond the islands is also coloured by Northern filters. Neither Conte nor Gauthier expresses any interest in the politics of the Republic except insofar as they relate to the situation in the North. Gauthier learns his first words of Irish from an electrician whom he suspects rather fancifully to be involved with the Provisional IRA, 'he is speaking to me at last the way you should speak to foreigner whose only desire is to learn: the IRA, the atrocities that are a daily occurrence in Northern Ireland.'[62] There is no interest in explaining to the reader the circumstances of political crisis and the encounter with the electrician is offered more by way of colourful anecdote than illustrative evidence. Conte reflects at greater length on the implications of protest in Ireland during his stay in Galway. He arrived in Ireland in 1981 in the middle of the hunger strikes and witnesses a silent protest in Galway after the death of Thomas McIlwee. He contrasts his experience of the Italian Left in the 1970s with Irish Republican politics and claims, 'I found myself for the first time face to face with a language in which political passion was also poetic.'[63] Conte cites as an example of this fusion of political and poetic passions, Bobby Sands's diary. However, he does not situate the hunger strikes in their precise historical moment but sees them as continuing a mythico-ritual tradition practised by Irish druids and Indian Brahmins. Indeed, Conte argues that he is beginning to understand Ireland's struggle through the 'spiritual legacy of its legends'.[64] Thus, Irish politics leaves history and enters the realm of the mythical, a transcendental entity that is essentially the stuff of spiritual fictions. The sentimental traveller is less concerned with attributing cause or offering explanation as assimilating the political experiences of travel into an intensely private catalogue of impression and conviction.

Conclusion

The purpose of this essay is to look at a number of post-1945 travel accounts of Ireland. The aim is not biographico-historical, to trace the changing fortunes of Ireland through the anecdotal illumination of the travel narrative but to consider the specificity of travel literature and how strategies of writing are related to experiences of Ireland. The pressure of intertextuality, questions of language and translation, the varying responses to the visual, the political, spatial and temporal dimensions of travel and the stratagems of renewal of the genre are among the aspects of travel literature on Ireland that we have discussed. The abundance of material not only in English but in other languages demands a necessary humility.[65] Questions such as the representations of the Irish language, the role of drink, the collective versus the romantic gaze, desire and sexual identity in travel accounts, the role of guidebooks, all invite comment and further research.[66] Jean-Didier Urbain speaks of the modern traveller's nightmare of degradation. The traveller as writer is cornered by the aggressive internationalisation and industrialisation of tourism, there is the painful 'dispossession of the symbolic territory of travel'.[67] Travellers in Ireland have seemed less conscious of their imminent extinction, of the threat of dispossession. There is no fear of the tyranny of repetition and the banality of precedent as they once again make their slow ascent up Croagh Patrick or head towards Dún Aengus under driving rain. The critics indeed have more to fear than the writers. It is important that travel writing on Ireland be re-annexed as the symbolic territory of literature rather than surrendered to history or journalism as an eloquent form of documentary witness. By recognising its difference, conventions and rhetorical devices, it then becomes possible to demonstrate how it triumphantly succeeds in giving 'universal significance to a local texture'.[68]

David Harvey sees changes in perceptions of space and time as the prerequisites of cultural evolution, 'Aesthetic and cultural practices are peculiarly susceptible to the changing experience of space and time precisely because they entail the construction of spatial representations and artefacts out of the flow of human experience. They always broker between Being and Becoming.'[69]

Brokerage implies transfer, movement and the history of modern travel in Ireland is intimately bound up with, among other things, differing notions of space and time and the negotiations between self and context. Implicit in the act of travel is that Being moves into a state of Becoming. It is in this dynamic, active sense that travel accounts are revealing. If writing is invariably associated with travel through postcards, letters home, the diary, it is partly because, as Fussell observes, the movement forwards is also a movement backwards. Writing on Ireland is, in this sense, travelling again, the recapitulation a second voyage that keeps the amnesia of return forever at bay.

NOTES AND REFERENCES

1   Paul Fussell (1982), *Abroad: British Literary Travelling Between the Wars,* Oxford University Press, New York, p. 41.
2   Fussell, p. 39.
3   Jonathan Raban (1988), *For Love and Money,* Picador, London, p. 68.
4   Jonathan Swift, *Gulliver's Travels,* vol. xi (revised ed.) in Jonathan Swift, *Prose Words,* ed. Herbert Davis et al. (1959), 16 vols., Blackwell, Oxford, p. 215.
5   Dervla Murphy (1978), *A Place Apart,* Penguin, Harmondsworth; Colm Tóibín (1987), *Walking Along the Border,* Queen Anne Press, London; Peter Somerville-Large (1982), *The Grand Irish Tour,* Hamish Hamilton, London.
6   Eric Newby (1987), *Round Ireland in Low Gear,* Viking, London; Rosita Boland (1992), *Sea-Legs; Hitching the Coast of Ireland Alone,* New Island, Dublin; John M. Feehan (1979), *The Magic of the Kerry Coast,* Mercier, Cork.

7   Gary Hogg (1950), *Turf Beneath My Feet*, Museum Press, London; Charles
    Graves (1949), *Ireland Revisited*, Hutchinson, London; Halliday Sutherland
    (1956), *Irish Journey*, Geoffrey Bles, London; Heinrich Böll (1957), *Irisches
    Tagebuch*, Kiepenheuer & Witsch, Köln.
8   Jean-Claude Guillebaud (1987), 'Une ruse de la littérature', *Traverses*, **41-2**:
    16. My translation.
9   Louis Gauthier (1984), *Voyage en Irlande avec un parapluie*, ULB, Montreál;
    Giuseppe Conte (1991), *Terre del Mito.* Mondadori, Milan.
10 John Urry (1990), *The Tourist Gaze: Leisure and Travel in Contemporary
    Societies,* Sage, London, p. 3.
11 Sara Mills (1991), *Discourses of Difference: An Analysis of Women's Travel
    Writing and Colonialism*, Routledge, London, p. 78.
12 Conte, op. cit., p. 9. My translation.
13 Newby, op. cit., p. 37.
14 Hogg, op. cit., p. 13.
15 Somerville-Large, op. cit., p. 67.
16 Graves (1949), op. cit.; Jan Morris (1986), *Among the Cities,* Penguin, Har-
    mondsworth, pp. 131-9.
17 Conte, op. cit., p. 14. My translation.
18 Fussell, op. cit., p. 45.
19 Gauthier, op. cit., p. 60.
20 Mary Russell (1992), 'Along the Edge', *The Irish Times,* 13 June 1992.
21 Newby, op. cit., p. 60.
22 Urry, op. cit., pp. 100-2.
23 For a discussion of post-Romantic disillusion see Margaret Sabin 'The Spec-
    tacle of Reality in *Sea and Sardinia*', in Philip Dodd (1982), *The Art of Travel:
    Essays on Travel Writing,* Frank Cass, London, pp. 85-6.
24 Gauthier, op. cit., p. 38. My translation.
25 Somerville-Large, op. cit., pp. 154-5.
26 Roy Kerridge (1991), *Jaunting through Ireland,* Michael Joseph, London.
27 Sabin, op. cit., p. 97.
28 ibid., p. 98.
29 Graves, op. cit., p. 18.
30 Newby, op. cit., p. 28.
31 ibid., p. 28.
32 Murphy, op. cit., p. 16.
33 Newby, op. cit., p. 250.
34 Gauthier, op. cit., p. 27. My translation.
35 ibid., p. 32.
36 See David Cairns and Shaun Richards (1988), *Writing Ireland: Colonialism,
    Nationalism and Culture,* Manchester University Press, Manchester, pp. 42-57.
37 Mills, op. cit., p. 90.
38 Graves, op. cit., p. 18.
39 Hogg, op. cit., p. 88.
40 Newby, op. cit., p. 47.
41 Jonathan Culler (1981), 'Semiotics of Tourism', *American Journal of Semiotics,*
    1: 127.
42 Mills, op. cit., p. 73.

43 Somerville-Large, op. cit., p. 52.
44 Martin Stannard, 'Debunking the Jungle: The Context of Evelyn Waugh's Travel Books 1930-9', in Philip Dodd (1982), op. cit., p. 112.
45 Mills, op. cit., p. 75; Edward Said (1973), *Orientalism,* Routledge Kegan Paul, London; M.L. Pratt (1985), 'Scratches on the Face of the Country: or what Mr Barrows saw in the Land of the Bushmen, *Critical Enquiry,* 12: 119-43.
46 See Urry, op. cit., pp. 20-1.
47 Newby, op. cit., p. 156.
48 Mills, op. cit., p. 89.
49 Gauthier, op. cit., p. 56. My translation.
50 ibid., p. 57. My translation.
51 Graves, op. cit., p. 69.
52 Murphy, op. cit., p. 19.
53 Fussell, op. cit., p. 210.
54 Graves, op. cit., p. 18
55 Christoph Wulf (1987), 'La Voie lactée', *Traverses,* 41-2: 124.
56 See Jenny Mezciems ' "Tis not to divert the Reader": Moral and Literary Determinants in Some Early Travel Narratives', in Dodd (1982), op. cit., pp. 5-6.
57 Mills (1991), op. cit., p. 3.
58 Murphy (1978), op. cit., p. 11.
59 Helena Sheehan (1992), 'The End of His Story', *Graph,* 12: 23.
60 Newby (1987), op. cit., p. ix.
61 Somerville-Large (1982), op. cit., p. 186.
62 Gauthier, op. cit., pp. 49-50.
63 Conte (1991), op. cit., p. 45. My translation.
64 ibid., p. 48. My translation.
65 Contemporary foreign travel accounts on Ireland are rarely translated into English. In this respect, Heinrich Böll's work is the exception rather than the rule. The absence of translations is presumably to do with assumptions made about the target audiences of travel accounts.
66 The image of Ireland in the modern travel literatures of Europe is to be the subject of a projected collective publication under the editorship of the author and Brian Rainey.
67 Jean-Didier Urbain (1987), 'Le Voyageur détroussé', *Traverses,* 41-2: 39.
68 Fussell, op. cit., p. 214.
69 David Harvey (1989), *The Condition of Postmodernity,* Blackwell, Oxford, p. 327.

The following works were also consulted in the preparation of this essay. C. Batten (1978), *Pleasurable Instruction: Form and Convention in Eighteenth-Century Travel Literature,* Univ. of California Press, Berkeley; S. Bochner, and A. Furnham (1989), *Culture Shock: Psychological Reactions to Unfamiliar Environments*, Routledge, London; M. Campbell (1989), *Writing about Travel,* A & C Black, London.

4

Myths and Mirrors: Tourist Images and National Identity

Barbara O'Connor

Questions and issues of national identity are of particular salience in a rapidly changing Europe — a Europe which is currently witnessing the processes of political fragmentation on the one hand and unification on the other. This climate of social and cultural flux and political re-alignment has major implications for the ways in which national identity is constantly being constructed and reconstructed within these boundaries. Irish society is no exception and is subject to social changes which will affect future constructions of cultural and national identity. Not least among these are the economic changes consequent on our membership of the European Community, specifically the emphasis given to the tourism sector as a target area of economic growth and the related production of tourist imagery for a growing European market.

Just as individual and personal identities are constructed through inter-action with others and determined largely by the ways in which we are perceived and treated by them, so too are cultural and national identities constructed from the representations which certain people both inside and outside our culture produce for us. The way in which we see ourselves is substantially determined by the way in which we are seen by others. Tourist images of Ireland and Irish people are just part of a panoply of other im-agery, political and social, which have diverse sources and which are influenced by a number of factors such as the historical relations with other countries and contemporary media representations amongst others. Tourist imagery can obviously vary in its effectiveness in determining identities in specific social and historical situations. In the case of Ireland, I would argue that it plays a significant role in providing a native self-image — a way of perceiving ourselves as an ethnic group and a way of relating to outsiders. There are a number of reasons why this is the case.

Firstly, Irish people have been exposed to tourist representations over a lengthy period of time, the country being involved in tourist promotion and development from the last century onwards. Since the Victorian era Ireland has been popularly regarded as a place of great natural beauty worthy of the traveller's gaze. Consequently it has occupied a central place in the Irish economy and has, to a large extent, been regarded as a panacea for economic problems. As far back as 1894, the first issue of *The Irish Tourist* expressed the hope that Ireland would 'attract multitudinous visitors to annually sojourn at our health and pleasure resorts, and thus leave us with that historic "plethora of wealth" which might act as a panacea for Ireland's ills'.[1] The same hope exists today as indicated by the amount of state funding going to tourism development (see Deegan and Dineen in this volume). The sustained and systematic state effort to develop tourism through national, regional and local initiatives (e.g. An Tóstal, the Tidy Towns Competition, the establishment of local speciality festivals such as the Wexford Opera Festival and the Galway Oyster Festival) has had the effect of making the majority of Irish people aware of the 'tourist gaze' and, hence, of the importance of their 'presentation of self' to others.

Secondly, there has always been a high level of contact between tourists and locals due to a combination of factors: the relatively small scale of the island and its population size, the nature and scale of many tourist services (e.g. bed-and-breakfast accommodation) and the large proportion of tourists who are in the 'visiting friends and relatives' category. This degree of interaction has helped to facilitate a local awareness of the ways in which they are constructed and perceived by outsiders.

The continuously abundant and widespread availability of visual tourist publicity on Ireland and the Irish must be acknowledged as influential in the available range of 'mirror images'. In fact, it has been argued that tourist imagery is the predominant form in Ireland. Gibbons, for instance, claims that 'the absence of a visual tradition in Ireland, equal in stature to its powerful literary counterpart, has meant that the dominant images of Ireland have, for the most part, emanated from outside the country, or have been produced at home with an eye on the foreign (or tourist) market.'[2] In addition, Irish people have long been exposed to media construction by outsiders, constructions which, while not being strictly 'touristy', have fed into and supported the tourist sector. These would include portrayals in Hollywood films such as *The Quiet Man, Finian's Rainbow* and *Ryan's Daughter* and French films such as *Le Taxi mauve*.

This article sets out to explore issues relating to national identity by investigating the dominant tourist images of Ireland and the Irish people. It raises questions about the relationship between the tourist markets, the images constructed for those markets, and the sense of identity which is engendered by such representations. The issue of identity is treated in a rather tentative and speculative manner. This is unfortunate given the importance of the issue but is necessarily so because of the paucity of tourism research specifically in the area of local/tourist interaction. It is hoped, however, that by using the limited ethnographic evidence available for Ireland, literary sources, and parallel evidence from other countries, that useful and suggestive comments can be made.

Tourist Images

The creation of tourist images is a complex process involving an interrelation between the needs of the tourists (market-driven) and what can reasonably be offered by the host country. But the process also involves selection from a range which already has a currency in the market countries. In some cases, such as the US, Irish tourist images are tapping into long established and relatively extensive imagery whereas in others, such as the more recently established Italian market, the associations with, and images of, Ireland are much more limited both in scope and in distribution. However, while a range of images of Ireland exists, depending on the market and source, a number of common themes and motifs have emerged and continue to be reproduced for tourist consumption.

Tourist imagery has been constructed by selecting and promoting certain aspects of culture as tourist 'markers'. The dominant motifs of this imagery — the view of Ireland as a country of 'shamrocks and shillelaghs', 'paddywhackery' and leprechauns are of common cultural currency and have been confirmed by writers on the subject such as Quinn,[3] and Peillon[4]. They agree that Ireland is represented as a place of picturesque scenery and unspoiled beauty, of friendly and quaint people, a place which is steeped in past traditions and ways of life. In short, it is represented as a pre-modern society. It is an example of what Horne sees as a process of spectacular inversion of modern industrial society which has turned parts of Europe into a museum of authenticated remnants of past cultures.[5] As one recent advertisement in a US travel magazine pronounces: 'In Ireland, we often find ourselves quite behind the times. And in no particular hurry to catch up.'[6]

The constraints on image production have been pithily commented on by Denis Donohue: 'Perched on the periphery of Europe we have long been accustomed to the sense that our destinies and our very descriptions are forged by persons of superior power elsewhere.'[7] Historically Ireland has been dependent on the British and US tourist markets with the result that the tourist images follow on from and link into pre-existing images in both of these countries. In Britain, the dominant stereotypes of the Irish had evolved from colonial rule and consisted of a number of both negative and positive putative characteristics, the more benign being selected for tourist purposes. The vast and continuous waves of emigration to the US throughout the nineteenth century gave rise to the establishment of dominant stereotypes through music, film and other forms of popular culture within the US.

Many studies of tourism in post-colonial countries, particularly in the Third World, draw attention to the connection between the two processes of colonialism and tourism. There is a view that 'international tourism recapitulates a historical process; areas of one's country are given over to the pleasure of foreigners, and the rhetoric of development serves as a defence'.[8] While we in Ireland do not suffer some of the extremely negative consequences of Third World tourism, there remain many parallels between the needs of the colonist and the tourist and hence, many similar kinds of representation. The representation of the specific territory as 'empty space' provides a case in point. Apologists for colonial expansion regarded the land marked out for plantation as empty and therefore available for stamping their own mark on 'virgin territory'. So, too, in a contemporary tourist context, areas and countries are represented as exclusively available as a pleasure paradise for tourists — a place in which they can engage in carefree play for the duration of their holiday.

The fit between colonial imperatives and the needs of the contemporary tourist also gives rise to similar stereotypes in other cultural spheres. The construction of work and leisure provides a good example. Giraldis Cambrensis in *The History and Topography of Ireland* (written c. 1187) recounted having visited the country in the entourage of Prince John of England. Regarding the natives he wrote: 'They are a wild and inhospitable people. They live on beasts only, and live like beasts. They have not progressed at all from the primitive habits of pastoral living . . . For given only to leisure and devoted only to laziness they think that the greatest pleasure is not to work and the greatest wealth is to enjoy liberty.'[9] It is striking that, apart from the the people being characterised as inhospitable, the positive side of the remaining putative traits are exactly those which are still in currency in the tourist promotion business 800 years later.

A break from the mundanity of everyday life, particularly a break from work, is a primary rationale for tourist travel. While this is a break from work for tourists, it entails the work of others to service and maintain their leisure and pleasure. Despite the reality, representations foreground a country which the work ethic has bypassed. What better place to be lulled into the desired mood of relaxation than a country where even the natives don't work? This leisurely pace of life is indicated in a number of ways

— from postcards which declare 'Rush Hour in Ireland', depicting a scene of a couple of cows on a road devoid of vehicular traffic, through to brochures and films which display the stock black-capped character in leisurely pose. To give just one example Quinn, in her research on Bord Fáilte brochures refers to a package option provided by Irish Ferries in which 'the scene . . . is set by a large photograph depicting two men attired in traditional dark clothing, boots and cap, in relaxed conversation by the roadside. Set in a remote undulating landscape, uninhabited except by some cattle in the distance, the photograph portrays a rurality far removed from any association with the stress of modern living. One man, carrying a walking stick, is travelling on foot, while his companion leans against an old black bicycle. The relaxed stance of both men indicates that the frenzied rush of city life is completely alien to this part of the world, with neither appearing to have any purpose likely to distract from their leisurely conversation.' [10]

When work is represented, it is transformed into something very different from the alienated experience which it very often is through the process of romanticisation. One way to romanticise work is to collapse it into nature — to suggest its organic nature and the ways in which it brings people closer to nature. Many and varied illustrations of this can be found in tourist brochures and postcards of people working on the land — engaged in tasks such as cutting the turf, saving the hay or bringing home the cows for milking. Or, alternatively, work is represented as the satisfying, creative and skilled activities of traditional craftsmen and women.

In addition to representations of a leisurely pace of life, leisure as an activity is also foregrounded. The Irish are seen as having a penchant for enjoyment — for talking, drinking, laughing and playing music. Leisure, then, is often represented in terms of the tourist joining in communal activities such as sports and musical events. 'A land of music and easy laughter' as an advertisement in a recent issue of a US travel magazine proclaims. [11]

One of the most striking features of tourist imagery is the way in which Irish people are represented. They are regarded as an essential ingredient in the publicity package. This is not to argue that this form of representation is unique to Ireland. In fact, objectification of the 'other' is an integral part of the entire tourist process and experience, whether in terms of landscape, architecture, artifacts, the past or the people. Tourists are generally coming from a world which is extremely individualistic, fragmented and anonymous. They live in a society which is characterised by highly specific and discontinuing relationships with other people. Simple people who live their lives in traditional ways far from the hurly burly of the city are sought out as an essential part of the tourist experience. However, there seems to be more emphasis on this aspect in societies which are more removed from the metropolitan centres of the western world, in societies

Figure 4.1   Turf Cutting near Achill, Co. Mayo (Bord Fáilte)

where the people are sufficiently different from the inhabitants of these centres to be regarded as either quaint or exotic and hence an object of curiosity for the tourist gaze. Because of this, I would like to suggest that there has been much more emphasis in tourist publicity material on the qualities of the people in Ireland than in other European countries which have not been colonised or are economically dependent and/or peripheral. Indeed, Ireland shares with many other 'peasant' and 'primitive' societies the setting up of the 'peasant' as a tourist attraction. One of the consequences of this emphasis on people as part of the tourist package is that Irish people become more inscribed within tourist expectations. Tourists expect a certain type of behaviour and are disappointed if these expectations are not met.

Historically, there has been yet another reason why people are such an important part of the tourist experience in Ireland. Because of the vast waves of Irish emigration to America, 'roots' tourism has been, and continues to be, of major interest to Irish-American tourists. They are particularly proud of their Irish ancestry, which may be accounted for in part by the relative succes of the Irish in US society. Much of their holiday may be spent in public records offices, graveyards and travelling the country in efforts to locate the ruins of the family castle or cottage. Attempts to locate relatives and forge links with them are often essential rituals of their holiday experience.

Hospitable, friendly, welcoming are three recurring and related epithets of tourist publicity. As early as 1840, the Halls were so laudatory as to claim that 'there is no country in the world so safe or so pleasant for strangers, so that for every new visitor it receives, it will obtain a new friend.'[12] It is no accident that the regular Bord Fáilte publication is called *Ireland of the Welcomes*. Quinn's analysis of Bord Fáilte brochures corroborates this claim to assurances of hospitality. She found that people were 'typically depicted in the service setting, aspiring tourists are assured that they will "be like a personal friend of the family" whose hosts will "be very sad to see them leave".'[13] Gallagher, too, in her analysis of Bord Fáilte films explores the representation of people and observes somewhat critically: 'Little freckled children and old men in peaked caps, the noble natives are a leisurely, hospitable, conversational and peaceful race, their collective identity based in the quasi-natural community.'[14]

Picturesque landscape and beautiful scenery constitute other dominant motifs in the tourist construction of Ireland. Again, these types of representation can be traced back to at least the Victorian era. The Halls waxed eloquent on the abundance of natural beauty which the country had to offer the tourist. For example, they open their section on Wicklow with the following fulsome remarks: 'To depict adequately half the delights of beautiful Wicklow would require a large and full volume. We must be content to stimulate the appetite of the tourist so that he may long for the rich banquet which nature has provided for him.'[15] And the foregrounding of scenic beauty continues in a more contemporary context. Quinn points to the fact that the highlighting of the natural landscape is a regular feature of tourist publicity campaigns. However, her study found a higher than average amount of space was devoted to the landscape theme — 39 per cent of Bord Fáilte brochure space as opposed to 32 per cent found in comparative study of twenty-one national tourist board brochures.[16]

One of the most striking aspects of the recent Bord Fáilte publicity in France is the visual and verbal emphasis on the uncrowded nature of the country — its depiction as empty space. As Robert Ballagh aptly observes on this aspect of representation: 'You have Bord Fáilte eulogizing roads where you won't see a car from one end of the day to the other: it's almost as if they're advertising a country nobody lives in.'[17] This is, again, very reminiscent of colonial constructions. In the contemporary tourist situation, however, there is a certain ironic truth in the claim since the remote grandeur and breathtaking beauty accorded to certain places (e.g. the West of Ireland) are precisely those parts where emigration has taken a heavy toll on the local population.

While Ireland has always enjoyed a 'green' image in terms of the colour and freshness of the landscape it has acquired an additional inflection in the recent past as an unpolluted land. Whatever the relative truth of this claim, the point worth noting in this regard is that tourism represents the demands of consumers who, having ruined their own environment, need to take over another.[18]

The attraction of the unspoiled nature of the country is not only an expectation of the contemporary tourist but has also been documented as a source of pleasure for the returning emigrant. Freitag, in an exploration of the returned in Anglo-Irish literature notes how 'the long absence from Ireland has transformed the island into a haven of peace and beauty. In the minds of many protagonists this little paradise has assumed almost magical qualities. It has become a 'Tír-na-nÓg', a purifying font out of which you drink to restore your health, to rejuvenate yourself.'[19] She cites numerous examples of such characters, one of whom is Mervyn Kavanagh who is leaving the 'smells and confusion of New York' and looks down from the plane on his homebound journey feeling that 'down there below the clouds the Shannonside air will still be clean and breathable: he'll be able to pump the gasolene and whatnot from his lungs.'[20]

In addition to the promise of 'empty space' tourists are also offered 'empty time' as a welcome release from the constraints of time which are imposed upon them in the course of their everyday existence (see article by Cronin in this volume). In discussing the form and content of Bord Fáilte films (1950s–70s) Gallagher looks at the way in which the portrayal of landscape as spectacle serves to down-play time. 'In landscape, time is absent. And so Ireland is endowed with "the gift of timelessness" (*Glamour of Galway*), "becoming a timeless land" (*Treasure Island*) "where today is

Figure 4.2   Donegal Bay from Kildorey Point (Bord Fáilte)

like yesterday'' (*Ireland Ours*).'[21]

The past is a motif not only in representing the general lifestyle, but also in terms of past glories and achievements. Castles, monuments and museums form part of the array of the heritage industry which is the fastest growing area of tourism in Ireland (see article by Brett in this volume). Quinn's research attests to the emphasis given to this area in the publicity brochures. She found that the choice of photographs depicting 'the Rock of Cashel, Glendalough, celtic crosses simultaneously establish the strong religious element which dominates Ireland's past, and the majestic and spectacular nature of Irish history. Evidence of a rich and cultural past can be found in the country houses and castles throughout the country, many of which are now hotels. All brochures emphasise this accommodation sector, inviting tourists to enjoy a stay in a luxurious and romanticised setting, reviving the gracious customs of life in Ireland of old.'[22] Gibbons, too, makes reference to the way in which the past is plundered in a discussion of industrialisation in general. His remarks are particularly appropriate to an analysis of the heritage industry. He notes that 'there is no genuine recrudescence of traditional values: rather ''traditions'' are manipulated and selected from the past according as they lend themselves to the dictates of the present.'[23]

This summary overview of predominant tourist images has shown the ways in which certain aspects of Irish culture, the people, the landscape, the past, work and leisure, have been selected and constructed as tourist 'markers' in a way which offers people an escape from the pressures of modernity to the simplicity and authenticity of the pre-modern. Tourist imagery has been instrumental in constructing Ireland and the Irish people as 'other' to the modern industrial metropolitan centres of Europe and the US. The ways in which Ireland is projected as a tourist destination must have implications for the ways in which tourists define Ireland and its inhabitants.

A Sense of Identity

When tourists and locals come into face to face contact with each other they will rely on stereotypes to structure their interactions, stereotypes which have been provided by publicity material. It is suggested that these stereotypes influence a sense of national identity in at least two ways: in terms of a general self-image as an ethnic group (whose fuller exploration would require a broadranging study) and, relatedly, in terms of local/tourist relationships both at the level of casual encounters and at the more formal level for that section of the population employed in the tourist sector.

What, then, is the nature of the local/tourist interaction? It is an impossible question to answer in the absence of detailed ethnographic studies of the relationship. To complicate matters further, social science research from other countries does not prove conclusive on this issue either. In fact, it consists of two opposing strands, one of which highlights the positive effects of tourism in terms of mutual benefits and cross-cultural understanding (e.g. the United Nations Conference on International Travel and Tourism in 1963 promoting both in the rather clichéd terms of travel broadening the mind) and the other coming from a radical Leftist tradition and drawing on theories of colonialism and/or underdevelopment, which emphasises the negative aspects. Many of the more critical studies tend to concentrate on tourism in the Third World, and while there are a number of differences between the tourist sector in Ireland and the Third World, I feel that there are also many parallels and that the theoretical framework would be useful for applying to the Irish situation given our economically dependent and post-colonial status.

It was noted earlier how the construction of tourist imagery is influenced by historical representations. This is no less the case for the way in which local people respond to tourists in that their behaviour, too, is determined by contact with strangers in previous historical periods. As Crick observes, in some cultures 'there may be an explicit parallel drawn to the colonial era, which may significantly affect the way tourists are treated.'[24] The emic classification of tourists is instructive in this regard. In the Seychelles the word tourist was heard as 'tous riches' (all wealthy).[25] The people of Clare Island refer to tourists as 'Praegers' following the visit of the famous naturalist Robert Lloyd Praeger to the island as director of a geological survey in 1911. Apart from the abundance and diversity of flora and fauna on the island, one of Praeger's main reasons for choosing this location was the availability of comfortable accommodation in the form of the island hotel. One can imagine the vast disparities in living standards between the naturalist and the islanders and the ways in which his visit may have served to reinforce stereotypes on both sides.

The inherent sense of superiority of the colonist and the Victorian traveller is equally a hallmark of the contemporary tourist since the directional flow of tourists is, by and large, from the wealthy centres of the world to the poorer, peripheral regions. There is a tendency in tourism, as Hiller notes, to represent the way the powerful nations perceive and relate to the rest of the world.[26] MacCannell, too, proposes that people in urban capitalist society can feel a superiority over the traditional, at the same time as they seek 'authentic experience' in it — an 'authenticity' which is no longer possible in their everyday life.[27] In a Third World context he suggests even more forcefully and specifically that 'the relationship between the tourists and the local people is temporary and unequal. Any social relationship which is transitory, superficial and unequal is a primary breeding ground for deceit, exploitation, mistrust, dishonesty and stereotype formations.'[28]

While these generalisations and analytic frameworks are useful, caution needs to be exercised in discoursing on the nature of the tourist/local relationship. It seems likely that people will place tourists in different categories and treat them accordingly (e.g. the 'independent traveller' may be accorded more hospitality than the American coach tourist) and that different sectors of the population will respond differently to the same tourist (e.g. the owner of the local bed-and-breakfast establishment may be more amenable to the tourist than the publican in whose bar s/he sits for the evening enjoying the music and the ambience, taking up space and sipping the one glass of Guinness!).

While taking the dangers of theoretical generalisation into account, there is still ample empirical evidence to support the argument that tourism can act to perpetuate negative stereotypes rather than to eradicate them. Pi-Sunyer demonstrates how national stereotypes of mass tourists in Catalan deprive them of an essential human status and this, in turn, legitimises hostility towards them and allows for cheating and charging higher prices. 'Contacts between villagers and outsiders have never been greater, but the barriers to understanding have probably never been higher . . . If tourism commodifies cultures, natives categorise strangers as a resource or a nuisance rather than as people.'[29] Cohen's work, too, on host/tourist interaction in developing countries suggests that locals respond to tourists in a double-edged manner — servility on the one hand and resentment on the other.[30]

In the absence of empirical evidence for Ireland, it is impossible to assess the quality of the local/tourist relationship. Doubtless, there are many documented cases of mutually pleasurable and beneficial encounters and there is definite evidence of the pleasures of interaction for tourists. The warmth and friendliness of the Irish people is consistently high on the list of attractions to visitors as evidenced by Bord Fáilte surveys. There is also a wealth of anecdotal material to corroborate these findings. Thomas O'Murchadha refers to some of the qualities which appeal to tourists. 'It's not the pretty scenery they remember, so much as the crazy guy they asked for directions. "'Go down past Mickey Pat's pub', he said", they will chortle, reliving their incredulity, " 'and turn left where the old school used to be . . .' " It is the wit, the courtesy, the informality, that staggers them. They are touched by something ancient in the manner of the old josser who spoke to them, and are amazed to find that he is interested in them.'[31] Finlan, too, attests to the high quality of the interaction between local and tourist in relating the case of a Northern Protestant on holiday in the South and recounting the incidents in which he was involved: 'And so it went for the three weeks — a non-stop procession of minor culture clashes that baffled and bemused. Though an abstemious man who barely ventured beyond a glass of stout, he found himself trapped in pitch darkness in an upstairs bedroom of a pub one late night with a group of men, all listening to each other holding their breath while a guard inspected the premises downstairs . . . At the end of it all, his bemusement had turned to delight. It was, he assured me, the best holiday of his life, despite appalling weather, and its single greatest attraction was the people he met.'[32]

But there in also evidence to support a less than favourable view of the relationship between locals and tourists. There are indications of feelings of insecurity, servility and resentment on the part of locals. The Victorian postcard entitled 'Bewildherin' the Tourists' provides an amusing testimony to the idea of the tourists as 'fair game' for cheating and swindling.

The desire to please tourists appears to be one characteristic response to their presence. Undoubtedly, this response springs partially from the most genuine of motives — a politeness and helpfulness which is still part of a cultural repertoire for dealing with strangers and which could be regarded as a valuable cultural asset. However, the desire to please seems to be partially sourced in anxiety. This sentiment was encapsulated well in the remarks of Nuala O'Faolain: 'When foreign journalists and particularly English journalists turn up and ask to have this or that about Ireland explained to them, I'm on the defensive at once. I'm afraid that they're going to say something hurtful. It's the same with giving lifts. I give lifts to tourists and go miles out of my way so that they'll think Irish people are nice, and won't be disappointed. You can't love somewhere as problematic as Ireland without being anxious.'[33] Deference towards tourists is another embodiment of the desire to please. Curtin and Varley in a study of Dutch anglers have drawn attention to the deferential manner in which anglers were customarily treated in South Mayo and that typically the older generation of boatmen still address their anglers as 'Sir'.[34]

Resentment and counter-stereotyping of tourists is well represented in popular culture, both verbal and written. It is evidenced in the myriad jokes and anecdotes in circulation about returned 'Yanks'. It is also a theme in the literature on returning emigrants. An example of this antipathy is provided by an Irishman writing in 1911: 'considering all they do for us, we are not fond of the Irish Americans. We do not, as a rule, much like them either as settlers or visitors. Their ways of life are a continual reproach to our easy going habits. We . . . feel we should get on better without them. They impress on us that we ought to "hustle round a bit", a thing we detest doing, and tell us that a year in America would "speed us up". We know it would, but we have not yet accepted speed as one of the ideals of life.'[35] The behaviour of the returned emigrant is not only resented but, as P. O'Farrell points out, the resentment is 'laden with hostility and intolerance and contempt'.[36]

This sense of resentment is also supported by the limited sociological writing which is available on the topic. Peillon makes an interesting observation on the nature of the interaction between locals and visiting Americans:

Lawrence, Publisher, Dublin

` BEWILDHERIN' THE TOURISTS. (*A scene at the gap of Dunloe, Killarney.*)
The various solicitations with which we were beset, to taste the "Mountain
Dew," to hear the "Wonderous Echos," to buy bog oak, and arbutus
ornaments, or to invest in "The Photographs" of "The Colleen Bawn"
or "The Colleen Das," composed a scene neither to be described nor
forgotten.   *Vide-Diary of a Bewildered Tourist.*

Figure 4.3   Bewildherin' the Tourists (Lawrence)

The visit of American distant relatives has provided a rather typical comedy situation and such tourists have been transformed into figures of fun. Their openness and their interest in things Irish, the goodwill that they manifest and the easy-going character of their behaviour are easily seen as evidence of naivety and credulity. They are often anxious to emphasise an Irish connection, to claim a particular link to Irishness, however indirect. The only grounds on which American tourists, self-confident representatives of a prestigious civilization, can be made inferior to the Irish are those of Irishness itself. Their claim to Irishness does not carry much weight and theirs remains at best a pseudo-Irishness. It places them in a position of inferiority, for what is pseudo does not match what is "genuine" and is easily ridiculed. The self-proclaimed pseudo-Irishness of many American visitors makes it possible to discard them as carriers of a potentially threatening otherness. The contact with different ways and different beliefs is neutralized.[37]

In a somewhat contrary argument Brody claims that rural farming communities are dependent on tourists for a sense of reassurance. But he also notes the same lack of confidence in their own community and way of life which had been remarked upon by Peillon. Brody goes on to suggest that tourists by visiting these rural communities are indicating approval of the rural way of life. But this provokes an ambivalent response on the part of locals. He states that 'often this approval is not taken for granted. That local people are often unsatisfied by a show of mere interest is indicated by their anxious questioning of the tourist — questioning which aims at defining the approval. In this respect tourists can be compared to an audience which the actors are never sure of.'[38]

In the wider public sphere, too, there is often an anxiety expressed about the way others, particularly tourists, will perceive us. Many arguments for civic and environmental development and amenity provision, and, indeed in some instances, destruction, are made in terms of the benefits to the tourist rather than for their value to the local population. In this regard it is instructive to note that local civic and social initiatives such as the Tidy Towns Competition and the activities of An Tóstal were encouraged, co-ordinated and in some cases funded by Bord Fáilte. It is not the beneficial effects of these projects which are in dispute but rather the political motivation for them which attaches more importance to the perceived opinions and needs of tourists than to those of the local population. The current plans of the Office of Public Works to give away ninety acres of the Killarney National Park to a private golf club could be viewed as indicating the determination to cater for tourist needs regardless of the consequences for the people of the area. In a newspaper article on this issue, Fintan O'Toole highlights the uncritical pandering to tourist development on the part of some state institutions: 'The justifications given for the handover of the land to the golf club are, firstly, that a third course will help tourism . . . Tourism development is not an end in itself: it is worth encouraging only when it has obvious and sustainable long-term benefits.'[39]

Changing Markets, Changing Images?

Tourism is not a static phenomenon and is, perhaps, more than other sectors of the economy, subject to rapid and major changes. The Gulf War, for example, resulted in a massive downturn in the number of US tourists visiting Europe in 1990. The tourist sector in Ireland has been changing in recent times. There has been a relative decline in the North American market and an increase in the continental European market (predominantly from France and Germany and Italy) and of tourism promotion in these countries (see article by Péchenart and Tangy in this volume). International tourism is also undergoing a shift from the tourism of modernity (mass tourism) to that of post-modernity (niche markets). In the light of these changes, a pertinent question to be addressed is the extent to which changes in markets will affect image production, if at all. An adequate answer to the question would require a comparative study of images over time.[40] However, some general comments can be made based on the data used for this article.

There does not appear to have been any significant change in certain images and motifs. Ireland continues to be represented as a land of natural beauty and tranquillity and as a pre-modern society. This is likely to remain a prominent feature of tourist publicity since the attractions of the countryside continue to appeal to the 'romantic gaze' of the tourist, in particular, as Urry points out, to the 'new service classes' who are currently exercising such a strong influence on the provision of tourist services.[41]

Having suggested earlier that historically there had been an emphasis on people as part of the tourist package, it seems to me from a limited perusal of the material that this emphasis has been lessening somewhat in recent years. A number of possible reasons could be offered for such a decrease in emphasis. There has been an increase in emphasis on other aspects of the tourist product, in particular on quality. Fresh, natural, and high quality food has become a strong selling point to the continental European market and is at least as important as hospitality *per se*.

There is also a current emphasis on activity holidays which means that tourists will be more independent in actively creating their own leisure. The relative decline in the US market also means that there is a corollary decrease in roots tourism and the opportunity which it provided for contact with locals. Roots tourism itself has become partially computerised, so that information which would previously have been substantially available through local contacts is now available through other channels. Recent years have also witnessed an increase in crimes against tourists, making it more difficult for image producers to credibly promote the friendliness and hospitality of the people.

The broader question which needs to be addressed is to what extent can we be self-determining in our efforts to develop tourism and tourist imagery in a sector which is undergoing increasing commercialisation and commodification? Policy statements are in the direction of what is referred to as sustainable tourism: small scale, ecologically sound, special interest and with an eye to maintaining local rural communities. These statements appear laudatory and welcome but it is difficult to assess what their implementation would mean in practice. For instance, what might the declared aspiration to maintain local rural communities entail for those communities? For farmers, agri-tourism, a subsection of rural tourism, is presented as the means by which the stated goals will be achieved. It is an open question as to whether this kind of strategy can be seen as a way of revitalising areas of rural Ireland or, conversely, as a mere construction for tourists. Irish agriculture has encountered major problems in recent years. Within the framework of the Common Agricultural Policy a large proportion of Irish agricultural production goes into intervention. Increasingly, farmers will be paid not to use a proportion of their land for agricultural production. Current changes in the CAP will result in the need for farmers to seek alternative sources of additional income. Agri-tourism is seen by government as one of the main sources of this additional income. But could the scheme for the development of agri-tourism be an indication of the process of hyper-reality in action: a sad case of people playing at being farmers for the benefit of tourists?

The extent to which changes in tourist policy and practice will effect changes in imagery and identity is something which needs to be established by further empirical work on tourism. This article has sought to open up the debate on the topic. It set out to explore some of the dominant representations of Ireland and the Irish people in tourist imagery and to address the possible relationship between imagery, tourist expectations and responses of locals to those expectations. There has been a critical emphasis throughout in claiming that Ireland has been, and continues to be, constructed as 'other' to cater for the leisure needs of the metropolitan centres of Europe and North America. This construction has, I have argued, a number of negative implications for the local population in terms of their sense of identity and self-worth, and in terms of their interaction with tourists. In adopting this approach, I do not wish to suggest that development of the tourist sector is necessarily or exclusively detrimental. But in the light of the relative neglect of the critical approach by policy makers to date, there would appear to be an urgency about addressing some of the possible negative consequences of tourist development in Ireland.

NOTES AND REFERENCES

1   Quoted in Brody, H. (1972), *Inishkillane: Change and Decline in the West of Ireland*, Penguin, Harmondsworth, p. 161.
2   Gibbons, L. (1986), 'Alien Eye: Photography and Ireland', *Circa*, **12**:10.
3   Quinn, B. (1991), 'The Promotion of Ireland as a Tourist Destination in Continental Europe', paper presented at the Institute of Irish Studies, University of Liverpool, Fifth Workshop on Social Science Research 'The Irish in the "New" Europe: Context, Trends and Issues'.
4   Peillon, M. (1984), 'Tourism — a Quest for Otherness', *The Crane Bag,* **8**(2).
5   Horne, D. (1984), *The Great Museum: the Re-presentation of History*, Pluto, London, p. 1.
6   *Traveller,* April, 1992.
7   Quoted in Kiberd, D., 'Decolonising our Minds as well as our Territory', *The Irish Times*, 11 August 1987.
8   Perez, L.A. (1973), 'Aspects of Underdevelopment: Tourism in the West Indies', *Sci. Soc.* **37**:474.
9   Quoted in Kearney, R. (1985), *The Irish Mind: Exploring Intellectual Traditions,* Wolfhound Press, Dublin, p. 311.
10   Quinn (1991), op. cit., p. 5.
11   *Traveller,* April, 1992.
12   Scott, M. (ed.) (1984), *Halls' Ireland — Mr and Mrs Hall's Tour of 1840*, Sphere Books, London.
13   Quinn (1991), op. cit., p. 5.
14   Gallagher, M. (1989), 'Landscape and Bord Fáilte Films', *Circa*, **43**:28.
15   Scott (1984), op. cit., p. 239.
16   Quinn (1991), op. cit., p. 5.
17   Ballagh, R., 'Getting away from Outworn Shibboleths of Irishness', *Sunday Independent,* 9 November 1980.
18   Bugincourt, J. (1977), 'Tourism with no Return', *Development Forum*, **5**(2):2.
19   Freitag, B. (1992), 'Come Back to Erin: the Returned Emigrant in Anglo-Irish Literature', *Journal of Irish Literature,* **2**(3):38.
20   ibid., p. 38.
21   Gallagher (1989), op. cit., p. 26.
22   Quinn (1991), op. cit., p. 5.
23   Gibbons, L. (1988), 'Coming out of Hibernation? The Myth of Modernity in Irish Culture', in R. Kearney (ed.), *Across the Frontiers: Ireland in the 1990s,* Wolfhound Press, Dublin, p. 217.
24   Crick, M. (1989), 'Representations of International Tourism in the Social Sciences: Sun, Sex, Sights, Savings and Servility', *Annual Review of Anthropology,* **18**: 330.
25   ibid., p. 330.
26   Hiller, H.L. (1979), 'Tourism: Development or Dependence?', in R. Millet and W.M. Will (eds.), *The Restless Caribbean,* Praeger, New York, p. 51.
27   MacCannell, D. (1989 2nd ed.), *The Tourist: A New Theory of the Leisure Class*, Schocken Books, New York, p. 83.

28 MacCannell, D. (1984), 'Reconstructed Ethnicity: Tourism and Cultural Ident-
    ity in Third World Communities', *Annals of Tourism Research,* **11:**375-91.
29 Pi-Sunyer, O. (1978), 'Tourists and Tourism in a Catalan Maritime Community',
    in V.L. Smith (ed.), *Hosts and Guests: The Anthropology of Tourism,*
    Blackwell, Oxford, p. 1.
30 Cohen, E. (1982), 'Marginal Paradises: Bungalow Tourism in the Islands of
    southern Thailand', *Annals of Tourism Research,* **9:**198-228.
31 O Murchadha, Thomas, 'The Secret Life of the Countryside', *The Irish Times,*
    8 November 1991.
32 Finlan, Michael, 'The Accidental Habitual Tourist', *The Irish Times,* 10 May
    1991.
33 O'Faolain, Nuala, 'Conniving with the Patriarchy just to Survive', *The Irish
    Times,* 2 March 1992.
34 Curtin, C. and Varley, T. (1990), 'Brown Trout, "Gentry" and Dutchmen:
    Tourism and Development in South Mayo', in C. Curtin and T.M. Wilson (eds.),
    Ireland From Below: Social Change and Local Communities, Galway University
    Press, Galway, p. 220.
35 Quoted in Schrier, A. (1970), *Ireland and the American Emigration, 1850-1990,*
    Russell and Russell, New York, p. 143.
36 O'Farrell, P. (1976), 'Emigrant Attitudes and Behaviour as a Source for Irish
    History', *Historical Studies,* **10:**112.
37 Peillon (1984), op. cit., p. 165.
38 Brody (1972), op. cit., p. 141.
39 O'Toole, Fintan, 'Destroying my Land and Woods for Golfers and Tourists',
    The Irish Times, 3 June 1992.
40 Unfortunately, Bord Fáilte's archival cataloguing system does not allow for
    a comparative analysis of campaign publicity material on an annual basis for
    specific markets.
41 Urry, J. (1990), *The Tourist Gaze: Leisure and Travel in Contemporary Societies,*
    Sage, London.

5

'Embodying the Nation' — The West of Ireland Landscape and Irish Identity

Catherine Nash

Introduction: Tourism and the West of Ireland; Contexts and Issues

The image of the landscape of the West of Ireland is central to a consideration of tourism and Ireland, in terms both of its use in the promotion of internal and international tourism and in the importance of travel accounts in establishing the cultural significance of the region. Images of the western landscape function in promotional publications as a shorthand notation for the landscape of Ireland in general. This article looks at questions of how and why the West has come to have this symbolic function, at what particular meanings were invested in this image to make it a desirable destination.

Though presented primarily in terms of its physical features, the West's image holds social and cultural meaning which has been significant in terms of Irish identity and involves issues of how the country has been presented to others and to the state itself. For an area to be valued as a potential tourist destination a sense of difference has to be established. This difference provides a reason for and gives value to the tourist visit. For the West of Ireland this difference was articulated against the Englishness of the colonial power. Yet it was also constructed as different within Ireland. The West came to stand for Ireland in general, to be representative of true

Irishness. It could be seen as a way of access into the Irish past through its language, folklore, antiquities, and way of life, yet also be conceived of as outside time, separated from normal temporal development, as evoked later by Seán Ó Faoláin as 'lost islands, lost consciousness, lost time'.[1] It stood for Irishness, yet it was simultaneously promoted as unique, special and desirable as a place to visit within Ireland.

This construction of the West as true Ireland depended on the relegation of the rest of the country to the status of the inauthentic, corrupted by anglicisation, urbanisation and industrialisation. In the context of Ireland's colonial history, the West functioned as a primitive 'other' against which the superiority of the colonial power could be measured. Yet the West continued to function as an internal 'other' through which to articulate difference, a difference valued in the national context, its cultural and racial purity and health, considered lost or declining in the rest of the country. It was constructed as both representative and different, its difference lying in its offer to the tourist of unique access to true Irishness. In terms of internal tourism the region offered the visitor both the attraction of the different and the security of the shared cultural values it symbolised. As representative of Ireland in general in tourist promotional literature it could, in the context of the new state, represent a cultural difference and independence with which to mirror the political.

This article then, is concerned with tracing the construction of the image of the West of Ireland, which rose to prominence in the first decades of the twentieth century. In this construction, the nineteenth-century, colonial image of the Celtic fringe was adapted by the writers of the literary revival and by the Irish-Ireland movement. The shift from Ireland as being the primitive 'other' of imperial discourses to the West as being the 'primitive within', an internal other, in early moves towards national self-determination, involves issues of gender and ethnic identity. The early image was linked to the colonial construction of the Celtic as feminine, and the discourses of cultural primitivism, which posited the West as the exotic periphery, appreciated, but ultimately relegated to a position of inferiority in relation to the dominant imperial centre. This 'West' was appropriated and refashioned by the Irish-Ireland movement into a masculine and Gaelic West, a refashioning of the image which continued to be influenced and constrained by the colonial construction of the West (see article by Cronin in this volume).

Yet in looking at the literary accounts of the West, both fictional and in the form of travel writing, to suggest a clear linear progression from the West as described in colonial accounts of the region to its representation by nationalist writers simplifies the contradictions and inconsistencies which are embedded in the writing. Though ultimately a shift did occur in the period concerned, in the way in which the West of Ireland figured in literature, topographical and travel writing, this article is concerned with exploring the continuities as well as the differences. It examines the way in which themes established in earlier writing were adopted, adapted or contested. It traces the ancestry of themes which, within the constraints of a post-colonial writing, functioned in a nationalist refiguring of the West. The landscape of the region, in the sense of its geology, climate and physical geography, was the base upon which themes of race, gender, spirituality, and the cultural politics of colonialism and nationalism were deployed. To trace the importance of the region is to understand its representations not as expressions simply of an already existing landscape with its pool of cultural symbols but as constituting the region and its significance, investing its iconography with layers of meaning.[2]

In 1892 the Congested Districts Board produced its first report on the regions in the West of Ireland, so designated after its formation in 1891.[3] While the term seemed anomalous in relation to the sense of emptiness and open space of the region, it was meant to denote an imbalance between the population and the use of or availability of resources and the subsequent poverty. The West was described by one writer in 1905 as 'a place that was not for man, and still was thronged by man. A congested district.'[4] Another West thus shadowed the celebration of the area: the West as a problem region. The West was an embarrassment to the British administration, as a region of poverty and underdevelopment so close to the heart of the empire, and later to the Irish government since both its decline and depopulation, or economic development, threatened loss of its cultural wealth, in particular the Irish language of the Gaeltacht regions. This tension between development and preservation was expressed in a report on the Connemara Islands to the Congested Districts Board in 1914.[5] In their concern to improve the region, a wish was expressed to conserve the simplicity of the life there, thereby preserving its cultural richness. This tension arose in travel writing also, which sought both to praise the region for its cultural and racial health and purity, and the industriousness of the people, yet also to illustrate the need to solve the problems of poverty, undernourishment and underemployment. As early as 1890, the contrast between the romantic tourist view and the awareness of the poverty had been expressed in an account of Achill:

> It is a fine place for the tourist in search of health and on pleasure bent during the holiday season, for if Nature has been niggardly in bestowing fruitfulness on the soil, she has richly endowed the island in scenic gifts, and the breezes that blow there have traversed that three thousand miles of ocean lying between Ireland and America. The tourist may indeed rhapsodise in language fine on the feasts for the eye and soul which the island affords. The people of Achill would be very happy if they could live on such food.[6]

The discordance of these different ways of seeing the landscape represents a clash between different versions of the West, which conflicted both within individual texts and between different travel writings on the region.

This chapter, then, is concerned with tracing the construction of multiple 'Wests', co-existing in conflict or accord. The term 'the West' generally denotes the western seaboard and the counties of Connaught. Like the term itself, sometimes expanding, sometimes contracting to contain a greater or lesser area in different contexts — the western seaboard, the land west of the Shannon, Connaught, Connemara, the western islands of Achill, Aran and later the Blaskets — the symbolic meaning of the term has also that shifting, fluid nature. The West stands as a cultural landscape of multiple meanings. Looking at the construction of these many 'Wests' is not to oppose them to a 'real' West using criteria of authenticity and truth, but to explore the ways in which the threads of themes became woven in the fabrication of its cultural symbolism, how and in what ways aspects of its distinctive landscape became loaded with this symbolism. This is not to depreciate the peoples' lived experience of the region and its cultural significance and the use of ideas of authenticity in the post-colonial re-writing of the nation, despite their post-modern destabilising.[7] Yet nor is it to ignore the politics of representation, in both the colonial and national contexts implicated in the imagery of the West.

The construction of the West must be seen in both the context of Irish history and culture and within a broader context; the context of the anti-modernism and romantic primitivism of early modernism, the context of European discourses concerning racial degeneration, eugenics, evolution and environmentalism, spiritualism and rural regeneration, and the particularity of these discourses in the context of Irish nationalist attempts to revitalise and revivify the nation. These discourses intersect with the idea of national identity and gravitate around notions of place and landscape.[8] The association between national identity and landscape, is manifest in the post-colonial literal and symbolic re-appropriation of place. In post-colonial literature, the development or recovery of an effective relationship with place, after dislocation or cultural denigration by a supposedly superior cultural and racial colonial power, becomes a means to overcome the sense of displacement and crisis of identity.[9]

In describing the development of post-colonial literature and its relationship to place, a three phase model has been suggested.[10] Its first phase covers the stage in which the colony is represented in travel literature which is written by and for the imperial power. The imperial centre remains the absent and enabling signifier and, despite the detailed reportage of landscape and customs, the superior imperial centre is privileged as the norm against which difference is measured and evaluated. In the second stage, the colonised writer uses landscape flamboyantly, assertively and selfconsciously to declare identity, worth and attachment to place. Finally, for those writers writing for the home audience, landscape becomes part of the common culture and milieu; it is absorbed as a familiar backdrop with its shared resonance, and is not stridently proclaimed. Though more helpfully viewed as a continuum, whose development is neither linear nor smooth, this model is useful in a consideration of the particular ways in which the landscape of the West was written about and what it could be used to signify. This discussion is framed by and grounded in two novels, between whose dates of publication lie the important years in the formation of this cultural landscape: *Grania — the Story of an Island* (1892) by Emily Lawless (1845-1913) and *Children of Earth* (1918) by Darrell Figgis (1882-1925).[11]

Though early accounts of the West exist, the region began to feature in travel accounts from the 1850s. This was due to the growing taste for the primitive as the region came to be the subject of travel literature, and the ethnographic, antiquarian and philologic interest of the nineteenth century. It was also the result of the development of transport links which facilitated the opening up of the region to tourists.[12] By the 1900s organised tours to Connemara were being advertised and a writer for *Ireland, An Illustrated Journal of the Green Isle*, a loyalist journal centred around the society of Dublin Castle, which featured reports and advice for the English or Ascendancy traveller, claimed in 1901 that 'Connemara and the Wild West have been so often the subject of newspaper articles, that we can hardly say anything about them that is new.'[13]

In the twenty-six years which separate the two novels, the region had risen to popularity, and cultural importance. Yet these and the other accounts of the West do not stand outside this popularisation, but are embedded within this process of symbolic formation. The literary and painterly representations of the West were not isolated from its tourist promotion, but intersected. Both novels are set on islands off the West coast; Inishmaan, of the Aran Islands, in *Grania*; in *Children of Earth*: Maolan, a fictional island, which though not clearly located is suggested in the novel to be north of the Aran Islands, off the Sligo or Mayo coast. Using these locations, both texts could employ and develop the symbolism of islands, in particular the symbolism of the Western island in Irish culture.[14] Both are love stories in a sense which deal with the fraught relationship of a couple; both end with the drowning of the principal female character. Themes of gender, environment and nature arise in both novels, though their treatment and significance differ. This difference must be understood in relation to both the context and the author's background. Emily Lawless was a member of the Anglo-Irish land-holding class and, however sympathetic to the Gaelic movement, was politically unionist. When Darrell Figgis wrote his novel, Synge had already published *Aran Islands*, and used the western setting in his drama. Figgis wrote as a nationalist and was politically active. He was a member of the Irish Volunteers and was involved in the Howth gun-running incident of 1914, and was imprisoned. He later headed the committee which drew up the Constitution of the Irish

Free State. This is not to say that his writing produced any more a 'true' account of the region and its people, nor was more free from the constraining influences of colonial writing. It is part of the argument of this chapter that writing on the West by the cultural nationalists could not escape from the discourses of earlier writing, since the negation of older Wests is still tied to the colonial influence.

The celebration of the West as an archetypal Irish landscape was part of an attempt to identify with a landscape which was a confirmation of cultural identity. It was not simply or only that the West was farthest from England and therefore most isolated from the cultural influences of anglicisation, but that its physical landscape provided the greatest contrast to the landscape of Englishness. In response to the cultural crisis of social change, industrialisation and later the First World War, Englishness was increasingly linked to the landscape of 'south country', that of rural, village England with its connotations of stability, continuity and tradition.[15] The landscape of the West, that of mountain, bog, lake and ocean, could be contrasted to the verdant richness of the landscape of English 'south country'. Its elemental bareness, vigour and vitality could be contrasted positively to the association of softness, shelter and fecundity of its 'other', the sublime in contrast to pastoral beauty, in addition to English urbanism. The sheer difference of the scale of its physical structure and the perception of its elemental power, were used to testify to the superiority of the Irish peasants to the special association of ideas which came to reside in the body of the individual 'man of the West' or 'woman of the West'. The particular racial and gender implications of this emphasis upon both the body of the land and the body of the peasant, will be dealt with in discussing both novels. By celebrating the West, a sense of Irishness could be linked to and reinforced by the idea of a quintessential Irish landscape. The ambivalent position of the Anglo-Irish, as the now indigenous descendants of the colonisers, heightened their eagerness to find a region of pure Irishness with which to identify, despite their class and religious differences. To writers of the Irish-Ireland movement also, the West could signify the source for the revitalising of Ireland, a landscape of both personal and national regeneration. Perceived as both a pool of cultural and racial strength and beauty, whether conceived of as a result of environmental influence, racial evolution or a combination of both, the West, in the sense of standing for the whole island and as a source of biological and physiological regeneration, could be seen as embodying the nation.

Grania — the Story of an Island
REPRESENTATIONS OF THE WESTERN LANDSCAPE AND PEOPLE IN THE LATE COLONIAL TEXT

This 'story of an island' is the story of Grania O'Malley who, orphaned, is brought up by her half-sister Honor, for whom Grania's lack of

conventional piety is a constant distress, despite their devotion to each other.
Grania, strong, vigorous and life-loving, attempts to find happiness with
the man she loves, Murdough Blake, who disappoints her in his lack of
emotion for her and his growing drunkenness. She eventually realises the
futility of her hopes for their happiness and finally drowns in an attempt
to fetch a priest for her sister's last rites. An indication of the audience
which Emily Lawless was addressing in the novel lies in the name itself:
'Grania' an anglicised version of the Irish name, Gráinne. Throughout the
text the author repeatedly directly addresses the reader, who is positioned
outside the context of the novel and that of Ireland. In describing the island,
the reader is called upon to contrast the area to their own locale: 'For,
be it known to you, oh prosperous reader — dweller doubtless, in a sleek
land, a land of earth and water, possibly even of trees — that these islands,
like their opposite neighbour, the burren of Clare, are rock, not partially
but absolutely.'[16] In identifying with the viewpoint, the gaze of the
English traveller for whom the author recounts the tale, she presents the
reader with scenes which stand outside the narrative, which position the
reader as the external viewer. The scenes are offered as subjects for the
travel writer, for the growing medium of photography, or painting, as scenes
to be appropriated, consumed and captured in representation. Her description of Murdough Blake is an invitation to do so:

> In his archaic clothes of yellowish flannel, spun, woven, bleached, made
> upon the island, in the cow-skin pampooties which give every Aranite
> his peculiarly shuffling and at the same time swinging step, he ought to
> have rejoiced the inmost heart of a painter, had a painter ever thought
> of going to the Aran Isles in search of subjects, a ridiculous supposition,
> for who would dream of doing so?[17]

Emily Lawless also disrupts this process. She oscillates between her position as insider and that of outsider. It is this ambiguity which characterises
the work and prevents the novel being read either as simply a patronising
account of the landscape and life of peasants on Inishmaan for an external colonial audience, as in the first stage of the developmental model,
or as a break from the traditions of representation of the Irish peasantry.
Perhaps the name 'Grania' provides again a useful indication of the
author's position. As a phonetic version of Gráinne, Lawless enabled the
English reader to pronounce the name as it would have been spoken in
Ireland. By adapting the name for an English readership, she renders it
in a way that is close to Irish speech if not to spelling.

'HUMAN TYPES' AND THE DISCOURSE OF PRIMITIVISM

There is a tension in the novel in relation to the caricature of the Irish
peasant which had been developed in nineteenth-century representation,
in particular through the 'stage Irishman'. In many ways Lawless presents

us with characters who conform to this characterisation as idle, savage, drunken, ugly, superstitious, loquacious, impractical, excessively religious peasants. Included in her cast are Shan Daly whose face 'above the rags was rather wilder, more unsettled, more restless than even West Connaught recognises as customary or becoming', who fishes with 'a sudden clawing gesture, expressive of fierce, hungry desire, his lips moving, his eyes glittering, his whole face working',[18] Murdough Blake, possessing 'one of the more distinctive gifts of his countrymen, and his tongue had a power of building castles in the air' with his 'good-looking, blunt-featured, thoroughly Irish face',[19] redheaded Teigh O'Shaughnessy 'extremely, almost painfully ugly, possessing one of those faces which confront one now and then in the West of Ireland, and seem to verge to such a cruel degree upon the grotesque'[20], and Honor, who claims 'a priest is not a man' but an apostle of Christ, and whose response to Grania's wish for happiness is 'Happiness? God love the child! What were any of us, and women especially, sent into the world for except to save our souls and learn to bear what's given to bear?'[21] Yet, Emily Lawless also undermines the stability which the idea of the typical affords. In the history of the relationship between England and the internal colonies, of Wales, Scotland and Ireland, attempts were made to defuse their radical potential to undermine the idea of a unified Britain. These efforts intensified after the rise of the idea of the nation following the French Revolution. Through the combined discourses of travel writing, ethnography and anthropology, and through satire, ridicule and humourous depiction, the other could be known and difference subordinated to a position of inferiority in relation to the English norm. In describing Con O'Malley, Grania's father, Emily Lawless ambiguously questions her own use of the idea of the typical, writing that he 'might have passed, in the eyes of an observer on the look-out for types, as the very picture and ideal of the typical Connaught peasant — if there are such things as typical beings, a point that might be debated'.[22] She thus undermines both popular and anthropological discourse which sought by scientific measurement and statistical method to establish racial characteristics with their implicit and explicit racial ranking. This concept of the typical survived, from the ethnographic study of the West in the late nineteenth century, to find its expression in representations of the West, the most obvious example being the 1934 film *Man of Aran*.[23]

This ambivalence extends to the figure of Grania who is presented as both the product of her environment, and an exotic outside her community. The repeated use of metaphors of animals and of the natural world in her description places her nearer to the organic, to nature and to the instinctive life and vitality of the animal. She is described as a child like 'some small marmoset or squirrel', 'a wild little face, and a wild little figure! Bare-headed, with unkempt hair tossing in a brown mane over face and neck'[24] who grew up 'as a seamew grows', into 'a tall, broadchested maiden, vigorous as a frond of bracken in that fostering Atlantic air, so cruel to weaklings, so friendly to those who are already by nature strong'.[25] In her distress at Murdough Blake's lack of affection for her, and his ignorance of her love or his lack, she cries out 'a low cry, half of anger, half of brain-tormented perplexity. It was like the cry of some dumb animal, vague, inarticulate, full of uncomprehended pain, and of still less comprehended dissatisfaction.'[26]

This association of Grania with nature and the landscape of the West was part of the ideology of primitivism which arose in the late nineteenth century, intimately linked with colonialism. It found expression in literature and in art, which in its use of tribal imagery sought to return to a raw, primal form of truth and a release of psychic energies, repressed by the restrictions of civilisation and modern society's separation from nature. It was an ideology which viewed the world not as composed of autonomous peoples but societies occupying levels of civilisation with Europe at the top of an evolutionary model of social development. The spatially distant came to be defined as temporally distant. While primitivism afforded the remote a limited positive evaluation with the associations of cohesion, simplicity, instinctiveness and organic relationship between lifestyle and environment, the primitive was ultimately considered lower in the hierarchy of civilisation. As constructions of the imperial centre, both art history and anthropology contributed to the production of primitivism as discriminatory discourse which posits the other as both an object for the aritist's gaze and for analytic scrutiny.[27]

Linked to the anti-urbanism and anti-industrialism of early modernism, in nationalist accounts of the West this primitivising continues. The idea of the primitive is appropriated but positively evaluated against the urban, industrial, colonial power. Yet while Grania is presented as an example of physical strength and beauty, closely in harmony with her environment, the degree to which she is representative of her community is fundamentally limited by her difference, attributed to her racial inheritance. Grania stands outside her community due to her mother's origins on the mainland of Galway and her Spanish blood. The novel opens with the assertion of Grania's element of the foreign — 'Seen against that indeterminate welter of sea and sky, the little brown face with its rapidly moving glances, strongly marked brows, vividly tinted colouring, might have brought southern suggestions to your mind. Small Italian faces have something of that same outline, that flash, that vividness of colouring; gipsies too' — explained by Lawless as 'that long-unrenewed, but still-to-be-extinguished streak of Spanish blood, which comes out, generation after generation, in so many a West Irish face.'[28]

This Spanish blood is explained as the result of trade links between Galway and the Iberian peninsula. The exoticism of this racial strain would be later rejected by nationalist writers for whom racial purity in the West

was profoundly important, whether conceived of as the result of descent
from the Firbolg tribe in early Irish history and legend, or from old Irish
clans driven west in the plantations of the sixteenth and seventeenth centuries. With less investment in the idea of racial purity, English and English
orientated Anglo-Irish accounts of the West repeatedly suggested an Italian
and, more commonly, Spanish strain in the people of the region. In the
novel, the very characteristics which would enable Grania to qualify as an
Irish heroine, her strength and endurance, beauty, self-sacrifice and love
of home place, separate her from her community, and are used to emphasise
her difference not her representativeness.

The elemental landscape of the island has trained Grania's natural
strength, yet in crossing the gendered division of work in the island she
is disapproved of and distanced. The vitalism of Grania, which later writers
would extend to the whole community, is a product of her invigorating
landscape, which Lawless recommends to her audience.

> Oh, troubled fellow mortals, self-tormented, nerve-ridden, live incessantly
> in the open air, live under the varied skies, heedless if you can, of their
> vagaries, and, if you do, surely sooner or later you will reap your reward!
> Grania O'Malley had reaped hers, or rather it had come to her without
> any sowing or reaping, which is the best and most natural way. She had
> a special faculty, too, for such living — one which all cannot hope to
> have or acquire. She could dig, she could chop, she could carry, she could
> use her muscles in every sort of out door labour as a man uses his, and
> moreover could find a joy in it all. For words, unlike Murdough, she had
> no talent. Her thoughts, so far as she had any conscious thoughts, would
> not clothe themselves in them. They stood dumb and helpless. Her senses
> on the other hand, were exceptionally wide awake, while for sheer muscular
> strength and endurance she had hardly her match amongst the young men
> of the three islands.[29]

Her disregard for the customary gender divisions evokes the censure of
the other women, one of whom exclaims

> I tell you there is no end to her queerness, and to the bold things she
> does be doing. It is well known to all Inishmaan, yes, and to Aranmore
> too, that she goes out to the fishing just like a man, so she does, just
> like a man, catching the plaice and the mullets and the conger eels, and
> many another fish beside I shouldn't wonder; and if that is not a bold
> thing for a young girl to do, then I don't know what is.[30]

Grania ultimately realises the restrictions and profound compromise of
negotiating her gender position. Later writers would extend the positive
evaluation of Grania as product of her environment to the wider community, but with loss of the value of the image, like her namesake, Grainnua
Uaile (Grace O'Malley 1530–1603), the sixteenth-century pirate queen, of
the strong independent woman.

RACE, PLACE AND EMIGRATION

Grania is deeply, instinctively attached to Inishmaan. For her

> Inishmaan was much more than home, much more than a place she lived
> in — it was practically the world, and she wished for no bigger, hardly
> for any more prosperous one. It was not merely her own little holding
> and cabin, but every inch of it that was in this peculiar sense hers. It
> belonged to her as the rock on which it has been born belongs to the
> young seamew. She was part of it, and it was part of her.[31]

In the context of large scale post-famine emigration, the deep bond of
Grania and her community to their home place, which featured strongly
in other writings, can be understood both as a compensatory response to
its apparent opposite — emigration, which was conceived as traitorship
to the nation. It also functioned as a prescriptive encouragement to remain. This organic link between environment and people was utilised in
discourses which employed scientific conceptions of current climatology
and anthrogeography to discourage emigration. European fears of cultural
degeneration of the 1890s, which continued into the first decades of the
twentieth century, employed ideas of environment either as a source of
degeneration in the growing industrial urban centres, or as its solution in
the reinvigorating value of rural life.[32] More generally, many racial
theorists supported a belief in each race having a natural home, which if
abandoned would lead to degeneration, either because climate produced
race, or because 'Nature' had created different races and placed them in
appropriate geographical areas.[33] While ideas of ethno-climatology were
used to express fears of loss of white racial supremacy in relation to the
colonies, the popular circulation of these ideas made them available to
be employed in the Irish context to discourage emigration. Fears of loss
of population were made more urgent by the associated loss of Irish
language speakers, culture bearers and vigorous genetic stock from the West
of Ireland. The association between the Irish landscape, in particular the
Western landscape, and climate and Irish national character was used in
this anti-emigration writing. In 1911 the relationship between emigration,
climate and race was summarised in *The Irish Review* as follows:

> 1. A race of mankind is the product of its environment, acting through
> the power of natural selection, for not less than 5,000 years.
> 2. No race can abandon its native environment and retain its specific
> character. If the emigration is into a climate fairly like the old one the
> race may in the course of time, at the expense of many family stocks,
> become acclimatised and transformed into a new race. If the new climate
> is considerably different from the old, and more especially if it is hotter
> or drier, the emigrant race will die out . . . .
> 3. Acclimation of a fair skinned race in any climate whose mean annual
> temperature exceeds 55 degrees F. is impossible; it is also impossible where

the mean maximum summer temperature exceeds 72 degrees F.; likewise it is imossible in any region whose natural rainfall is less than 20 inches, and whose normal sunshine is greater than 40 per cent of the possible.
4. The only parts of North America safe for Gaelic emigrants are Alaska, British Columbia and Newfoundland; in South America only the southern-most provinces of Chile; in the Antipodes only Tasmania and the southern island of New Zealand.
5. The best country for Irish men and women in the 20th century is Ireland itself.[34]

Frequently the results of emigration were characterised by the loss of the Irish complexion in Irish women, used to the rain and cloud of Irish and most especially West of Ireland weather. One writer described a 'young girl who left Queenstown, with the fresh bloom of health upon her cheek, with such a complexion only the genial Irish clime can give' who 'soon loses her colour and becomes a sickly, dried up, sapless creature'.[35] Similarly, concern over emigration fused issues of gender and race, as it was felt that loss of those who 'would have made the best mothers and wives' would leave 'at home the timid, the stupid, and the dull to help in the deterioration of the race and to breed sons as sluggish as themselves'.[36] Both ideas of racial pride and racial fears are projected on to the body of woman. The association between environment, in particular climate, and national character was linked to the Celticism of Matthew Arnold and his characterisation of the emotional Celt as forever between the tear and the smile, which was adopted, adapted or rejected by nationalist writers.[37]

The volatile emotional character of the Celt was linked to changeable weather conditions. The Western landscape and its weather, which was considered as a magnified version of the country's climatic conditions, was considered as 'a breeding ground for one of the picked races of the world'.[38] The sky which Emily Lawless describes

> as one must go to Ireland — nay, to West Ireland — to see; great rolling masses of clouds above, black or seemingly black by contrast with the pale opaque serenity beneath . . . Nowhere any direct sunlight, yet the play of light and shadow was endless, tint following tint, line following line, shade following shade in an interminable gradation of light and movement[39]

would be linked by later writers to the Irish temperament.

> It is in this striking effect of contrast in almost everything we looked at that the peculiarity of our scenery chiefly consists, and it appears to have stamped the character of our people with those contrasting lights and shades so well exhibited in our exquisite and strongly marked national music. In the loveliness of the landscape in Ireland, as in the character of the people who inhabit it, and in their music, the smile and the tear are ever close together.[40]

This conflation of landscape and national character was made explicit in an article of 1922, in which the 'Tears of Ireland' stood for both the racial character and Ireland's rainfall. First establishing the racial origin of this melancholia, the writer goes on to suggest that to the matter of race and history 'must be added the factor of climate and geographical conditions' which he describes as 'skies that often weep' and 'elements in Ireland's physical contour calculated to create serious moments in human lives. It is a well-watered land with many a hill-guarded rivulet reflecting the gloom of shadow-haunted skies and the melancholy of solitary ways.'[41] Linked to Celticism, the climate was seen as a source of national character.

THE VISITOR'S GAZE AND THE LANDSCAPE OF DESIRE

In perhaps the most significant scene in the novel, Grania confronts two English women visiting the island and their male companion. It is in this scene that the sense of Emily Lawless's own position, as ambiguously positioned in relation to her subject matter, and the tensions of race, gender, class and culture are most apparent. The colonised subject, especially the colonised woman, so often the object of the gaze of the traveller, is allowed to look back. In a rare account of the response of the peasant to the privileged, enquiring and appropriating eyes of the visitor, Emily Lawless allows the representation of the feelings of Grania, the sense of intrusion, the sense of being looked upon.

> A vehement feeling of annoyance made Grania long to rush away, to hide herself behind a boulder, to do anything rather than have to encounter these strangers — gentry, the sort of people that Murdough was always talking about and envying — people who lived in big white houses with staring windows like those she had seen in Galway. Pride, however and a sort of stubbornness hindered her from running away. She went on accordingly down the path, and when the contact became imminent, merely stepped in a little aside, on to a piece of flat rock beside a stunted thorn bush and stood there — her cumbersome burden rising behind her — waiting till the visitors had passed.[42]

The position is reversed and the visitors are afforded the descriptions usually given to the peasant woman, with its detailed reporting of dress and physical characteristics. 'There were three of them — two ladies and a young man escorting them. they came up laughing, evidently amused, and enjoying the sense of discovery — for Inishmaan was all but untrodden ground — a flutter of skirts and parasols, of hat-ribands and waterproof cloaks filling up the pathway.'[43] Lawless is aware of the mythic sense of discovery, part of primitivism, with its suggestion of the unchanging, isolated and pristine quality of the region prior to 'discovery', yet she is implicated in the position of the visitors. Though knowing the Aran Islands since her childhood in Co. Galway, her mother's home, she is separated by class, religion, and culture from the community she depicts in *Grania*. This distance would have been heightened in her tour of the Aran Islands with the English Sir Henry and Lady Blake while she was preparing the novel.

The reversal in this passage counteracts the repeated descriptions of the women of the West which recur with almost formulaic predictability in travel writing on the region, with varying degrees of sexualised content. While convergences can be mapped between the colonial appropriation of the landscape of the colony and the production of the subject woman, the codes of representation of the peasant woman were re-employed in nationalist writing on the West. In this writing the West features as a landscape of desire, cultural and sexual. In reaction to feminisation of the Irish character in Celticism, the Irish-Ireland movement asserted masculinity as the essential characteristic of the Gael.[44] Yet the shift from emphasis on Celtic to Gaelic did not make the use of the woman's body redundant as a signifier of meaning, though the feminine was rejected for the masculine as epitomising the national character. In this example from 1909, ideas of anti-urbanism, nationalism, concern abut the body, health and physique, and a thinly disguised eroticism are projected on to the woman's body, and against England as urban, industrial and debased.

> Poorer than Donegal, poorer than Kerry — yet how infinitely better is life there than in the crowded slums. There rises to my mind the figure of a young girl whom I passed on the lovely shore of Kilkieran Bay — she stepping along beside an older woman, bareheaded, barefooted, her young breasts showing graciously under her light blue bodice; very young, untouched by care, but glorious in the strength and symmetry of her unspoilt beauty. Compare her with the factory-hand, beribboned, over-balanced with the feather in her hat, her figure deformed by bending over a machine, its deformity emphasised by a hideous copy of some demoded fashion; and how your peasant outshines your cockney . . . The strident coarseness of towns is remote from all this range of existence.[45]

The emphasis on dress in the description of the people of the West corresponds to the importance of dress as a marker of national identity. Its importance was testified to in the concern over national costume in the Gaelic revival movement, which amounted to a 'national dress debate' in the 1910s.[46] As a volatile marker of national and sexual status and visible sign of difference 'the (ad)dress of the national subject may identify, disguise, distort or enhance the desired body politic'; as part of a 'variable cultural nexus constructed from such elements as race, class and geography, dress can indicate the seams within a national culture where several of these elements are stitched together'.[47] The emphasis on the red skirts of the women was tied to the symbolism of the colour as an indication of vitality, and to the belief in the national love of colour, evident from ancient costume.[48] In *Grania*, a starving family, who appear like 'some earth or rock emanation', rather than 'things of living flesh and blood, so grey were they, so wan, so much the same colour, so much apparently the same texture as what they leaned against', are contrasted to Grania's vividness and vigour and her strength and potential biological productiveness.[49] The 'deformity' of the factory hand through 'bending over a machine' is also a deformity considered to be the product of modern fashion which was considered to restrict the female reproductive functions. The concern over dress can be understood in the context of the cultural and biological role which was afforded to women within Irish nationalism.[50] The celebration of the women of the West intersects with issues of concern over degeneration, anti-urbanism, the moral economy of the body, and the sexual politics of representation.

However equivocal was the position of Emily Lawless in relation to these codes of representation, in allowing Grania an acknowledged subjectivity in response to the visitors, she de-stabilises these codes while implicated in the primitivising of the region and its people. That Grania's confrontation is with women travellers raises the issue of women's travel writing and their position within their own patriarchal and racist society and their approach to the cultures and people they encountered.[51] In this passage of the novel Grania is both presented for view, and most significantly looks back:

> Grania stood doggedly waiting — her head a little thrown back; something of the storm and stress that filled her visible in her whole look and bearing, a wild, untamed vision of strength and savage beauty, standing beside that crooked and stunted thorn-bush. The visitors to the island were a little taken by surprise by it. One of the two ladies put up an eye glass to look at her, at the same time touching her friend's arm so as to call her attention. With an angry sense that she was being stared at, Grania on her side turned and gazed fiercely at them, her great slumberous eyes, so southern in their darkness, filled with a curious lowering light.[52]

Grania, though primitivised and exoticised, the red-skirted woman of the West, as both woman and colonial subject, for one moment at least returns the gaze.

Children of Earth

REGENERATION FROM WITHIN: THE WESTERN LANDSCAPE IN A NATIONALIST TEXT

In *Children of Earth*, Maolan, the western island, whose name Figgis derived from the Irish word *maolan,* meaning 'something bare', or 'a bleak eminence', is isolated, austere and demanding, and provides the environment in which to dramatise the relationship between the island people and the Earth Mother, and their steadfastness, endurance, dignity and strength.

The story recounts the relationship between Eoghan O'Cleary, 'an Earth-child more consciously than any of those others who yet bore her imprint' and Nancy O'Flatherty, and the conflict between their love with his 'counter-fidelity' to nature.[53] Again, the title of the novel provides an initial starting point and a clue to the context of ideas in which the novel was written. The importance of the notion of 'Earth', which is used as a personal name for a personified and feminine nature, emerges strongly in the text. Yet, while Darrell Figgis was writing *Children of Earth* he published an appreciation of George Russell, *Æ: A Study of a Man and a Nation,* and it is within this work that the author elaborates on his concept of Earth. George Russell was a mystic, artist, writer and organiser of the Irish co-operative movement. It is against the mixture of pragmatism and spirituality, of anti-urbanism, and ideas of regeneration of and through the rural, which were interlaced in the co-operative movement, that the novel can be read.[54] Both Figgis and Russell shared in a lament for a loss of spirituality which separation from nature had entailed, and the belief that a return to the land would enable spiritual and physical regeneration. Linked to legend and folklore, Earth for Figgis was Dana, the ancient goddess, of whom modern urban dwellers were unaware, 'thinking nothing of the great life, the deep knowledge, the throb of power beneath them; or the joy of the great Shining Ones that are housed within her or that throng the heavenly places in hierarchy on hierarchy of brightness and beauty and power.'[55]

The title *Children of Earth* implies not only the sense of offspring, nurtured, tended and disciplined by a loving, yet stern Earth as mother, but also the sense of innocence, security and simplicity before separation from the mother. It evokes the 'youngling joy' which Figgis claims is 'our true heritage' in discussing George Russell's essay 'The Renewal of Youth'.[56] The title also echoes the term 'Children of the Fields' which Russell used to describe the rural population in his essay on 'The Building up of a Rural Civilization' of 1912.[57] The novel stands in relation also to the West of folklore, constructed by Yeats, Lady Gregory, and other folklorists, in the way the idea of Earth is linked to the folklore of the *sidhe*, the 'bright ones' of the Irish underworld. The sense of the display of the landscape for an external audience, which was overt in Lawless's novel, is not present in Figgis's. Figgis taps the shared resonance of the Western landscape, yet in his emphasis on the power of the Earth the landscape figures more importantly than is suggested in the final phase of the three-stage model of post-colonial fiction. As in *Grania*, the bond between the community and its landscape is significant in the context of attempts to prevent emigration. Like *Grania,* the novel must also be seen in relation to theories of the relationship between human life and the environment, in particular, in this case, the role of the environment in evolution. The West provided again the focus for the intersection of these ideas with conceptions of national identity.

LANDSCAPE AND PEOPLE; REVERSAL OF COLONIAL EQUATIONS

Like Grania, Eoghan is presented as possessing a deep and instinctive love of and closeness to nature, and like Grania is distanced from his community. Yet the positive evaluation of Grania as close to nature in Emily Lawless's novel is extended to the rest of the community in *Children of Earth*. Eoghan's dignity, reserve, pride and sympathy with the rhythms of nature are simply a heightened manifestation of the community's characteristics. James Burke is sent as a village schoolmaster to the island, and falls in love with Nancy. They marry after a matchmaking in which Nancy feels powerless to intervene, but which brings her to a realisation of her love for Eoghan. James Burke is presented as isolated from the temperament of the people and in discord with their natural environment; 'There was none of that fixed unrelenting pursuit of his object that seemed to be demanded by this portion of the face of Earth. There was no strength, no calm, no fixed resolve; and even his passion seemed of another order, less deep, more whimsically cast.' The people of Coisabhaun and Islean, villages on the island, are described as 'more abiding'.[58] Maurya, Nancy's mother who had opposed their match, comes to love and respect Eoghan, as she works with him and sees 'the love he had for the land, as one who was part of it, grown out of it, and thinking for it', bound in simple unity in the recognition that their 'flesh came from Earth, and their sweat watered it again'.[59] In *Grania,* closeness to nature is presented as wildness. In *Children of Earth* it is a source of stability, constancy and strength. The colonial equation of wild landscape with 'wild Irish' is reversed. The environment is powerful but its energy in Figgis's novel is directed, controlled and understandable in its seasonal cycle. Eoghan's quiet dignity, strength, endurance and affinity with the land are characteristics shared by the rest of the community in Figgis's depiction of the island. This counteracts the negative stereotype of the Irish people as voluble and shiftless; the colonial image which Figgis had rejected explicitly in his article on Irish nationality in the *English Review* in 1913.[60] The community is presented as in accord with and respectful of this varying environmental energy, the exertions of earth.

GEOGRAPHY AND DEMOGRAPHY: THE NATIONAL LANDSCAPE AND NATIONAL HEALTH

At the beginning of each of the three sections of the novel is a chapter solely devoted to description of the seasonal characteristics of Earth. While indicating the passage of time, in these accounts Earth becomes a character in the text, and her realm the setting for the story. The landscape in the novel acts as both agent and arena. In counterposing an Irish national identity, based on rural life and spirituality to that of an English urban, industrial materialism, the landscape of the West could be invested with symbolism based on the physical geography of the region and its social significance. Other Irish landscapes did not provide the degree of difference from the image of English 'south country', to enable them to stand as national landscapes. The scale of the topography and the weather conditions, the degree to which the geological and structural formations of the region were visible in the region with its sparse vegetation and open vistas, emphasised the natural forces and suggested the limits of human endeavour in relation to these natural conditions. The sense of large scale forces, of ocean, of wind and mountain is used in *Children of Earth* to convey an idea of a purposeful nature. The novel opens with a description of a storm, 'a night of revelry for Earth herself. She in whose setting their little affairs were rehearsed, who bent and shaped them and their doings, dismissed them now and took uninterrupted possession of her spaces', 'Earth who moulds and builds the destinies of those who lean on her bosom, stretched her power to the utmost . . . Earth rose in dominance over the life she had bred and, in hardihood nurtured.'[61] Earth is presented as an active, conscious, purposeful agent, 'ever present, attuning and tempering her sons of men when they were least aware of her, or of her strong knowledge of them'.[62] The Western landscape becomes the arena in which the natural forces condition, harden and breed the people to physical and spiritual perfection, 'She bred her children, and those that leaned on her bosom, she tutored to the strength and fierceness she herself knew.'[63]

In the novel this sense of environmental determinism is presented as the deliberate result of a divine will and plan. In describing the coming of winter, Figgis uses the language of Darwinian evolutionary theory, but connects it to the purposeful actions of Earth rather than a random process.

> She the creator of life, and its suckler, was showing how she could kill, select, harden and discipline. She who fed and fostered gave no heed now either to stiffening limbs or whimpering complaint. Her infinite cruelty became like her infinite tenderness, an influence while on her way to a further goal. She killed as she created, making the one deed an immolation as the other was a gift offering, while a larger purpose shone like a crown above the seeming medley of her fortunes. And always she was beautiful; divinely not malignly so. She justified herself by the perfect justification, beyond all schemes of intellect; divine beauty.[64]

Natural selection, and the survival of the fittest, is linked to earth's 'larger purpose'.

In the late nineteenth and early twentieth century, evolutionary theory was employed in debates concerning human degeneration.[65] In both Darwinian and Lamarckian theories of evolution, the role of environment was stressed. In both, degeneration could result from lack or lessening of environmental stimulus. Linked to fears of racial degeneration consequent on urban growth and the regenerating potential of rural life, these discourses circulated in both scientific and popular publications. The construction of the West was linked to these wider discourses, but was imbued with nationalist implications. It could be conceived of as a national landscape which, due to its demanding and difficult environment and the challenge presented by its natural topography and weather conditions, was productive of a people celebrated for their physical perfection. These people, hardened by the environment were considered the model of excellence for a national population. The conflation of body and nation, in national discourse, which found its most extreme expression in the contemporaneous British eugenics movement, was a concern with the 'body politic' — the nation and the national population. George Russell, in 1912, writing on the role of women within the co-operative movement, interweaves themes of spirituality, anti-urbanism, health, bodily perfection, and nationalism with its implications in terms of gender. Women, according to Russell

> will bring home to the long drugged and long dulled national conscience that the right aim of a nation is the creation of fine human beings, and not merely the production of national wealth. Women, however they may err as individuals, are concerned collectively far more than men about the character and well-being of a race. It is a divinely-implanted instinct with them, and this instinct must be liberated and let work its will.[66]

The emphasis on bodily excellence as a product of environment was a reaction to nineteenth-century simianisation of the Irish peasant in the English press. It was also linked to the concern over cultural and racial preservation and reproduction in nationalist discourse. For Russell, unsanitary conditions have caused the population to

> become so unhealthy and ugly, so distorted from the divine image, that beautiful women and shapely men who ought to be normal are abnormal. All the strings of our being are being grayed or flaccid, or hanging loose, or are too tight, and there is no health in us; and rarely do our eyes light up at a beautiful and healthy human being with the perfect modelling and sweet curves which denote perfect health.

He suggests the selection of 'half a dozen people of both sexes, beautiful and healthy persons' and their exhibition in every village in Ireland, with accompanying dictum, 'To aspire to have a nation of people like these is the right aspiration of a great nationality.'[67] It is within this context that the symbolic significance of the western landscape can be understood, as a landscape productive of national health.

Embedded within the discourses of anti-urbanism and celebration of the rural, which figured strongly in the writings of George Russell, the landscape of the West in *Children of Earth* features as both a landscape of the sublime, in the extremity of the natural forces, whose evolutionary role has been discussed above, and as an Irish pastoral, a hard pastoral, without a sense of leisure or easily won productivity. Working the land, the people are presented as in tune with a life which is deeper and more spiritual, as the 'great stable element in the life of the nation'. In Darrell Figgis's account of the early summer work of the people in the fields, the sense of the harsh but divine power of nature remains.[68] The sense of the West as an exacting landscape of mountains, of tiny fields reclaimed from the bog and of Atlantic storms, is contrasted with the fecundity and richness of the English pastoral. It shared with this image the glorification of rural toil, yet the arduous nature of agriculture and its vulnerability to damage by natural forces make this hard pastoral a source both of spiritual and corporal health and power.

In Synge's account of the Aran Islands of 1907, a similar theory of environmental influence is suggested. The danger involved in fishing, for Synge, had considerable influence on the local character, since those unable to survive due to awkwardness, cowardice or stupidity would have been eliminated in the survival of the fittest.[69] The rocky terrain, for which pampooties, the local footwear, were most suitable, he suggests has preserved for the people the 'agile walk of the wild animal, while the general simplicity of their lives has given them many other points of physical perfection'.[70] To this link between environment, lifestyle and physique is added the stimulus of a lifestyle in which the variety of activity due to the absence of any division of labour is considered to be a source of intelligence.[71] This way of life, like their implements, which for Synge 'seem to exist as a natural link between the people and the world that is around them' is presented as in an organic relationship to environment.[72] While this environment is personified into a deeply elemental divine female goddess in *Children of Earth,* the conception of the evolutionary power of the Western landscape is reiterated. It is partly this divine purpose behind the austerity of the landscape that allows the landscape to be considered stern yet beautiful, in contrast to the description of Inishmaan by Lawless as 'the most retrograde spot, probably, within the four seas' with an 'ugliness enough to sicken not the eyes or the heart alone, but the very stomach'.[73] With the shift in its symbolic meaning is the shift in the perception of the Western landscape.

SPIRITUALITY, SEXUALITY AND THE WESTERN LANDSCAPE

Eoghan's relationship with Earth has implications in terms both of gender and national identity. His closeness to nature counteracts the usual conception of women as close to nature through their biological reproductive ability. It also differs from folkloric accounts of the 'wise women' recorded in Lady Gregory's *Visions and Beliefs in the West of Ireland.*[74] Yet not only is nature feminised, and presented as a mother figure, but also the author's description of Earth, and Eoghan's relationship to Earth, slips from the maternal to the sexual. Earth 'stands before him', 'reveals herself'. Eoghan lies in the heather 'as though he were taking an enormous caress and revelling voluptuously in it.'[75] In his mind, the land and the body of Nancy become merged. He leaves her after a meeting on the heath 'dimly perceiving the rolling masses of dark earth that seemed to him as much the living pressure-giving and pressure-taking flesh of her whose embrace was yet warm on his body.'[76] While away from the island after Nancy's marriage to James Burke, he begins to 'want the mountains there with a terrible passion, with a thirst that subdued all his thinking till he became less a man than an absorbing desire.'[77] He has visions of Earth as 'a strong masterful shape, woman-like in face and roundness of limb, darkly red of hue, with great round eyes, dark and deep into which he had perforce to look', described later as 'a dark face with dark skin and dark eyes over full breasts'.[78]

This sense of love for the feminised landscape yet fear of its power is repeated in the account of the feelings of another islandman toward nature, in which the sexual element of the love is cast in Oedipal terms with its mixture of guilt and fear. 'He looked on Earth as a son may look on his mother, loving her, proud and glad in her, yet more than half ashamed at the strength of his affection. The life pulsed from earth to him in the one vein, and astonished him with joy till he defended himself against himself.'[79] Like the Oedipal love of the mother, love of Earth has become a source of shame. The desire for loss of self in experience of nature, with its echoes of Synge's account of his experience on Aran, becomes in Figgis's account of Eoghan's ritual on the heath an orgasmic loss of consciousness of self.[80] Eoghan often leaves Nancy after their marriage and its first passionate weeks to wander the hills at night. Nancy, distraught and uncomprehending, searches for him on the hills which she fears and finds him one night at a stone circle, turning towards each stone to 'kiss the earth at his feet with the same self-forgetful ecstasy that she herself so well knew'.[81] Though a sense of closeness towards nature is projected on to the whole community, the conscious relationship to female Earth is presented as gender exclusive, described in terms of a heterosexual or Oedipal mother-son relationship. Though Eoghan inherits this feeling from his mother, who dies in an asylum, having been abandoned by Eoghan's father because of her wanderings on the hills when Eoghan was a baby crying for her at night, this fact is subordinated in the novel to the emphasis on Eoghan's masculine relationship with feminised Earth, which conforms to the nationalist rejection of the feminisation of Irishness in Celticism.[82]

The West as a region of people, spiritual and superstitious, and keenly aware of the supernatural, presented by folklorists, is rearticulated in *Children of Earth* into a region in which this spirituality is on a much deeper level, linked to reverence for nature and ancient wisdom. This version of the West as Celtic, feminine and superstitious, had its precedent in Arnoldian colonial construction of Irishness. In the novel it is replaced with a West in which the landscape rather than the population is feminine, the domain of a people whose strength and virility were a product of the strength of earth and whose spirituality is not superstition but deep awareness of larger powers. In *Grania,* folklore functions to provide humorous subject matter, and is linked to the primitive, as Lawless suggests the Celt's awareness of the supernatural is akin to that of sensitive animals. An account of a woman's opposition to the local belief that her baby has been taken and replaced with a fairy child presents the people as illogical and ignorant, cruel as well as comic. In *Children of Earth* the people's sense of a supernatural world is an extension of their corporal experience of their environment. Eoghan's repeated bending low to embrace the wind becomes a reverential ritual of homage to the power of Earth.

This sense of the spiritual in nature is consistent with a growth in mysticism, which had its adherents in the theosophical movement in Dublin led by George Russell.[83] This sense of spirituality was discordant with Catholic conceptions of Irish life which rejected the notion that orthodox religion was a thin veneer over an innate paganism. The degree to which passionate love and its physical expression feature in the novel was also in conflict with the emphasis on the family and the subordination of sexuality by Catholic nationalists. Yet Figgis's emphasis on sexuality appears not as a rejection of the restrictions of Catholic teaching but as a reaction to the colonial image of the peasant as devoid of romantic feeling. In *Grania,* Lawless's frequent assertion of the lack of a conception of romantic love amongst the people implies the instinctive nature of their sexuality, which is controlled by the rigid norms of the island community. It is against this image that Figgis writes. In *Children of Earth,* Eoghan and Nancy's love appears as an emanation from the powerful, procreative energy of Earth. Their cycle of passion and tenderness follows the alternating storm and calm of the weather after their marriage. The description of the Western community in *Children of Earth* is deeply structured by the rejection of the negative aspects of the colonial image.

Despite the difference in the authors' backgrounds and contexts, it is within *Grania* that Catholicism is most overt. However, the representation of Irish religious devotion, through the figure of Honor, in Emily Lawless's novel, suggests that it functions as a display both of its excesses and its superficiality. In *Children of Earth* orthodox religion plays a minor role. Its ceremonies are presented as part of the cycle of births, marriages and deaths of the island community. Its minor role suggests its accepted significance, and its presence in harmony with reverence to Earth. Though the depiction of Eoghan's worship of earth conflicts with writings on the

West which emphasise the Catholic piety of the people, in its reframing of peasant superstition, *Children of Earth* does represent a nationalist appropriation of the symbolism of the Western landscape. The West as land of fairy and folk tale and of people whimsically superstitious, becomes the West of a deep spiritualism based on love of the landscape and its power. Again it is a rejection of the Celtic and feminine for the Gaelic and masculine, employing gendered ideas of male and female to support expressions of national identity. It is only the curse which Eoghan put on Nancy's marriages which threatens to upset this rewriting.

Yet the author leaves the reader to decide whether it is the curse or their belief in it which eventually causes Nancy's death. In this recasting of Western spirituality in terms of love and recognition of the powers of nature, the West becomes, in the author's words, an expression of, 'the spiritual world, of which the world of landscape is an appearance'.[84]

In both colonial and nationalist writings, the land and the body featured in the construction of Irishness and Irish national identity. The physical geography features as both a symbol and a source of the social geography of the region. Differences between the varied versions of the West lie in the degree to which the landscape and the people, considered as product of the landscape, were positively viewed. The links believed to exist between the human geography and the environment made the West and its symbolism central to debates concerning the political, cultural and demographic nation, in the context of Irish nationalism. Emily Lawless's novel represents both a colonial text and one which subverts the colonial ideology. The popular image of the West of Ireland has emerged from its appropriation as a national landscape of regeneration, against the landscape of Englishness, as in *Children of Earth*, but it remains shadowed by its colonial representation and context of European romantic primitivism. It is against this background that the symbolic value of Paul Henry's paintings can be understood. In 1912 Darrell Figgis moved to Achill Island. Paul and Grace Henry also moved to this island in the same year. Influenced by their reading of Synge, they followed in the tradition of moves to the peripheries by Synge, Paul Gauguin and the artists of the painting colonies of Brittany.[85] The construction of the West was part of both an Irish national and a wider European context. This article has been about different versions of the 'West'. It is perhaps this multiplicity of meaning which gives the West its symbolic power. It stood for Irishness, yet its uniqueness was utilised in promoting its suitability as a tourist destination. Experience of the West meant and continues to mean contact with Irish landscape and life, and in visits to the Gaeltacht regions, the Irish language. While remaining an important tourist destination, its cultural centrality is being undermined by those who question its masking of alternative versions of Irish national identity and its relevance to modern Ireland. Yet the amount of energy spent in contesting its ascendency in contemporary Irish culture suggests the strength and resilience of its symbolic power as embodying the nation.

NOTES AND REFERENCES

1   O'Faolain, S. (1940), *An Irish Journey,* ills. by Paul Henry, Longmans, Green and Co., London, p. 181.
2   Daniels, S. and Cosgrove, D. (1988), 'Introduction: the Iconography of Landscape', in Daniels, S. and Cosgrove, D. (eds.), *The Iconography of Landscape,* Cambridge University Press, Cambridge, pp. 1-10.
3   Congested Districts Board (1892-8), *Base Line Reports of Inspectors, 1892-8,* Dublin.
4   Kennedy, B. (1905), *The Green Sphinx,* London, Methuen, p. 202.
5   Green, A.S., Barbour, H., Hyde, D. and Wilson, A. (1914), 'The Connemara Islands', *Irish Review,* iv(39): 113-27, 124.
6   MacDonagh, M. (1890), 'Life in Achill and Aran', *The Westminster Review,* 134(2): 159-71, 161-2.
7   This issue is raised in Brydon, D. (1991), 'The White Inuit Speak; Contamination as Literary Strategy', in Adam, I. and Tiffin, H. (eds.), *Past the Last Post, Theorising Post-Colonialism and Post-Modernism,* Harvester Wheatsheaf, New York and London.
8   Smith, A.D. (1986), *The Ethnic Origins of Nations,* Basil Blackwell, Oxford, pp. 174-208.
9   Ashcroft, B. et al. (1989), *The Empire Writes Back; Theory and Practice in Post-Colonial Literatures,* Routledge, London.
10 Ashcroft, B. et al., op. cit., pp. 5-6, and Gray, S. (1986), 'A Sense of Place in the New Literatures in English', in Nightingale, P., *A Sense of Place in the New Literatures in English,* University of Queensland Press, St Lucia, New York and London, Queensland Press, pp. 5-12.
11 For biographical information see: Brewer, B.W. (1983), ' "She was part of it": Emily Lawless (1845-1913)', *Eire — Ireland,* 19(4): 119-31, Sichel, E. (1914), 'Emily Lawless', *The Nineteenth Century,* lxxvi, July: 80-100, Malone, A.E. (1926), 'Darrell Figgis', *Dublin Magazine,* xii, (3), July-September: 47-54.
12 For examples of writing on the Aran Islands see O hEithir, B. and R. (1991), *An Aran Reader,* Lilliput Press, Dublin.
13 Anon (1901), 'By the Atlantic Shore', *Ireland; an Illustrated Journal of the Green Isle,* 1(11), May. An example of an early tourist publication is Thomas Cook and Son (1900), *Tours and Excursions to and through the Emerald Isle,* London, Dublin and Belfast.
14 Foster, J.W. (1977), 'Certain Set Apart: The Western Island in the Irish Renaissance', *Studies,* 66(264): 261-74, and Foster, J.W. (1987), *Fictions of the Irish Literary Revival: A Changeling Art,* Syracuse University Press, New York; Gill and Macmillan, Dublin, pp. 94-113.

15   Howkins, A. (1986), 'The Discovery of Rural England', in Colls, R. and Dodd, P., *Englishness; Politics and Culture 1880-1920,* Croom Helm, London, pp. 62-88.
16   Lawless, E. (1892), *Grania: the Story of an Island,* Smith, Elder & Co., London, p. 27.
17   ibid., p. 60.
18   ibid., p. 3-4.
19   ibid., p. 13-4.
20   ibid., p. 47.
21   ibid., p. 175.
22   ibid., p. 21.
23   See for example, Browne, C.R. and Haddon, A.C. (1893), 'The Ethnography of the Aran Islands, Co. Galway', *Proceedings of the Royal Irish Academy,* **18**: 768-830.
24   Lawless, E. (1892), p. 5.
25   ibid., p. 59.
26   ibid., p. 199.
27   Goldwater, R. (1967), *Primitivism in Modern Art,* Random House, Vintage Books, New York; Hiller, S. (ed.) (1991), *The Myth of Primitivism, Perspectives on Art,* Routledge, London; Varnedoe, K., *A Fine Disregard: What Makes Modern Art Modern,* Thames and Hudson, London, pp. 183-215.
28   Lawless, E. (1892), pp. 5-6.
29   ibid., p. 66.
30   ibid., p. 144.
31   ibid., p. 61.
32   Livingstone, D.N. (1991), 'The Moral Discourse of Climate: Historical Considerations on Race, Place and Virtue', *Journal of Historical Geography* 17:413-34; Livingstone, D.N. (1992), ' "Never Shall ye Make the Crab Walk Straight": An Inquiry into the Scientific Sources of Racial Geography' in Driver, F. and Rose, G., *Nature and Science: Essays in the History of Geographical Knowledge,* Historical Geography Research Series, **28**:37-47; Pick, S. (1989), *Faces of Degeneration: Aspects of a European Disorder c. 1848-1918,* Cambridge University Press, Cambridge.
33   Stephan, N. (1985), 'Biological Degeneration: Races and Proper Places', in Chamberlain, J.E. and Gilman, S.L. (eds.) (1985), *Degeneration: The Dark Side of Progress,* Columbia University Press, New York.
34   McCarthy, G. (1911), 'Emigration, Climate and Race', *Irish Review,* **1**, July:209-14; see also Kelly, R.J. (1904), 'Emigration and its Consequences', *New Ireland Review,* **xxi**, July:257-67, O'Malley, A. (1916), 'The Effects of the American Climate on the European Immigration', *Studies,* 5:516-35.
35   Kelly, R.J., op. cit., p. 266. (Queenstown was the name for Cobh, Co. Cork under British administration.)
36   Russell, G.W. (1912), *Co-operation and Nationality,* Maunsel and Company Ltd., Dublin, pp. 67-8.
37   Cairns, D. and Richards, S. (1988), *Writing Ireland: Colonialism, Nationalism and Culture,* Manchester University Press, Manchester, pp. 42-57.
38   Gwynn, S. (1909), *A Holiday in Connemara,* Methuen, London, p. 312.
39   Lawless, E., op. cit., p. 121.
40   Flood, J.M. (1918), *In Five Provinces: a Journal of Wanderings in Ireland,* Thomas Kiersey, Dublin, p. 14.

41   Cassidy, J.J. (1922), 'The Tears of Ireland', *Catholic Bulletin*, **xii**, January:40-5.

42   Lawless, E., op. cit., pp. 272-3.

43   Lawless, E., op. cit., p. 273.

44   Butler Cullingford, E. (1990), ' "Thinking of her . . . as . . . Ireland' ': Yeats, Pearse and Heaney', *Textual Practice*, **4**(1): 1-21; Cairns, D. and Richards, S. (1987), 'Woman in the Discourse of Celticism', *Canadian Journal of Irish Studies*, **13**(1):43-60.

45   Gwynn, S. (1909), op. cit., pp. 91-2.

46   See, for example, Concannon, E. (1911), 'Our Dress Problem: a Proposed Solution', *Catholic Bulletin*, **1**(2):4-5, and Russell, G. (1910), 'Irish National Costume', *The Irish Homestead*, 29 January.

47   Parker, A., Russo, M., Sommer, D. and Yaeger, P. (eds.) (1992), *Nationalism and Sexualities*, Routledge, London, p. 10.

48   For a later example see: O'Byrne, C. (1936), 'Irish Love of Colour', *Irish Monthly*, **lxiv**: 179-82.

49   Lawless, E. (1892), op. cit., p. 38.

50   Yuval-Davis, N. and Anthais, F. (eds.) (1989), *Women — Nation — State*, St. Martin's Press, New York.

51   See Mills, S. (1991), *Discourses of Difference, An Analysis of Women's Travel Writing and Colonialism*, Routledge, London.

52   Lawless, E. (1892), op. cit., p. 273.

53   Figgis, D. (1918), *Children of Earth*, Maunsel, Dublin, p. 42. The story involves a curse of drowning which Eoghan puts on Nancy's marrying, in his distress at her matching to the local schoolmaster, despite their powerful love. Following the drowning of her husband, he marries her to take the curse on himself, feeling responsible for the man's death. Nancy learns of this and eventually drowns trying to prevent Eoghan's death from the curse.

54   Figgis, D. (1916), *Æ: A Study of a Man and a Nation*, Maunsel, Dublin and London.

55   ibid., p. 2.

56   ibid., pp. 48-9.

57   Russell, G. (1912), op. cit., pp. 98-9.

58   Figgis, D. (1918), op. cit., pp. 62-3.

59   ibid., p. 268.

60   Figgis, D. (1913), 'Irish Nationality', *English Review*, **xiv**, April–July:456-68.

61   Figgis, D. (1918), op. cit., p. 1.

62   ibid., pp. 4-5.

63   ibid., p. 302.

64   ibid., pp. 75-6.

65   Bowler, P. (1989), 'Holding your Head up High: Degeneration and Orthogenesis in Theories of Human Evolution', in Moore, J. (ed), *History, Humanity and Evolution*, Cambridge University Press, Cambridge, pp. 329-53.

66   Russell, G. (1912), op. cit., pp. 71-2.

67   ibid., pp. 71-2.

68   Figgis, D. (1918), op. cit., p. 122. For a discussion of the symbolism of rural labour see Barrell, J. (1980), *The Dark Side of the Landscape, the Rural Poor in English Painting, 1730-1840*, Cambridge University Press, Cambridge and Gibbons, L. (1988), 'Romanticism, Realism and Irish Cinema', in Rockett, K., Gibbons, L. and Hill, J., *Cinema and Ireland*, Routledge, London, pp. 194-257.

69   Synge, J.M. (1907), *The Aran Islands,* Maunsel, Dublin; Elkin Mathews, London, p. 215.

70   ibid., pp. 178-9.

71   ibid., p. 260.

72   ibid., p. 168.

73   Lawless, E. (1892), pp. 14, 75.

74   Gregory, A. (1970, first published 1920), *Visions and Beliefs in the West of Ireland,* Colin Smythe, Gerrards Cross.

75   Figgis, D. (1918), op. cit., pp. 65-6.

76   ibid., p. 53.

77   ibid., p. 131.

78   ibid., pp. 116, 122.

79   ibid., p. 123.

80   Figgis had written of this idea of unity with the landscape through a loss of a distinct and separate sense of self in his account of Synge's work; Figgis, D. (1911), 'The Art of J.M. Synge', *Fortnightly Review,* **DXL**, NS, December: 1056-68.

81   ibid., p. 273.

82   ibid., p. 141. The connection between his mother's insanity and her rejection of her mothering role may follow the popular and medical notions of the relationship between the reproductive, emotional and mental functions of the woman's body; see Showalter, E. (1987), *The Female Malady, Women, Madness and English Culture 1830-1980,* Virago, London.

83   Matless, D. (1991), 'Nature, the Modern and the Mystic: Tales from Early Twentieth-Century Geography', *Transactions of the Institute of British Geographers,* **16**:272-86; Gibbon, M. (1957), 'Æ and the Early Days of Theosophy in Dublin', *The Dublin Magazine,* **3**, xxxii, (July-September):25-37.

84   Figgis, D. (1918), p. 151; for a discussion of the use of folklore by the revival writers see: Foster, J.W. (1977), *Fictions of the Irish Literary Revival,* pp. 203-18; for an example of Catholic nationalist representation of the West see Bulfin, W. (1979, first published 1907), *Rambles in the West of Ireland*, Mercier Press, Dublin.

85   Knapp, J.K. (1989), 'Primitivism and Empire: John Synge and Paul Gauguin', *Comparative Literature,* Spring, **1**, 2: 53-68; Orton, F. and Pollock, G. (1980), 'Les Données Bretonnantes: La Prairie de représentation', *Art History,* **3**, 3, September:314-44; Paul Henry recalls in his autobiography the influence which reading Synge's work had on him: Henry, P. (1951), *An Irish Portrait,* Batsford, London.

PART III
Tourist
Policy

6

Irish Tourism Policy: Targets, Outcomes and Environmental Considerations

James Deegan and Donal Dineen

Introduction

In the 1980s policymakers in Ireland have been preoccupied with the twin problems of the public finances and the high rate of unemployment. The improvement in the former in recent years has not had a proportionate impact on the latter so that current unemployment rates now stand at 17 per cent[1] with little prospect of falling within the foreseeable future. Sectoral industrial policies have been a major plank in the government's strategy of reducing unemployment but the limited flow of foreign investment in the 1980s (which was in marked contrast to the significant inflows in the previous decade, coinciding with Ireland's initial period of membership of the EEC) and the failure of the indigenous sector to generate sufficient net new jobs has shifted the focus somewhat towards other sectors, one of which is tourism. It is only over the last three to four years that this sector has received the same intense interest as other sectors of the economy in terms of the expectations to deliver jobs. A similar focus on tourism as a key sector for economic regeneration and development has been noted in several of the less-developed and declining regions of the European Community.

Tourism is not a neatly defined sector within the economy, which may partly explain the lack of attention to it in the past. Though the principal sub-sectors are international carriers and accommodation providers several other sub-sectors are affected by the fortunes of the industry either through indirect purchases of goods and services (food, drink, craft goods, financial services) or through the incomes generated in shops, bars and restaurants frequented by tourists.

An additional reason for the relative neglect of tourism as an income and job generator has been the actual and perceived constraints operating to limit the growth of the industry; constraints such as poor image, poor climate and the dearth of cultural attractions which are available in alternative destinations. Haahti refers to a ranking of twelve European countries according to a variety of attributes as perceived by international holidaymakers.[2] Ireland was ranked last, i.e. offered least, on three attributes — accessibility, facilities for sports and activities, and cultural experience — and second last on a fourth — night life and entertainment — while Finland was ranked first on three attributes, two of which have been identified frequently as offering a competitive advantage to holidaying in Ireland — peace and quiet and friendly, hospitable people. These data refer to 1979.

The quality of jobs in tourism is often associated with atypical or precarious work forms having a heavy concentration of relatively low-paid, temporary, part-time and seasonal workers. Placing a heavy emphasis on a sector with such characteristics did not seem attractive as a palliative to mass unemployment.[3] The focus on tourism in recent years may well have been predicated on a simple exhaustion of the job creation alternatives which coincided with the opportunism presented by the doubling of the EC Structural Funds and winding down of the Common Agricultural Policy within the 1992 context. Set against the background of Edwards' forecasts for tourism growth to 1995, Ireland could not afford to lose out on the anticipated boom.[4]

In recent years concern for the environment has made it somewhat more fashionable to consider Ireland as a holiday destination among the internationally mobile community. The growth of 'alternative tourism' has also been strong though its encouragement, however well-intentioned, may lead to its own demise through the attraction of the mass tourist markets.[5] There is an inherent conflict between the policymaker's need to maximise the employment impact of tourism growth, through substantial increases in tourism numbers, and environmental conservation. Short-term objectives need to be tempered by consideration of longer term consequences.

The plan of this chapter is as follows: the first section deals with the objectives of Irish tourism policy and evaluates performance in the light of these objectives, with particular emphasis on government targets of doubling tourism numbers between 1988 and 1992; this is followed by a critical analysis of Irish tourism policy; the following section addresses the environmental impact of present policies and relates this to the debate on sustainable tourism; the final section offers some brief conclusions.

Tourism Policy Objectives and Performance

Following a decade of decline in real terms in externally generated tourism revenue between 1969 and 1979 and a somewhat erratic performance up to the mid–1980s, the government published a White Paper on tourism policy in 1985.[6] This was the first official attempt to clarify government thinking on tourism in a focused manner and to specify the broad objectives of policy.[7] The White Paper outlined the national objective as follows:

> To optimise the economic and social benefits to Ireland of the promotion and development of tourism both to and within the country consistent with ensuring an acceptable economic rate of return on the resources employed and taking account of:
>
> — tourism's potential for job creation,
> — the quality of life and development of the community,
> — the enhancement and preservation of the nation's cultural heritage,
> — the conservation of the physical resources of the country, and
> — tourism's contribution to regional development.[8]

Though characteristically vague, the White Paper nevertheless placed job creation high on the agenda as the desired outcome of tourism development in Ireland. It also recognised the difficulties of measuring the employment attributable to the sector.[9] The 'proportional method' of employment measurement in tourism was the preferred method recommended by the working group on tourism and employment.[10] This method measures the proportion of total expenditure in each expenditure category derived from tourism and applies this proportion to total employment in the relevant sectors; it takes account of indirect and induced employment arising in other sectors, derived from initial tourism spending. Indirect employment refers to the employment in sectors supplying goods and services to the tourism sector itself while induced employment is created through the spending of incomes earned by those employed in tourism or in sub-supply sectors. If employment generation is the principal objective of tourism policy then it was (and is) of the utmost importance that no ambiguity should arise in the measurement of this variable, notwithstanding any data deficiencies which remain.

The period since 1985 has been characterised by a plethora of reports on the tourism sector.[11] These reports generally focused on the opportunities and potential of the sector, the external threats arising from completion of the EC's internal market and the investment programme planned as part of the structural funds made available to Ireland. The importance of the sector to the economy in revenue generation, balance of payments and employment terms was also highlighted, particularly in the Tansey Webster report.

The government also refined its policy objectives into more specific targets in both the *Programme for National Recovery* (1987) and the *National Development Plan, 1989-93* which was published in 1989.[12] Substantial funds to develop the sector were now available from the European Regional Development Fund (ERDF) — the total investment was expected to be of the order of IR£300m. from 1989 to 1993. The breakdown of this total was IR£138m. from the ERDF, IR£152m. from the private sector and the remaining IR£10m. from the public sector. These increased structural funds represent the most important source of finance ever made available to the tourism sector. The demand-side targets which were set projected both the number of visitors and expenditure by those visitors to double over the period 1988-92. This implied an annual compound growth rate of 15 per cent. The government estimated that in order to fulfil these ambitious targets the required number of visitors would be 4.2m. per annum by 1992, with an additional 25,000 jobs in the sector (compared with 2.8m. visitors and 69,000 jobs in 1988).

INDUSTRY PERFORMANCE

Though employment growth is the ultimate objective of government policy, and with it the improvement in living standards, more immediate measures of industry performance may be used to demonstrate tourism's changing contribution to the economy. The number of tourists and the revenue generated by the tourist sector (both domestic and out of state) are two key variables used in this context. Figure 6.1 provides a schematic outline of the various performance measures relevant to the tourism sector.

The focus in this section is on tourism numbers, expenditures and employment. Tourism numbers, especially foreign visitors to Ireland, represent a key initial target of tourism policy. The trends and composition of overseas tourists are examined since the early 1980s, according to origin country/zone and reason for visit. The total number of overseas visitors to Ireland increased by 84 per cent over the period 1981-90 i.e. from 1.668m to 3.069m. Table 6.1 shows the annual average growth rates for specific sub-periods.

The acceleration in overall growth rates is noted in the latter years of the decade with the compound annual 15 per cent growth rate target almost being achieved. The dramatic substitution of mainland European for North American visitors is evident in this period. Britain is still the principal market for overseas holidays to Ireland though its share declined from 63 to 58 per cent between 1983 and 1990. Comparisons with a number of popular European country destinations (Greece, Portugal, Italy, Spain, UK) shows that Ireland has had more rapid growth in foreign visitor numbers since 1985 and particularly since 1988.

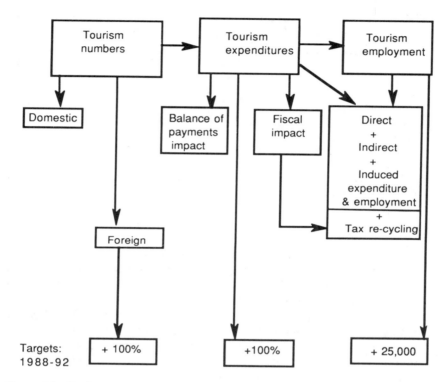

Figure 6.1   Performance measures in the tourism sector

In 1991 total overseas numbers fell by 2.6 per cent. Major declines in visitors from North America (down 20 per cent) and from 'Other Areas' (down 13 per cent) were partially compensated for by an increase in European tourists of 13 per cent.

Table 6.1   Annual Average Percentage Change in Visitor Numbers to Ireland by Area of Residence 1981-91

	1981-85 %	1985-90 %	1988-90 %	1990-91 %
UK	- 1.1	10.1	10.4	- 4.2
Other Europe	4.6	17.5	35.5	13.0
N. America	17.6	1.4	4.0	-19.6
Other areas	14.0	8.6	20.0	-12.9
Total	3.7	9.9	14.4	- 2.6

Sources: Derived from CSO, *Tourism and Travel,* (various years), Stationery Office, Dublin; Bord Fáilte, *Tourism Facts* (various years), Bord Fáilte, Dublin.

Table 6.2   Annual Average Percentage Changes in Visitor Numbers to Ireland by Reason for Journey 1981-90

	1981-85 %	1985-90 %	1988-90 %
Business	-7.3	11.8	7.6
Tourist	5.1	10.9	30.0
VFRs	5.7	8.3	7.3
Other	-3.0	8.4	-0.8
Total	3.5	9.9	14.4

VFRs = Visiting friends/relatives
Source: CSO, *Tourism and Travel,* (various years), Stationery Office, Dublin.

REASON FOR VISIT

The growth rate of tourist numbers is explored in Table 6.2. The VFR (Visiting friends and relatives) category is quite important to the Irish tourist trade where the proportion varied between 32 and 41 per cent of overseas visitors and averaged 37 per cent in the 1988-90 period.

The sustained growth in 'pure' tourist numbers is noted from 1985-90 with particularly dramatic growth in the years 1987-90. VFRs continued their steady growth throughout the decade but expanded at a less than proportionate rate from 1985. Thus Ireland appeared to be gaining market share among non-ethnic tourists which could be critical to longer term development of the sector.

TOURIST EXPENDITURES BY RESIDENCE AND REASON FOR VISIT

Before analysing total expenditure figures it is interesting to compare average spending by the different categories of visitor. The principal Continental European country markets for overseas visitors to Ireland are France and Germany followed by Italy, the Netherlands and Spain, with both Italy and Spain exhibiting particularly strong growth over the latter part of the decade. British based visitors are by far the lowest spenders per capita and their average length of stay tends to be substantially shorter than that of tourists from further afield. North American visitors have traditionally been the highest spenders and this is confirmed when adjustments are made for average duration of stay. Since 1984, the variation in average spend across different origin countries has narrowed. A tourism policy strategy which aims to attract both high spending and long stay visitors is sensible compared with the converse. For this reason concentration on visitor numbers alone as a policy target is inappropriate.

Short stay business visitors tend to spend more on a daily basis per person. While tourists and VFRs stay for similar time periods the lower spend of the latter reflects the absence of accommodation costs in their holiday expenditure. It is likely that VFRs spend more on non-accommodation items (food, drink, retail purchases) than their tourist counterparts, as the difference in average spend (IR£80 in 1990) is too low to be explained by accommodation cost differences alone. Based on patterns over the last five years Table 6.3 shows the average number of visitors required from different origin countries to generate IR£1,000 of foreign exchange earnings (figures exclude access costs).

While the tourist board needs to be aware of market demand trends these figures suggest that the return from marketing expenditure may be more effective in some source markets than others. Environmental concerns would suggest that it is more appropriate to have smaller numbers of high spending tourists rather than large volumes of low spending tourists.

TOURISM EXPENDITURES

The revenue receipts from foreign visitors to Ireland have shown significant fluctuations over a long time span. The steady growth in real terms in the 1960s was followed by a 30 per cent reduction over the 1969-72 period — the start of the Northern troubles. The remainder of the 1970s was characterised by steady recovery especially in the Continental European market. The pattern in the 1980s was one of continued fluctuations up to 1986, partly due to the international recession and dollar exchange rate changes. A steady improvement in real terms was experienced from 1987 to 1991 (Table 6.4).

Domestic tourism revenue varied from 33 to 42 per cent of foreign revenue over the period 1985-91. This puts domestic tourism at approximately one quarter of the total size of the sector. These tourism expenditures (or revenues) may be segmented into payments to Irish carriers and spending on accommodation and other tourist goods in the economy. They may be augmented by domestic tourism expenditures to measure the total

Table 6.3   Number of Tourists Required to Generate IR£1,000 Expenditure (1986-90)

British		5.6
North American		2.3
Other		2.4
Cont. European		3.2
of which		
French	3.8	
German	3.2	
Italian	2.9	
Dutch	3.7	
Other European	2.8	

Source: Derived from CSO, *Tourism and Travel,* (various years), Stationery Office, Dublin.

**Table 6.4   Tourism Revenue* from Overseas Visitors to Ireland
1970, 1975 and 1980–91**

	IR£m.**	Yearly % Change
1970	725	–
1975	617	–
1980	774	–
1981	727	– 6.1
1982	708	– 2.6
1983	702	– 0.1
1984	733	+ 4.4
1985	806	+10.0
1986	735	– 8.8
1987	803	+ 9.3
1988	904	+12.6
1989	1,024	+13.3
1990	1,139	+11.2
1991	1,213	+ 6.5

* Total expenditure (excluding international fares) plus passenger fare receipts of Irish
carriers from visitors to Ireland.
** In constant 1990 prices (except for 1991).
Sources: *White Paper on Tourism Policy* (1985), Stationery Office, Dublin; CSO (1990),
Tourism and Travel, Stationery Office, Dublin; Bord Fáilte (1991), *Tourism Facts,* Bord Fáilte,
Dublin.

initial impact of the sector and its contribution to economic growth. The
volume growth in tourism revenue is shown in Table 6.5 for recent years
together with its principal components. The significant contribution of
foreign revenues to total tourism revenue growth is highlighted in the table
though problems with data collection and interpretation for domestic
tourism suggests that these figures may be less reliable.

The first-round effects noted above do not measure the full impact
on GNP of foreign and domestic tourism. To uncover the latter it is
necessary to estimate the indirect purchases made by sub-suppliers to the
prime 'tourist' providers. These include food and drink, craft and souvenir
goods and any other goods and services supplied to hotels, guesthouses,
tourist amenities and so on. An additional impact arises from the re-
spending of incomes generated in hotels and other tourist suppliers and
in the sub-supply firms, i.e. the induced spending. An input-output
framework is used to estimate the relevant proportions of purchases between 'tourist' and other sectors and the ultimate impact of the induced
effects. Henry provided such a framework and used it to estimate tourism
multipliers, both expenditure and employment.[13]

Table 6.5   Growth in Irish Tourism Revenues 1985–90 (In constant 1990 prices)

	IR£m.						% Annual Average Growth	
	1985	1986	1987	1988	1989	1990	1985–1990	1988–1990
Out of state	609	556	619	704	779	876	7.5	11.5
Carrier receipts	196	178	183	200	245	263	6.0	14.7
Sub-total								
Foreign ex-change earnings	806	735	803	904	1024	1139	7.2	12.2
Domestic tourism revenue	316	246	320	334	342	413	5.5	11.2
Total tourism revenue	1124	981	1123	1238	1366	1552	6.7	12.0

Source: Derived from Table 2 of Tansey Webster and Associates (1991), *Tourism and the Economy*, Report for the Irish Tourist Industry Confederation, Dublin.

The expenditure multipliers are as follows (1989):

Out of State and Carrier Receipts
Direct   0.64
Direct + Indirect   0.77
Direct + Indirect + Induced   0.99
Domestic
Direct + Indirect only   0.81
Overall
Domestic + Foreign   0.94

Thus every IR£1m. of tourism export earnings contributes IR£0.99m to GNP while domestic tourism expenditure contributes a lower amount of IR£810,000; the average impact works out at IR£940,000. Tansey Webster applied these multipliers estimates of tourism expenditures for the 1985–90 period so as to determine the contribution of the sector to the economy.[14] Their summary figures are reproduced in Table 6.6. This table highlights the steady expansion in the importance of the tourism sector in terms of its contribution to GNP, rising to almost 7 per cent by 1990. Export tourism was the principal contributor to this relative expansion while domestic tourism more or less maintained its share of GNP at 1.4–1.5 per cent.

Thus, in expenditure terms and in its impact on GNP the performance of the Irish tourism sector has been impressive especially since 1987. Since the upsurge in growth preceded the establishment of the five year targets under the Programme for National Recovery, this begs the question as to the underlying causal influences on the performance.

TOURISM EMPLOYMENT

As illustrated in Figure 6.1 above, the third indicator of sectoral performance and a clear objective of government policy is employment gener-
tion. Earlier difficulties with exaggerated employment claims arising from
tourist expenditures in Ireland led to attempts to agree a common
methodology. The report in 1988 of a joint inter-departmental and inter-
agency working group on tourism and employment outlined the rationale
for choosing the 'proportional' method of employment measurement.[15]
A similar approach has been adopted in the UK.

This approach converts the expenditures estimated above (direct, indirect and induced) into employment numbers on a pro-rata or proportional basis. For example, if 5 per cent of the food sector's output is supplied
to the 'tourist' sector, then it is assumed that 5 per cent of employment
in the food sector is tourism dependent. Essentially the methodology relies
on an input-output framework which throws up the expenditure figures
in the first instance. Though by no means a completely accurate method
it does have the advantage over other methods of being able to incorporate
up-to-date information.

Measurement problems arise from the heterogeneous nature of the
industry and the attribution of output to tourist and non-tourist demand
sources, for example in hotels. The treatment of the tax recycling issue,
whereby the employment gains arising from the re-spending of tax revenues
generated by tourists are counted, may present some difficulties also.
Displacement effects which arise particularly from domestic tourism (where
tourism expenditure may be simply a diversion from spending elsewhere
in the economy or a diversion of tourism expenditure within the country)
need to be noted in any attempt to measure the true employment effects
of the tourism sector.

Table 6.6   Impact of Tourism on Ireland's GNP, 1985–90

	(% of GNP)					
	1985	1986	1987	1988	1989	1990
Foreign	4.3	4.0	4.1	4.5	4.9	5.1
Domestic	1.4	1.1	1.3	1.4	1.3	1.5
Total	5.7	5.0	5.5	5.9	6.2	6.7
GNP growth rate	−0.4	−0.7	4.6	3.3	4.4	6.0
Growth rate of tourism's GNP contribution		−12.1	13.1	10.8	10.6	13.1

Source: Tansey Webster and Associates (1991), *Tourism and the Economy*, Report for the
Irish Tourist Industry Confederation, Dublin.

Henry used the input-output method to estimate tourism employment for 1989 and Tansey Webster added 1990 estimates using the same methodology.[16] This approach parallels the expenditure estimates methodology above by which the direct, indirect and induced expenditures are converted into employment data. The Department of Tourism, Transport and Communications also provided estimates using the proportional method; indirect employment was adjusted downwards because intermediate demand tends to be lower for sectors of most relevance to tourism, and induced employment was estimated rather arbitrarily by multiplying direct jobs by a factor of 0.3. Other derived tourism employment data, which incorporate 30 per cent of tax recycling employment from overseas tourism expenditure in the estimates, in addition to the employment data estimated from the input-output approach, provides a third measure of employment in the sector. This rather arbitrary figure of 30 per cent acknowledges the presence of some re-cycling effect of taxes generated from overseas tourism revenue. The various estimates are brought together in Table 6.7. The breakdown of these employment estimates between direct tourism jobs and other jobs gives a ratio of 2:1, using the input-output approach and 1.5:1 using the proportional method. In other words, for every 1.5-2 persons employed in direct tourist businesses (hotels, carriers, etc.) one additional job exists elsewhere in the economy.

Table 6.7 Alternative Estimates of Tourism Related Employment in Ireland 1982, 1985–90

	I-O Method (1)	Proportional Method (2) (000s)	Derived (3)
1982	49.1	60.5	—
1985	51.9	65.0	—
1986	—	55.6	—
1987	—	63.5	59
1988	—	69.0	65
1989	64.5	75.0	73
1990	72.8	80.0	82

Sources:
(1) E.W. Henry (1991) 'Estimated Employment and Gross National Product Impacts of 1989 Tourism in Ireland', paper read before the *Statistical and Social Inquiry Society of Ireland, Dublin, 9 May; quoted and extended in Tansey Webster and Associates (1991), Tourism and the Economy,* report prepared for Irish Tourist Industry Confederation; no tax recycling is included.

(2) This method is outlined in the report of the inter-departmental committee contained in Minister of Tourism and Transport (1988), *Report of Working Group on Tourism and Employment,* Stationery Office, Dublin.

(3) Tax recycling at 30 per cent of total is included here but in other respects is similar to (1).

Focusing on the three years to 1990 in relation to employment changes we find, using the third column in Table 6.7, that the annual increase in numbers was 6,000 (+10 per cent) in 1988, 8,000 (+12 per cent) in 1989 and 9,000 (+12 per cent) in 1990. Thus, tourism employment increased from 6 per cent of total in 1985 to slightly over 7 per cent in 1990. Given the established target of an increase in numbers employed of 25,000 over five years, more than 90 per cent of this had been achieved in the first three years of the programme.

SUMMARY REVIEW OF PERFORMANCE

The performance of Irish tourism since the mid-1980s has been impressive relative to the remarkably weak performance of the previous 25 years. Table 6.8 shows that Ireland's market share of world tourism declined from the late 1960s through the 1970s, stabilised in the early 1980s and began to improve in the late 1980s. As a result, Ireland's share of world tourism has grown from 0.75 per cent in 1986 to 0.84 per cent in 1989. European tourist arrivals grew from 1.17 per cent (1986) to 1.34 per cent (1989). The improvement in numbers of tourist arrivals, at least until recently, masks a rather worrying trend in Irish tourism. Ireland's share of both world and European tourism receipts has been consistently lower than its equivalent share of tourist arrivals. Table 6.9 shows that real expenditure by overseas tourists grew steadily throughout the 1960s reaching a peak in 1969. Only since 1985 has real expenditure consistently exceeded the level achieved in 1969. In addition there has been a long term decline in the real inflation-adjusted spending per foreign tourist; by 1989 such spending was at its lowest level in thirty years. Recent improvements, while encouraging, would need to be sustained over several years to arrest this long-term decline.

CRITICAL APPRAISAL OF RECENT PERFORMANCE AGAINST TARGETS

It was earlier noted that targets for Irish tourism were established in 1987. While the setting of targets is to be welcomed in principle the underlying rationale for the specific targets chosen was neither explicit nor necessarily correct. Nonetheless target setting does allow one to evaluate outcomes against specific benchmarks. The outcomes were as follows:
   — for the first sustained period for almost twenty years Irish tourism increased its overseas market share;
   — specific targets to double foreign tourist numbers over five years (i.e. a 15 per cent annual compound growth rate) were marginally exceeded in the first two years, increased by 10 per cent in 1990 and declined by almost 3 per cent in 1991; the shortfall from the projected target in the latter year was 18 per cent or 654,400 fewer overseas tourists;
   — over the four year period (1988-91) the revenue targets from overseas tourists were more or less achieved; performances in 1990 and particularly

Table 6.8   Tourist Arrivals 1960-89 (millions)

Year	World	Europe	Ireland	Ireland's Share of	
				World Market	Euro Market
1960	69.3	50.1	1.37	1.98	2.74
1965	112.7	83.0	1.73	1.54	2.09
1970	159.7	112.0	1.76	1.10	1.57
1975	214.4	151.6	1.69	0.79	1.11
1980	284.8	193.6	2.26	0.79	1.17
1981	288.8	192.7	2.19	0.76	1.14
1982	286.8	195.2	2.25	0.78	1.15
1983	284.2	189.9	2.26	0.79	1.19
1984	312.4	204.2	2.58	0.83	1.26
1985	322.7	210.0	2.54	0.79	1.21
1986	330.5	211.4	2.47	0.75	1.17
1987	356.8	226.0	2.66	0.75	1.18
1988	381.9	233.4	3.01	0.79	1.29
1989	414.2	260.5	3.48	0.84	1.34

Source: Hawkins, D., and B. Ritchie (1991), *World Tourism and Travel Review: Indicators, Trends and Forecasts* Vol. 1, C.A.B. International, Wallingford.

Table 6.9   Tourist Numbers and Revenues (excluding Republic of Ireland and N. Ireland)

Year	Tourist numbers (000s)	Revenue at current prices (IR£m.)	Revenue at constant 1990 prices (IR£m.)	Real revenue per tourist (1990 prices)
1960	941	27.1	330.5	351
1965	1260	40.8	408.0	324
1970	1459	59.9	457.3	313
1975	1289	98.1	395.6	307
1980	1731	233.7	467.4	270
1981	1680	251.5	420.6	250
1982	1719	301.4	434.9	253
1983	1714	335.3	439.4	256
1984	1903	384.2	468.5	246
1985	1951	459.0	537.5	275
1986	1881	436.5	493.3	262
1987	2095	504.3	553.0	264
1988	2425	593.8	631.0	260
1989	2804	687.4	705.0	251
1990	3096	795.8	795.8	257
1991	3015	855.9	829.4	275

Source: Hawkins, D. and B. Ritchie (1991), *World Tourism and Travel Review: Indicators, Trends and Forecasts* Vol. 1, C.A.B. International, Wallingford.

in 1991 suggest that Ireland attracted more high spending tourists than previously;

— employment targets on a pro-rata basis appear to have been achieved in the 1988-91 period;

— apart from the increased EC Structural Funds available, government expenditure on tourism promotion and development (through Bord Fáilte) declined in real terms over the decade of the 1980s and particularly since 1985;

— indications from the preliminary results of the first six months of 1992 suggest a recovery from the depressed 1991 level (overseas visitors up 4.3 per cent) to return more or less to the numbers in 1990; revenues continued to improve more than proportionately and increased by 5.1 per cent in nominal terms over the 1991 level.

The favourable outcomes for Irish tourism are due to several factors such as liberalisation of air fares, the shift away from traditional sun-spots and overcrowded/polluted resorts in Spain and Italy, the environmental image of the country and the push towards alternative tourism — all of which are largely outside the scope of direct promotional campaigns; while difficult to apportion cause, the low inflation of recent years will have helped correct the image of Ireland as a high cost holiday destination.

While welcoming recent developments, it is necessary to assess what influence, if any, Irish tourism target setting and policy has had on the outcomes. If this is minimal, or non-existent, and principally subject to international fashions or events, then Irish tourist numbers and revenues could just as likely decline over the next few years. This raises the question of the role of government, longer term strategic planning for the tourism sector and environmental issues affecting tourism which are addressed in the final sections of this chapter.

Irish Tourism Policy — A Wider Perspective

This section addresses key issues affecting the contribution of tourism to economic development, specifically, government support for tourism, tourism planning and the relationship between this planning, or lack of it, and the environment.

GOVERNMENT SUPPORT FOR TOURISM

The tourist industry in Ireland as elsewhere is not without its proponents of further government support. In particular it has frequently been observed that the industry receives rather less support than similar industries domestically and internationally.[17] The argument is then usually advanced that, on the grounds of equity, further government support should be given to tourism. Reference is usually made to the employment-generating and balance of payments effects and the growth potential of the industry. Such pleas for support possess a superficial attraction. In a market economy there may well be instances where government intervention is justified, but the specific reasons usually put forward for financially encouraging tourism may not be economically sound.

Apart from policy measures designed specifically to improve the workings of the market economy to increase competitive pressures, it is widely accepted that government intervention is justifiable in conventional economic terms in the following.

Social costs and benefits (externalities)
There are many cases where the actions of one individual or firm affect other individuals or firms. Instances where one individual's actions impose a cost on others are referred to as negative externalities. But not all externalities are negative. There are some important instances of positive externalities where one individual's actions confer a benefit on others. If a person creates a beautiful flower garden in front of her house, her neighbours may benefit from being able to admire it. Whenever externalities exist, the resource allocation provided by the market may not be efficient. Since individuals do not bear the full cost of the negative externalities which they generate, they tend to engage in an excessive amount of such activities; conversely, since individuals do not enjoy the full benefits of activities generating positive externalities, they will engage in too few of these. Thus, for example, there is widespread belief that without government intervention of some kind the level of pollution will be too high. To put it another way, pollution control provides a positive externality so that without government intervention there would be an under-provision of pollution control.

Public goods (special case of externalities)
These refer to the provision of goods that confer positive externalities but would be under-provided by the market economy (e.g. public parks, national monuments), and

Merit wants
These relate to commodities or services which the state wishes its citizens to consume but would be under-consumed in a free market. The most notable examples of merit goods are health and education services.

In these instances the public sector may be obliged to intervene in the free enterprise economy even where competitive forces are considered to be at a 'desirable level'.[18] A consideration of public goods, externalities and merit wants reveals that a case may be made for public sector intervention in tourism. The strength and virtues of the case may be debatable but it is clear that the discussion is of a form different from that which usually occurs when government support for tourism is considered. Current government policies may be interpreted as enabling enterprises that could not survive by themselves to continue in existence. This view may be especially true of the Section 4 grants in the UK, suspended in 1989. The main aim of the scheme was to bring forward capital expenditure and jobs in tourism projects that could not have gone ahead as fast or to the same standard and size without assistance.

A comprehensive appraisal of the scheme by PA Cambridge Economic Consultants concluded that the scheme is a low additionality scheme, and it did not adequately address the major issue of the sector, that of market failure in innovative development. To do so, assistance would need to be more targeted on the relevant aspects of market failure (e.g. market appraisal and information and at certain times only on funding).[19] While the Irish Business Expansion Scheme differs somewhat from the Section 4 scheme certain parallels are inescapable.[20]

It may well be the case that tourist projects experience particular problems of seasonality, of fixed and inflexible supply, of volatile demand, of short-term risk and loss but long-term profitability, and so on, such that commercial sources may be reluctant to lend in adequate amounts. Pump-priming finance may well be appropriate in such cases but not in the form of grants which distort the true cost of the enterprise and transfer part of the cost to the taxpayer. It may be more appropriate to move the emphasis to commercially-based loans from 'sympathetic' financial institutions.

Currently, subsidies are given directly to producers (whether in the form of grants or tax allowances). Costs are thus transferred from the producer to the taxpayer according to criteria which have little to do with the wishes of the consumer or the efficiency of resource allocation or utilisation. Such policies have, of course, been evident in Ireland for manufacturing industry for many years. Those who seek further government support for tourism do so on grounds of equity with manufacturing industry and may appear reasonable. However, in the current political environment where the merits of the free enterprise system and state disengagement from industry are emphasised it may be more pertinent for those in tourism to shift their emphasis from employment and balance of payments to externalities, public goods and merit wants. Such criteria for government intervention have a sounder economic base and are more consistent with a free-enterprise philosophy than employment and balance of payments effects.

In addition to the foregoing, structuralist theorists argue the need for government intervention on slightly different grounds. Their argument centres on deficiencies in the structure of the economy in many countries which makes it extremely difficult to develop. The structural problems are usually associated with late economic development and government intervention is required to stimulate development.[21]

A prime objective of any economy is to achieve a production system that satisfies consumer demands (the ultimate objective of all production) and does so in the most efficient manner. Appeal to employment and balance of payments effects in itself does not help satisfy this objective, neither does a system that operates through direct grant payments. There is an appeal to the 'wrong' criteria and implementation through 'inappropriate' policy.

TOURISM PLANNING

As Braddon and others have argued, planning for tourism at the national level, as at other levels, should be undertaken in the light of broader national development goals and objectives.[22] In some cases these may be stated explicitly or there may be firm government direction. Elsewhere they may not be clearly articulated and the tourism planner has little guidance as to what overall goals should be pursued through the development of tourism. In many instances tourism plans focus specifically on tourism goals with little direct reference to broader issues, thus lessening the likelihood that tourism will contribute effectively to national development. Tourism policy in the Netherlands in the 1980s has stressed the need to mitigate the large adverse balance of international tourism payments by the stimulation of four aspects of the tourist industry:

— the capturing of a larger share of the high-spending inter-continental trade to Western Europe;

— the diversion of part of the Dutch market from foreign to domestic destinations, as a form of import substitution;

— the encouragement of near-neighbourhood holidaymaking especially from the West German market, in order to exploit trends either to more off-season holidays or summer holidays close to home;

— more profitable exploitation of European transit tourists.[23]

Many other countries have also initiated deliberate tourism objectives. Irish tourism policy does not appear to follow such a structured approach. The most innovative feature associated with recent policy has been the objective of doubling numbers and revenues. The question arises as to why the objective of doubling tourism numbers was adopted. If, as stated, the aim was to increase employment and improve the balance of payments position, could other means not have been employed? Could an attempt not have been made to target high spenders in smaller numbers who would have brought the same benefits and fewer associated costs, both economic and environmental? Perhaps there were serious impediments but the available literature emanating from the tourist industry does not give us any insights. It certainly appears that the objective of doubling revenue was simply translated into doubling numbers. In addition the objective of doubling tourism numbers does not appear to have been grounded in a strategic policy. In particular, it was assumed that there would be a 15 per

cent annual increase across all countries. Such an approach bears little relation to elementary demand on other economic considerations. Recent
reports that objectives were achieved in relation to target markets appears
more of a post-hoc rationalisation than anything else.

PLANNING AND THE ENVIRONMENT

Since the publication of the world conservation strategy by the International
Union for the Conservation of Nature in 1980 many countries have begun
working towards the goal of sustainable resource development.[24] Increasingly, sustainable management of resources is being accepted as the logical
way to match the needs of conservation and development. The new era
of environmental concern is of immediate relevance to tourism. Tourism
development and success are inextricably tied to the environment. There
are a number of views on the relationship between tourism and the environment as illustrated in Figure 6.2 below. Figure 6.2(A) represents a
malign view of the relationship: as tourism development occurs there is
a significant decline in environmental quality. Figure 6.2(B) suggests that
there is only a minor decline in environmental quality for a large increase
in tourism development and Figure 6.2(C) suggests a benign relationship.
The extent to which one or all three relationships occur will depend critically
upon tourism planning and the associated development. The beneficial environmental improvement usually associated with tourism is related to the
improvement or maintenance of old buildings, museums, and the provision
of parks and so on that might decay or not be provided in the absence
of tourism. The detrimental effects relate to negative externalities associated
with tourism development, e.g. pollution, traffic congestion, damage to
old buildings. Examples of traffic congestion, overcrowding and litter pollution are already a feature of Ireland's premier tourist destinations at peak
season. While the tourism lobby has traditionally been vocal in outlining
the benefits of tourism such as foreign exchange and employment, it has
(at least until recently) downplayed the costs. The challenge that the industry must confront is to balance the immediate economic gains with the
long-term goal of protecting the environment that ultimately will dictate
its survival.[25]

Tourism markets are likely to be characterised by externalities. A region
whose comparative advantage depends on outstanding natural beauty may
attract too many tourists, leading to congestion, overcrowding, pollution
and the destruction of the environment which formed the basis of the area's
competitiveness. Similarly, this can occur and has occurred with ancient
buildings, footpaths, cliffs and waterways. Some environmentalists suggest that these problems are beginning to emerge in Ireland. Destruction
of certain plants in the Burren and pollution of the inland waterways
associated with rapid mariculture are cited as examples. Where property
rights are well defined the private markets can easily solve such problems

EQ = Environmental Quality

TD = Tourism Development

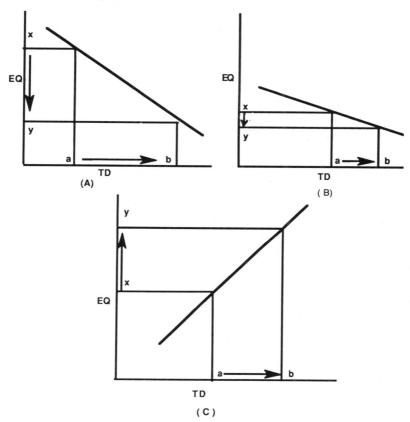

Figure 6.2   Relationship between environmental quality and tourism development

by charging a price, thus excluding those unwilling to pay and using some of the income to maintain the asset. This implies setting prices that reflect the real cost of a visit to an area, taking account of environmental considerations. Charging such prices allows re-investment in the asset for preservation purposes.

The reason why the destruction of natural resources and the pollution of the environment have proceeded apace is that they do not show up in the accounts of those responsible. This is because substantial parts of the tourism market are based on common property such as scenery, coastlines and mountains. In other words, parts of the tourist market are characterised by property rights which are ill-defined, unenforceable or not worth policing and enforcing. Increasingly, however, there is acceptance of the need to take account of the costs both of using environmental inputs in production and of damaging the environment through pollution. In tourism development, the cost of protecting the environment needs to be treated as an internality, i.e. as a cost of doing business. Developers with longer term time horizons will see it as necessary to absorb such costs (e.g. construction of a sewerage plant rather than using a sea outfall). Unfortunately, these costs will not be 'calculated' by the user unless an external authority forces them to do so, usually by means of taxation or incentives and disincentives.

The Irish Context

The first sections of this chapter dealt with the performance of Irish tourism during the 1980s. The relative improved performance could be attributed to improved marketing and targeting of areas. An alternative view might suggest that a good deal of the improvement has more to do with international demand factors than anything else. The improved performance can be traced to an easing of demand for sun holidays and an increasing demand for environmentally friendly and relaxed holidaymaking. If this scenario is correct it has significant implications for past and future development of Irish tourism policy.

According to Plog, 'We can visualise a destination area moving across the spectrum, however gradually or slowly, but far too often inexorably towards the potential of its own demise. Destination areas carry with them the potential seeds of their own destruction, as they allow themselves to become more commercialised and lose their qualities which originally attracted tourists.'[26] Ireland has been promoted as a quiet, unspoilt country with friendly people. The policy over the last four years has emphasised the doubling of tourism numbers. There would seem to be a contradiction between the promotion and the policy implementation. The question arises as to the appropriate policy for a small country to adopt. For example, tourism policy adopted in Cyprus aims to attract tourists from the high and middle income groups.[27] Not only are the economic benefits from these groups perceived to be greater but a low-volume high-spending market is believed to be more in keeping with a small island where mass tourism would have adverse effects both on the environment and the social fabric of the country with a consequential deterioration of all tourist attractions.

The evidence to date would suggest that Ireland has decided to adopt mass tourism as a policy objective. Adherents would argue that the country can absorb much greater numbers without causing environmental damage. The empirical evidence is not available but more importantly the fundamental debate on carrying capacity has not even begun. In addition there is increasing evidence that some scenic areas and attractions are reaching bottleneck proportions at certain times of the year. Traffic jams in the Burren and Killarney are testament to the concentrated nature of Irish tourism. Perhaps we are far from the boom-bust cycle of tourism that has beset some Mediterranean countries but current policy can only exacerbate emerging problems and concerns. The prime concern must be to identify and rectify bottlenecks and deficiencies in the national tourist system rather than promote new areas. This is especially important in a country such as Ireland where the emphasis for overseas visitors at least is on touring rather than destination-oriented tourism. Bottlenecks in one or two key places may effectively limit the growth of tourism throughout the country as a whole.

Conclusion

In this chapter Irish tourism policy has been critically appraised. It was found that the funding, strategy and emphasis of the policy are not consistent with tourism making a long-term contribution to economic development. The current cash grant system is producer-oriented rather than consumer-oriented; it may serve to keep prices down marginally but the payment is not related to consumer usage. The strategy to double tourism numbers with emphasis on mass tourism is seen as being desirable neither in economic nor environmental terms. The analysis would suggest it might be more pertinent for those in tourism to shift their emphasis from employment and balance of payments to externalities, public goods and merit wants. This conclusion is not specific to the Irish situation as many other countries have and continue to pursue tourism policies which are not consistent with long-term economic development. We can only hope that myopic employment gains and foreign exchange earnings do not blind policymakers to the need for long-term planning with environmental considerations that will ultimately determine the contribution which tourism can make to economic development.

NOTES AND REFERENCES

1   Prior to June 1992 unemployment rates were averaging 20–21 per cent; due to a change in the classification of those appearing on the Live Register of Unemployment the June unemployment rate is much lower.
2   Haahti, A.J. (1986), 'Finland's Competitive Position as a Destination', *Annals of Tourism Research,* **13**:11–35.
3   However, Williams, A.M. and G. Shaw (eds.) (1988), *Tourism and Economic Development: Western European Experience,* Belhaven Press, London and New York, point out that though direct jobs may be of poor quality the jobs

generated indirectly through second round purchases, such as food, are likely to be of higher skill and quality.

4   Edwards, A. (1985), *International Tourism Forecasts to 1995,* The Economist Intelligence Unit, London.

5   For an extended discussion on this see Wheeler, B. (1991), 'Tourism's Troubled Times: Responsible Tourism is not the Answer', *Tourism Management,* June.

6   (1985), *White Paper on Tourism Policy,* Stationery Office, Dublin.

7   This is not to suggest that earlier references to tourism policy did not implicitly identify its role in terms of income generation, contribution to the balance of payments and employment results.

8   (1985), *White Paper,* p.8.

9   Arising out of the White Paper, a working group of civil servants and state agency personnel was established to review the measurement of employment in tourism and reported to the Minister for Tourism and Transport in May 1988. A critical element of the debate on measuring employment was the inflating of numbers employed arising from the respending of taxes raised from out-of-state tourists. This assumed a balanced budget policy stance which is clearly untenable when large budget deficits exist. The working group suggested these be excluded from the employment supported by the sector though some recent employment estimates in tourism include a proportion of the 'tax respending' employment.

10 Minister of Tourism and Transport (1988), *Report of Working Group on Tourism and Employment,* Stationery Office, Dublin.

11 Among these are: Price Waterhouse (1987), *Improving the Performance of Irish Tourism,* Price Waterhouse, Dublin; (1990), *1992 and the Tourism Sector,* A Report for the European Bureau, *Department of the Taoiseach,* Stationery Office, Dublin; (1990), *The Operational Programme for Tourism,* Stationery Office, Dublin; Tansey Webster and Associates (1991), *Tourism and the Economy,* Irish Tourist Industry Confederation, Dublin; SKC, Peat Marwick and DKM (1987), *Tourism Working for Ireland: a Plan for Growth,* Dublin.

12 (1987), *Programme for National Recovery,* Stationery Office, Dublin; (1989), *National Development Plan, 1989-93,* Stationery Office, Dublin.

13 See Henry, E.W. (1991), 'Estimated Employment and Gross National Product Impacts of 1989 Tourism in Ireland', Paper read before the Statistical and Social Inquiry Society of Ireland, Dublin, May 9. In economic terms, multipliers refer to the total impact of a given level of investment or expenditure once various 'rounds' of spending induced by the initial amount have worked through the economy. Thus overseas tourists who spend in restaurants lead the restaurants to buy food, pay wages and purchase electricity which in turn leads to purchases by those employed in these 'sub-supply' firms and so on. Earlier attempts to estimate export tourism multipliers appeared seriously to over- estimate the impact of tourism on the economy. For a brief review of the Irish literature on this see Deegan, J. and Dineen, D.A. (1992), 'The Employment Effects of Irish Tourism Projects — A Microeconomic Approach', Johnson P. and Thomas, B. (eds.), *Perspectives on Tourism Policy,* Mansell Publishing Co., London, pp. 137-56.

14   See Tansey Webster and Associates (1991), op. cit. A fourth stage induced effect has been identified also which measures the impact of re-spending the taxes generated from tourism through an increase in government expenditure. This presumes a balanced budget policy stance which is not generally considered plausible in the Irish economy context with its widespread experience of deficit financing throughout the 1980s. The effects of this fourth stage are ignored in this paper in measuring the expenditure impact.

15   (1988), *Report of Working Group on Tourism and Transport*, Stationery Office, Dublin.

16   See Henry, E.W. (1991), op. cit. and Tansey Webster and Associates (1991), op. cit.

17   See Tansey Webster and Associates (1991), op. cit.

18   Brown, C.V. and Jackson, P. (1983), *Public Sector Economics*, Martin Robertson, Oxford, pp. 22-39.

19   PA Cambridge Economic Consultants, (1990), *Additionality in Section 4 Projects*, Final Report.

20   The Business Expansion Scheme was introduced in 1984 to encourage investment in manufacturing industry. It was extended to the tourism sector in 1986 and several schemes were developed for this sector. For an extended discussion of its impact see O'Keeffe, R.A. (1992), 'The Impact of the Business Expansion Scheme in Improving the Accessibility of Long-Term Risk Capital to Small and Medium-Sized Enterprises in the Mid-West Region', unpublished MBS thesis, Department of Business Studies, University of Limerick.

21   For further discussion on the structuralist alternative see Chenery, H. (1975), 'The Structuralist Approach to Development Policy', *American Economic Review*, **65**(2): 310-16.

22   Braddon, C.J.H. (1982), *British Issues Paper: Approaches to Tourism Planning Abroad*, British Tourist Authority, London.

23   Ashworth, G.J. and Bergsma, J.R. (1987), 'New Policies for Tourism: Opportunities or Problems?', *Tijdschrift voor Economische en Sociale Geografie*, **87**(2): 151-5.

24   World Commission on Environment and Development (1987), *Our Common Future*, Oxford University Press, Melbourne.

25   See Deegan, J. (1991), 'Environmental Problems Associated with Tourism: Is Alternative Tourism the Answer?', *Irish Business and Administrative Research*, **12**:104-113.

26   Plog, S.C. (1973), 'Why Destination Areas Rise and Fall in Popularity', *Cornell H.R.A. Quarterly*, November: 13-16.

27   See Andronicou, A. (1983), 'Selecting and Planning for Tourists — the Case of Cyprus', *Tourism Management*, **4**(3):209-11.

7

Tourism, Public Policy and the Image of Northern Ireland since the Troubles

David Wilson

This paper investigates the effect of the 'troubles' on tourism in Northern Ireland (NI) over the last two decades, and looks at some of the ways in which the tourist industry has tried to counter the negative image of the North as a country torn by civil strife. ('The North' and 'The South' are local expressions for Northern Ireland and the Republic of Ireland respectively.) The following sections provide a brief survey of existing source material available in the public domain and probably raise more research questions than are answered. After a review of the available statistics on tourism the paper then considers the response of the Northern Ireland Tourist Board (NITB) to the difficulty of marketing tourism during the troubles, looks at the growing critique of its activities, and concludes with an attempt to reconcile the conflicting NITB and media images of the North.

Tourism Trends in Northern Ireland

First of all, what are the 'facts' about tourism in recent years, and what explanations have been offered to account for them? The following tables are taken from NITB *Visitor Reports*. Some of them go back to 1959 thus conveniently showing the tourism trends immediately prior to the onset of the present conflict in 1969. These tables can at the same time, along with other reports and brochures published by the NITB, be treated as 'texts' in which a number of themes can be discerned and analysed.

One key indicator of changing tourism patterns is the number of people leaving NI by air and sea shown in Table 7.1.[1] The total number of passengers grows annually until 1969, fluctuates around this level until the late 1970s, then continues to increase again steadily throughout the 1980s. However, these overall statistics conceal some dramatic changes in the number of tourists visiting NI since the troubles. Tourists slump from a high point of 792,000 in 1969 to a figure around 300,000 until the late

Table 7.1 Passenger Traffic out of Northern Ireland by Air and Sea

	Total passengers	NI Residents travelling	Tourists to N Ireland	In-transit visitors and others
1959	766,000	323,000	413,000	30,000
1963	892,000	354,000	488,000	50,000
1967	1,106,500	350,700	698,000	57,800
1968	1,184,000	377,000	742,000	65,000
1969	1,245,000	393,000	792,000	60,000
1970	1,170,000	426,000	684,000	60,000
1971	1,180,000	662,000	462,000	56,000
1972	1,146,400	738,400	275,500	132,500
1973	1,241,600	787,200	305,800	148,600
1974	1,245,500	793,800	292,000	159,700
1975	1,260,200	782,000	298,300	179,900
1976	1,169,600	767,100	267,600	134,900
1977	1,243,000	801,600	304,200	137,200
1978	1,379,400	865,900	375,100	138,400
1979	1,463,900	858,200	447,600	158,100
1980	1,494,400	851,500	446,800	196,100
1981	1,343,200	831,700	357,800	153,700
1982	1,343,300	817,300	370,100	155,900
1983	1,445,800	871,200	408,700	165,900
1984	1,557,600	919,300	431,200	207,100
1985	1,658,000	947,800	463,200	247,000
1986	1,820,100	1,048,000	513,800	258,300
1987	1,981,000	1,174,700	537,700	268,600
1988	2,085,000	1,167,000	570,400	347,600
1989	2,234,000	1,240,800	642,600	350,600
1990	2,346,000	1,340,000	703,200	302,800

Table 7.2   Cross Border Traffic out of Northern Ireland

	NI originating day-excursionist & tourist traffic	Irish Republic day-excursionist traffic returning	Staying visitors to NI returning to or exiting via ROI	Total
1969	14,099,000	7,419,000	222,000	21,855,000
1970	11,059,000	5,388,000	267,000	16,740,000
1971	8,060,000	3,830,000	337,000	12,098,000
1972	6,760,000	3,191,000	160,000	10,111,000
1973	7,436,000	3,497,000	181,000	11,114,000
1974	8,101,000	3,415,000	205,000	11,721,000
1975	8,106,000	3,436,000	231,000	11,773,000
1976	8,121,000	3,429,000	164,000	11,714,000
1977	8,127,000	3,474,000	199,000	11,800,000
1978	8,162,000	3,435,000	253,000	11,850,000
1979	7,626,000	3,253,000	286,000	11,165,000
1980	8,873,000	3,389,000	267,000	12,529,000
1981	8,451,000	3,220,000	232,000	11,903,000
1982	8,273,000	3,900,000	342,000	12,515,000
1983	8,652,000	5,500,000	459,000	14,611,000
1984	8,947,000	5,500,000	480,000	14,104,000
1985	8,700,000	5,000,000	404,000	14,104,000
1986	7,681,000	5,000,000	319,000	13,000,000
1987	6,546,000	5,000,000	413,300	11,960,000
1988	7,652,900	3,412,500	360,800	11,426,200

1970s when they slowly begin to pick up again, although they have yet to regain their previous high point. Conversely, the number of NI residents travelling outside NI has grown steadily, increasing three-fold over the same period.

A second key tourist indicator is the number of people leaving NI across the land border with the Republic of Ireland (ROI). Although the figures in Table 7.2 do not distinguish between road and rail traffic, the vast majority of these travellers cross by vehicle. With the onset of the troubles the number of NI people visiting the South fell by nearly 50 per cent and has oscillated around this figure ever since. Visitors from the ROI to the North also fell by around 50 per cent but increased substantially in the mid-1980s for reasons to be examined later. The only category showing an overall increase (after declining during the height of the violence in the 1970s) is that of the actual numbers of tourists crossing the border. The evidence thus suggests, somewhat paradoxically, that once tourists are persuaded to visit NI, they are less concerned about the presence of the border than the local inhabitants who live on either side of it.

Table 7.3   Total Tourist Trips

	Great Britain	Irish Republic	Overseas	Total
1959	382,000	200,000	51,000	633,000
1963	405,000	246,000	54,000	705,000
1967	645,500	340,000	95,000	1,080,000
1969	674,000	300,000	92,000	1,066,000
1970	634,000	263,000	80,000	977,000
1971	417,000	181,000	72,000	670,000
1972	254,000	134,000	47,000	435,000
1973	279,000	150,000	58,000	487,000
1974	266,000	169,000	52,000	487,000
1975	270,000	202,000	57,000	529,000
1976	245,000	135,000	52,000	432,000
1977	280,000	158,000	65,000	503,000
1978	349,000	194,000	85,000	628,000
1979	379,000	227,000	104,000	710,000
1980	403,000	217,000	90,000	710,000
1981	343,000	167,000	78,000	588,000
1982	352,000	277,000	83,000	712,000
1983	377,000	390,000	98,000	865,000
1984	405,000	412,000	91,000	908,000
1985	419,000	331,000	113,000	863,000
1986	453,000	262,000	109,000	824,000
1987	480,000	347,000	116,000	943,000
1988	512,000	297,000	121,000	930,000
1989	612,000	342,000	137,000	1,091,000
1990	610,000	357,000	186,000	1,153,000

A third key indicator provided by the NITB is their estimate of the total number of tourists visiting NI shown in Table 7.3. Again, the figures tell their own story. All three categories of tourist — from Great Britain (GB, note that this refers only to England, Scotland and Wales), ROI, and overseas — increase steadily throughout the 1960s then decline sharply in the early 1970s. Whereas the number of tourists from GB have yet to regain their 1970 highpoint, visitors from both the ROI and overseas had by 1983 overtaken their 1970 figures. In 1989 the total number of visitors passed the 1969 mark for the first time in two decades. In general, tourism from overseas seems to have been the least affected by the troubles. However, a significant change has taken place with regard to the country of origin of these overseas visitors. In 1967, 60,000 visitors came from the USA, 15,000 from Europe, and 20,000 from other overseas countries. By 1988 the figures were 52,000 from the USA, 39,000 from Europe, and 30,000 from other countries. Not only that, in 1988 nearly 40 per cent of the USA visitors and 32 per cent of the European visitors were taking the major part of their holiday in the ROI, crossing into the North for relatively short periods of time.

This last point draws attention to the fact that tourism developments in NI and the ROI are not independent of one another. In the South some debate has surrounded the decline in American visitors, whose main route of entry into the Republic has been Aer Lingus flights landing at Shannon airport. The ROI government's insistence that all international flights land at Shannon (in order to bolster the economy of an outlying region) may be one reason why most of the major American carriers do not fly to Ireland. Other explanations for the fall in numbers may be the resulting high cost of flights to Ireland (because of the necessity of transfers), poor service offered by Aer Lingus on its transatlantic services (which in any case only serve the North-Eastern seaboard), coupled with inadequate standards of food and accommodation for tourists when they reach their destination, all of which were suggested in a recent TV documentary.[2] Which, if any, of these arguments are significant is not an issue here. The point is to emphasise the fact that changing tourism patterns in the ROI have a direct influence on visitor numbers in the North (which at present has no regular transatlantic services operating at all).

Still on the subject of tourist numbers, care must be taken when interpreting the figures shown in Table 7.3, especially with regard to the reasons why people visit NI. Again, there have been significant changes over the last two decades. Of the total number of visitors in 1969, 38 per cent were visiting friends and relatives (VFR), 36 per cent were on holiday, 25 per cent were on business, and 1 per cent had other reasons for being in NI. In 1988 the figures were as follows: 49 per cent VFR, 14 per cent on holiday, 4 per cent shopping, 24 per cent on business, and 9 per cent other. The category 'other' as used by the NITB includes cultural and educational visits. The most striking change is in the number of people actually visiting the North as independent holidaymakers — a decline from 36 per cent to a mere 14 per cent of the total. These statistics, perhaps more than any others, indicate the impact of the troubles on the popularity of NI as a tourist destination.

A recent report on tourism by the Department of Economic Development entitled *A View to the Future* has looked closely at this aspect of tourism in the North, and points out that its structure differs fundamentally from that of either GB or the ROI, as can be seen from Table 7.4.[3] The report draws a number of interesting conclusions from these statistics. It suggests that the low numbers of actual holidaymakers in NI reflects the violent image of the North in the outside world. If this is so, it asks, why bother promoting tourism at all until an end to the troubles is in sight? Why bother spending money on marketing and infrastructure if the

Table 7.4

Reason for Visit (1987)	NI %	ROI %	GB %
Holiday	13	49	44
Visiting friends & relatives (VFR)	50	21	20
Business	22	18	23
Shopping	5	–	–
Other	10	12	13

majority of visitors (VFR + business) will continue to come to NI regardless of whether or not tourism is promoted? These arguments are considered both defeatist and unconvincing (remember this is a government report). Instead, the contribution of increasing tourist numbers to both employment and wealth are emphasised (how the NITB is attempting to attract more tourists is a question to be addressed shortly). The report also features an intriguing little diagram indicating the relationship between tourism and violence in Northern Ireland:[4]

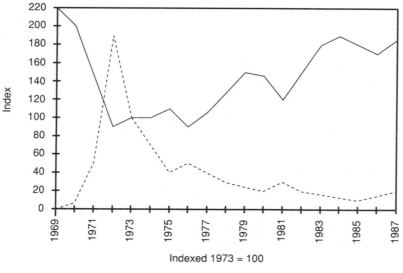

Indexed 1973 = 100

Key

——— Staying Visitors

- - - - Terrorist Incidents

Figure 7.1   Tourism and violence in Northern Ireland, 1969-1987

A number of points can be made about this chart. First, it is not at all clear what the common index on the vertical axis is supposed to indicate. Second, no definition of 'terrorism incident' is given (are murders, bombings, riots, kidnappings and punishment beatings all included?). Third, the way the diagram is constructed seems clearly to be suggesting that the troubles have all but disappeared (again, an appropriate image for a NI government department to be projecting). Finally, there may be other reasons for a decline in tourist numbers other than local violence (world recession, changing tastes, or international events such as the aircraft hijackings of the mid-1980s or the recent Gulf War). That said, the relationship between tourist numbers and terrorist incidents is a striking one. The upsurges of violence in 1976 (which led to the formation of the Peace People), in 1981 (the year of the hunger strikes), and in 1985 (following the signing of the Anglo-Irish agreement), events which all gained international publicity, were all followed by a decline in tourism. However, there are signs that this inverse relationship may be weakening in the concluding figures for 1986–87 when tourist numbers increase despite a rise in the level of violence.

Events since then would seem to confirm this hypothesis, as tourist numbers fell only slightly in 1988, the year of the Milltown massacre and the killing of the British army corporals during the subsequent funerals, two particularly gruesome incidents (all the more so for taking place in front of the TV cameras). As can be seen in Table 7.3, this fall was due solely to the reduction in visitors from the ROI, numbers from both GB and overseas actually increasing. One factor contributing to the weakening of the inverse ratio may lie in the policy of the Provisional IRA, who for some years have publically claimed not to be targeting the civilian population of NI. Moorhead, who makes this point, suggests that this was because the killing of civilians was losing them support, especially in America.[5] Nevertheless, they were still trying hard to dissuade Americans from visiting NI:

> Noraid, Sinn Fein and the IRA have worked hard, and in most cases have been successful in persuading Irish Americans not to support the 'British Occupation' of Northern Ireland. Holidaying in the Province is often regarded as an act of traitordom, an act which contributes to the Northern Ireland economy, and so supports the status quo. Such activity is totally contrary to the revolutionary ethos of these nationalist organizations.[6]

The weakening of the correlation between violence and tourist numbers in recent years could also reflect the fact that terrorism in the North has ceased to be as newsworthy as it once was and that many incidents are no longer recorded in the international press. Alternatively, it might indicate that an 'acceptable' level of violence has now been reached which no longer deters the prospective visitor. Finally, perhaps an increasing number of tourists are being drawn to NI because of, rather than in spite of, the troubles. Whilst impressionistic evidence would support this view, the author has not been able to uncover any statistics indicating its extent. However, this issue has been rather contentiously raised in the recent NITB corporate plan. Among the strengths of NI tourism listed such as scenic beauty, cultural heritage and the warmth of the people, it also states the following under the heading of 'Curiosity':

> Many people around the world have heard of Northern Ireland but often for the wrong reasons. They may be motivated to visit simply to see why there should be such conflict in a modern society. The opportunity to harness this 'curiosity factor' should not be overlooked as a positive factor in encouraging people to visit and understand Northern Ireland.[7]

This statement unleashed a storm of protest the day the corporate plan was published, largely from Protestant politicians who objected to the implication that the misery and destruction caused by the troubles were to be turned into a tourist attraction. Ken Maginnis, for example, argued that: 'The real cynicism of the board's promotion centres around the suggestion that the suffering of the people of Northern Ireland can be packaged as a tourist attraction. It is disgusting beyond words.'[8]

On the debit side the corporate plan lists the following weaknesses still inherent in NI tourism: the negative image of the North, the lack of distinctiveness between NI and other nearby resort destinations in the ROI and Scotland, the lack of international air services (only Paris and Amsterdam currently maintain direct links), poor quality and quantity of accommodation, lack of investment in the tourism sector, and, finally, another statement which caused an angry response from some members of the Protestant community:

> Over 80 per cent of holiday visitors access Northern Ireland from or through the ROI. Entry this way is not infrequently an off-putting experience to tourists because of ugly and forbidding checkpoint structures. It is to be hoped that arrangements can be made to minimise the impact on the visitor and thereby assist the development of the all-Ireland tour which is of such importance to future tourism growth.[9]

One local newspaper responded to this seemingly innocuous suggestion in the following terms:

> Precisely how that might be done is not explained . . . The cynic will see merit in this section of the corporate plan. If the border checkpoints could be removed presumably terrorism would increase and if the authors of the plan are right in their first submission (that terrorism could prove an attraction to tourists) then the tourist industry would benefit![10]

A fourth and final indicator of the importance of tourism in NI is the estimated revenue generated by the industry shown in Table 7.5.[11]

Table 7.5   Tourism Revenue (£m. sterling)

	GB	ROI	Overseas	Total	Total in 1973 prices
1973	8.21	0.59	3.43	12.23	12.23
1974	8.88	0.85	3.41	13.14	11.31
1975	9.58	0.97	4.30	14.85	10.31
1976	10.40	0.92	4.39	15.71	9.36
1977	13.56	2.26	7.85	23.67	12.18
1978	18.95	2.98	8.64	30.57	14.53
1979	21.72	7.93	12.93	42.58	17.84
1980	29.92	9.62	14.51	54.05	19.20
1981	24.30	7.16	10.80	42.26	13.42
1982	23.11	12.50	12.39	48.00	14.03
1983	30.60	27.49	14.10	72.19	20.18
1984	34.26	27.43	16.05	77.74	20.69
1985	34.30	23.03	21.20	78.53	19.70
1986	43.77	19.23	18.84	81.84	19.86
1987	46.32	22.99	22.08	91.38	21.28
1988	54.06	23.56	19.38	97.00	21.54
1989	82.78	27.68	25.85	136.31	25.09
1990	83.25	26.31	45.53	153.09	25.82

Curiously, given the period covered in the preceding tables, this one starts in 1973. Could this be a deliberate ploy to minimise the extent of the damage caused to this sector of the NI economy by the troubles? Revenue falls in real terms until 1976, after which it steadily increases apart from slumps during the periods 1981-2 (the time of the hunger strikes) and 1985-6 (following the outbreak of Protestant violence after the signing of the Anglo-Irish Agreement). Particularly noticeable is the dramatic increase in money spent by residents of the ROI in the North, especially in the years 1983-4.

In the mid-1980s existing price differentials between North and South were further increased by hikes in the rate of Value Added Tax (VAT) in the ROI. The cross-border trade generated by these fluctuating differentials has recently been studied by T.M. Wilson who states, using Fitzgerald's estimates, that in 1986 southerners could be spending anything up to IR£300m. in the North, mainly on alcohol, tobacco, petrol and household appliances such as TVs, videos and washing machines. With regard to alcohol, 'spirits were up to a third cheaper than in the South, and beer was often priced at 40 per cent less.'[12] In Newry, for example, this new demand was met

> by an influx of British chain stores (e.g. Texas Stores) who set up
> warehouse-style centres at the fringe of the town, complete with their own

carparks. Town centre retailers campaigned for and achieved the creation of a town pedestrian mall shopping zone. Newspaper ads in southern newspapers drew consumers to these locations simply by advertising their normal discounted prices. Their goal was to keep the consumer in their town and prevent him/her from going further into the province. No price war was ever needed. Normal UK prices were incentive enough.[13]

Because many of these items were over the import tax free limit they were smuggled back into the ROI, often along the 'unapproved' roads crossing the border. However, a combination of factors led to the disappearance of this cross-border trade by the end of the 1980s, namely the increasingly severe legislation imposed by the ROI on the importation of goods from the North, stricter enforcement of the law by ROI customs officers, and rising prices in the North resulting from higher inflation rates and an increase in VAT. Massive bomb attacks by the IRA on the security checkpoint just outside Newry on the main Dublin/Belfast road and the constant disruption of the Dublin/Belfast railway line in the same area must also have made a contribution to the decline in the business fortunes of largely Catholic Newry.[14] One final point: the attempt to compare Wilson's figures with those in Table 7.5 raises the interesting question of just what the NITB means by 'tourism revenue', for this is nowhere made clear, although it apparently refers to the estimated revenue from visitors staying a minimum of one night in the North. In 1986 £19.23m. was spent by such visitors. The extent of the revenue generated by day-excursionists from the South is thus indicated by comparison with the other estimates above.

The NITB and the Marketing of Tourism

How has the NITB responded to the challenge of marketing the North in the face of terrorist activity and adverse media publicity? The main sources of material used in this section are the annual reports of the NITB. The NITB was in fact the first regional tourist board to be established in the UK, by means of the Northern Ireland Development of Tourist Traffic Act 1948, the objectives of which were:

> An Act to provide for the establishment of the Northern Ireland Tourist Board, the registration of certain catering establishments, the giving of financial and other assistance towards the provision of amenities and services calculated to promote the development of tourist traffic and otherwise to make provision for the encouragement and development of tourist traffic.[15]

The NITB is run by a government-appointed board of business, trade union and community leaders, and is answerable to the Department of Economic Development which also provides most of its funds. By 1958 the main 'problems' with tourism had been diagnosed by the NITB as the shortness of the holiday season, lack of comfortable coaches (also criticised for being without couriers and PA systems), poor access to many of the attractions (such as the Giant's Causeway), inadequate signposting at road junctions, beauty spots ruined by litter, lack of knowledge about the North on the part of local people themselves which prevented them becoming 'the Province's best ambassadors', and a shortage of hotels and restaurants especially in Belfast.[16]

A specific section on 'marketing' first appears in the report for 1969, the year the present troubles began. By now the NITB was actively involved in a whole range of promotional activities which included co-operation with local authorities, resorts, hotels and caterers; stands at various GB exhibitions such as the International Boat Show; bringing travel agents and writers over to NI on promotional visits; improving booking and information services; employing 'personality girls' to travel on ferry services across the Irish Sea to distribute information to travellers; collaborating with the British Travel Association and Bord Fáilte in joint advertising campaigns; seeking to establish a new hotel grading scheme; and extending research to identify the most suitable kinds of visitors to try and attract.

The severe civil disturbances in the early 1970s began to affect the marketing strategy of the NITB which, whilst continuing to advertise in GB, cut back on overseas promotion — 'it is plain that press advertising overseas would be a waste of money in the present circumstances'.[17] The following year a 'low profile was adopted towards press and TV coverage' as the media seemed more interested in the political situation.[18] In 1973 'no major advertising was undertaken', and the tourism infrastructure itself was beginning to suffer as 'no fewer than 27 hotels, guest houses and restaurants were destroyed or damaged by terrorist activity'. This was a substantial loss when added to the forty-odd establishments destroyed, damaged or closed during previous years.[19] Between 1974 and 1981 the NITB published figures in its annual reports showing the extent of the damage being done to the hotel industry (see Table 7.6), after which it ceased to publish such information (again for policy reasons perhaps?).

In 1974 the North was again considered almost 'unsaleable' as a tourist destination, although increasing numbers of Dutch and German tourists

Table 7.6

Hotels	1974	1975	1976	1977	1978	1979	1980	1981
Destroyed	2	2	1	6	1	5	1	1
Damaged	3	1	11	3	2	2	3	1
Closed	4	1	1	–	1	–	–	–

were recorded, attracted by fishing and hire cruising, mainly around Lough Erne.[20] The NITB began to target this potential market in 1975 whilst again deciding against a national campaign as its 'research indicated that big advertising expenditures would be wasted money'.[21] The following year the first signs of optimism appear when 'after years of almost continuous bad headlines, it was noted in 1975 that much of the continental news media had dropped Northern Ireland and become preoccupied with other (bad) news stories', and a 'hard sell' drive was mounted on the continent.[22] In 1977 further encouraging news is reported. The number of European travel agents selling NI holidays had risen from 12 to 6,000 in three years, and serious marketing efforts were renewed in America.[23] As can be seen from the total number of visitors in Table 7.3, the worst years were now over, although it was not until the early 1980s that the depressed day-excursionist traffic from the South was to increase.

In 1980 the first direct air service was opened to a continental destination (Amsterdam) although nearer home the on/off saga of the Belfast to Liverpool ferry service (Belfast's last direct service to the British mainland) was beginning. An interesting list of figures appears in another NITB publication that year showing how overseas visitors spent their time (visitor numbers in brackets):

— dining out (100,000)
— day excursion (68,000)
— forest park visits (48,000)
— visits to places of historical interest (46,000)
— hillwalking/climbing/caving (21,000)
— golf (20,000)
— visits to stately homes and gardens (15,000)
— freshwater fishing (10,000)
— attending festivals (6,000)
— cruising (5,000)
— sea fishing (4,000)
— car touring (3,000)
— visit to American heritage homes (1,000)
— equestrian (1,000)[24]

These figures clearly show the small scale of overseas tourism in NI, and it is significant that one issue not encountered in the literature is any suggestion that tourist numbers are having detrimental effects on the quality of life of the local inhabitants.

The NITB's reaction to the hunger strikes of 1981 was quite different to its response to the civil disturbances of the early 1970s, and the following quotation also shows an awareness of the effect of general economic trends on tourism:

Against a background of world-wide recession, rising prices at home and wide media coverage of the hunger strikes in late spring and early summer, the Board nevertheless carried out a programme of intense overseas marketing and public relations activity aimed at tour operators, travel agents, travel writers — both trade and consumer — and representatives of the air and sea carrier companies. The object was to try and maintain our position and keep the confidence of the overseas travel industry who had invested in the country by including Northern Ireland in their published Britain/Ireland tour programmes.[25]

To review the NITB's activities for each year during the 1980s would add little to the general picture that is emerging, one of steadily increasing confidence along with the gradual expansion of the marketing 'net'. Although more extensive criticisms of the NITB are dealt with in the next section, their marketing efforts during this period have been described as 'too vague and too narrow', this 'poor marketing' being attributed to 'lack of co-ordination by all concerned'.[26] Also of note during this period was the growing co-operation between the NITB and Bord Fáilte, and also with Aer Lingus, in the promotion of all-Ireland holidays, especially in the United States. However, this co-operation was for economic reasons as well as for marketing ones: 'Without the resources needed to conduct our own self-contained promotional campaigns in such a large market place we have always depended upon Northern Ireland being included in all-Ireland or all-Britain-and-Ireland packages.'[27]

The NITB has always been enthusiastic about its links with Bord Fáilte. However the converse is not necessarily the case, as Moorhead has suggested. In the 1970s Bord Fáilte was trying to avoid being identified with the troubled North, whereas today 'one of the concerns that Bord Fáilte must have is that international visitors who traditionally went to the ROI may now be enticed north for part of their holiday, so losing tourism revenue to the ROI.'[28]

The home market became another focus of the NITB's attention as it tried to encourage more visitors from the South as well as to persuade local residents to take holiday breaks in their own country. In 1985 its 'operational plan' defined the Board's current objectives as follows:
— to maximise external currency earnings, and to distribute those earnings as widely as possible around the province;
— to maximise domestic tourism expenditure;
— to extend tourist traffic to a point where year-round tourism becomes possible;
— to seek visitors and develop products which generate high per capita spending.[29]

The dip in tourist numbers which took place in 1986 was blamed by the NITB on two factors: uncertainty in the ROI over civil unrest in the North (this time the main source of the troubles was the violent Protestant backlash to the signing of the Anglo-Irish agreement in November 1985), and the reluctance of Americans to travel to Europe as a result of the Libyan crisis and Chernobyl.[30]

Promoting special interest activity holidays became a feature of NITB policy in the late 1980s, and as tourist numbers steadily approached their 1969 high point concern was expressed about the need to provide an adequate tourist infrastructure. Increased funding for tourism development projects became available from the European Regional Development Fund and also from the International Fund for Ireland. These sources, along with the Board's own tourism development scheme were estimated to be generating a 'total gross investment of over £100 million in tourism infrastructure, accommodation and amenities during the next three to four years.'[31]

Tourism in Northern Ireland today is thus becoming an increasingly diversified industry, as can be seen in the wide variety of attractions[32] as well as in the range of 'special interest' brochures now published by the NITB.[33] The industry would appear to be entering the 1990s well placed to capitalise on a steadily increasing demand for a growing range of holiday activities, many of which reflect the NITB's efforts to extend the range of the tourist season. However, all is not quite as rosy as this conclusion might appear to suggest.

Critics of Tourism Development and the Role of the NITB

Taking a roughly chronological approach to the literature, the work of the NITB is reviewed fairly positively by Griffith-Jones.[34] After summarising its marketing strategies he argues that one of the major difficulties still to be overcome is the region's poor transport links, especially to the European and North American markets. Advantages possessed by the tourist industry include the existing infrastructure, spare hotel capacity, the small scale of tourism in NI which facilitates co-operative marketing arrangements involving the NITB and the private sector, the system of compulsory hotel registration, close co-operation between the NITB and local councils (who have control over tourism development in their own regions), and the fact that unlike their English, Scottish and Welsh counterparts, the NITB has direct control over the allocation of government funds placed at its disposal (in GB the government itself allocates grants for specific projects recommended by regional tourist boards).

A more critical review is offered by Smyth, who concludes that 'public policy towards tourism in Northern Ireland lacks co-ordination, purpose and direction'.[35] The thrust of his argument is that there is a serious conflict of interest between the main public agencies involved in tourism. In spite of its high public profile, the NITB is only one among several organisations involved in the promotion of tourism in NI. There are also the Department of Economic Development (DED), the 26 local councils, and other government departments such as the Department of the Environment (when historic buildings and monuments, and conservation issues are involved) and the Department of Education (responsible for sport and recreation facilities as well as museums and the arts, although quangos such as the Sports Council and Arts Council must also be included here). To this must be added other government bodies concerned with 'regulatory controls such as town and country planning, liquor licensing, shop hours and employment legislation', not to mention roads, transport and policing.[36] Smyth continues:

> The provision of these tourist facilities, services and resources was seldom their primary intention. Given then that the policies and activities of a wide range of bodies impinge on interests which are of paramount importance to the tourist industry the question must be asked as to how their role is integrated within the role of the DED, NITB and the local authorities — the answer is quite simply that their activities are not integrated in any meaningful way.[37]

This failure to co-ordinate is blamed on 'the lack of any effective forum which would allow the representation of all tourist interests in the province and provide a means by which the tourist board could obtain feedback on their activities and plans'. Suggestions for such a consultative organisation had been made by NITB consultants Horwath and Horwath in 1980, but had not been implemented. Smyth concludes that 'no coherent policy towards tourism is likely to evolve until some powerful and integrative institution is created'.[38]

Leslie also considers the role of government in the development and control of tourism which he describes as central.[39] Although his dissertation is primarily a case study of Carrickfergus, he deals with some more general issues in his conclusion. He suggests that in the 1970s the weak link had been 'the apparent lack of commitment from the hospitality industry and other organisations such as local authorities and regional associations, towards the NITB and the promotion of tourism'. This relationship improved during the 1980s, although he argues that the government itself appears to have become less supportive, preferring instead to focus on industrial development and small-business incentive schemes. He is also critical of the private sector 'which shows little private enterprise and innovation'. This could be due to apathy, a lack of necessary skills, or 'a reflection of low levels of demand thus suggesting that new ventures would be too risky'. The private sector has been most active in the accommodation field, but the system of grant aid has arguably disadvantaged smaller operators. He also criticises standards of management, service and value for money. There is a lack of budget accommodation, wet weather facilities, signposting and toilets. The small scale of tourism in NI, along with its environmental resources, should be seen as a potential strength, leading to the development of 'green' or 'alternative' types of tourism. Like Smyth, Leslie finds a lack of co-ordination between sectors and advocates the establishment of a new organisation 'perhaps one which is independent of any one sector though supported by all'. Moorhead also makes a substantial number of recommendations for improving the marketing of tourism in NI, including greater emphasis on the youth market and on wet weather facilities.[40]

Attempts at seeking wider consultation had in fact been initiated by the NITB in 1985 when it sought responses to its discussion paper on Northern Ireland Tourism, and proposals for a new appointed body were put forward officially in 1989, this time in the DED's report on tourism *A View to the Future:*

> It has been decided that the most effective approach would be the creation of a Northern Ireland Tourism Development Organization with responsibility for both marketing and product development, bringing together the present promotional role of the Northern Ireland Tourist Board and the grant-aiding functions of the Department of Economic Development. This body will be an agency outside Government, with a Board appointed by the Minister, and will be able to recruit staff directly.[41]

However, at the time of writing the new organisation had not yet been established, although new legislation is apparently at the planning stage. One can perhaps discern some antipathy towards these proposals on the part of the NITB in its apparent lack of response to them. After all, the proposals would appear to be aimed at curtailing the powers of the NITB.

The conservation lobby has also criticised the DED for failing to include 'green' tourism in its report. Milton suggests that conservation interests are threatened by the proposed new body because of the need to ensure a 'good return' on any investment of government funds. She further notes that

> certain kinds of tourist development, which benefit some sectors of the market, are clearly detrimental to conservation interests. Current proposals to develop a marina complex at Killyleagh on Strangford Lough have been opposed on the grounds that it would detract from the scenic quality of the area. In Fermanagh, wildlife interests have been threatened by a proposed marina at Lough Head, and by plans to open the Arney River to pleasure boats.[42]

Increasing conflict of this kind can clearly be expected over the next few years as the Northern Ireland community becomes more alert to the ambivalent relationship between tourism and conservation.

As pointed out earlier, the NITB's corporate plan for 1992 makes it clear that the Board is aware of some of these perceived problems of the tourist industry in Northern Ireland. The Horwath report on tourist accommodation, commissioned by the NITB, has been partly resonsible for alerting it to some of the shortcomings in this particular sector. The report found that many hotels in the North were failing to satisfy their guests. Among the reasons for this were an inadequate hotel grading system, old and dated furnishings and décor, poor service, unimaginative restaurants and menus, hotel guests alienated by other customers attending 'functions' in the same building, and unprofessional operations showing a lack of training and inadequate knowledge of modern service standards generally.[43]

In passing, it is interesting to note that Bord Fáilte has not been immune from similar criticisms. Pearce, for example, has pointed to the ambivalent relationship and conflicting interests between Bord Fáilte and the Regional Tourist Offices in the ROI.[44] O'Rourke also has blamed the centralised approach of Bord Fáilte for its failure to halt the declining contribution of tourism to the economy of the South.[45] In GB conflict has also been noted between public national and regional tourism institutions as well as between these two and the private sector at the local level.[46]

Thus tourism at both the substantive and policy levels in Northern Ireland today is not without its critics in spite of the steady growth of the industry over the last decade. However, it is interesting to note that the objections discussed in this section are of a qualitatively different kind to the critique which usually develops in larger resort areas where the focus tends to be on the disruption caused to the traditional way of life by the intrusive presence of too many tourists and large hotel complexes. With the exception of the small conservationist lobby the literature concentrates on the organisational structure of the industry itself, and especially the role of the NITB within this structure. The NITB, which during the worst years of the troubles was a lone voice attempting to counter the adverse image caused by the civil disorders, has come under increasing attack of late. Notwithstanding this, the presumption remains in almost all quarters that tourism is good for Northern Ireland, bringing in money and stimulating economic growth in an otherwise industrially depressed corner of Britain and Ireland.

Tourism and the Image of Northern Ireland

The main theme running through this paper has been the impact of the troubles on tourism in NI. The statistical trends have been reviewed, along with the marketing strategy of the NITB as it struggled to present NI as an attractive holiday destination. Perusing the list of leading tourist attractions enables a picture to emerge of the tourist 'experience' in NI today, and looking at the inventory of NITB publications illustrates how special interest rather than mass tourism is now being promoted.[47] This final section returns once again to the relationship between tourism, terrorism and the image of Northern Ireland.

It had been the author's intention to analyse in some detail the promotional literature to see whether it was possible to correlate any changing images they contained with the political events of the last two decades. However, it proved impossible to locate any NITB guides published prior to the 1980s, and so this plan had to be abandoned, although glimpses of what might have been found are contained in an undergraduate dissertation by Houston, who had been able to uncover some relevant material before it had been disposed of by the NITB. She considers the stereotypes of NI embedded in past brochures by looking at the frequency of references to various types of activity, as well as the content of their photographic material. An interesting series of transformations emerges from her analysis.

> In the 1950s brochures, the main image of Northern Ireland is one of paradise and also wildness . . . Northern Ireland was being portrayed as an idyllic, natural environment where calmness and tranquility prevailed. In the 1960s serenity was a dominant component of the image . . . in the 1970s we see the dominant component this time is scenery . . . in the brochures of the 1980s we see a return to people as a dominant component of the stereotypic image.[48]

The change in focus in the 1970s is attributed to the troubles during which, in the face of adverse media publicity, the only positive asset remaining to be marketed was things rather than people. 'During this period people were regarded as nasty, ruthless, callous, etc., and would therefore add little, or nothing, to the positive image which was being transmitted by the Tourist Board.'[49] Houston suggests that the return to people in the early 1980s reflected a growing need to highlight people, as well as scenery, in a positive light. She continues: 'This is most likely due to the fact that the Tourist Board has recently found a greater need to promote the province as a popular holiday destination and in so doing found it necessary to highlight people, as well as scenery, as a positive aspect of Ulster.'[50]

Moorhead also refers in passing to the changing image of NI presented by the NITB. She observes that when serious marketing activity was resumed in the late 1970s 'no longer was Northern Ireland portrayed as a destination for a seaside holiday, but rather as a location for certain activity holidays, i.e., fishing, cruising, sailing, etc.'[51] This of course made sense given the targeting of German and Dutch tourists at the time.

The photographic illustrations contained in the current (1992) NITB brochure[52] break down roughly as follows (although many of them are difficult to place in specific categories):

— scenic views (incl. coastal and mountain views, many with
   holidaymakers)   24

- buildings (incl. historic monuments, stately homes, traditional cottages   20
- sport and recreation (incl. fishing, sailing, walking, golf, equestrian)   19
- arts and crafts (incl. pottery, glass, textiles, music, theatre)   11
- pubs, hotels and restaurants   9
- natural history (incl. birds, flowers, fruit)   8
- churches (incl. interiors)   7
- city views   3
- portraits of local people (young child in costume, locals in pub) 2
- Celtic images (stone cross, round tower)   2

The most striking features of the brochure is found in the last three items, which suggest that images of local people (cf. Houston), the urban environment and certain aspects of Irish history are (intentionally or otherwise) being played down by the NITB. This apparent desire to convey a totally sanitised impression of NI is also reinforced by its written contents. There is not one single reference to the troubles in the entire booklet, nothing to reassure the traveller that he or she will be safe, no hints at all as to what parts of Belfast and NI it might be advisable to avoid on certain occasions (Belfast like any other large city has its dangers, not all of which are related to the troubles, such as theft and mugging), and no suggestion that there is anything worth seeing in the more notorious parts of the city like West Belfast (such as the wall murals).

This pretence of the non-existence of the troubles is also to be found in some of the more established 'respectable' independent guidebooks. The 1992 *Michelin Guide*, for example, contains no reference to the troubles in its section on NI, although a few political events are briefly listed in its 'historical table' at the beginning of the volume. Its description of Belfast also contains no reference to West Belfast, covering only the city centre, the University area and some local excursions.

Moorhead takes the tourist industry to task for ignoring the political and security situation: 'If these incidents are not discussed openly or placed in context, they portray an even more negative image of Northern Ireland than already exists. As research among ROI visitors revealed, genuine fear keeps people from holidaying in the Province, as 53% stated that "fear of personal safety" prevented them from travelling North.'[53] She suggests that 'literature explaining the NI security procedure should be made available' and that 'staff should be given training in how to deal with enquiries regarding the political situation'.[54] The following points could be stressed:

- tourists are not targets;
- terrorist incidents do occur but usually far from tourist regions;
- security checks will take place by army/police; they are a regular

occurrence . . . a road checkpoint does not mean that the visitor is in a dangerous area; they take place all over the Province;
— it should be emphasised that terrorist activity takes place in a few areas and that a small percentage of the population is actually engaged in such activity.[55]

Ryan also has argued that brochures in general should contain this type of information, although he acknowledges that there is often a time lapse between events and the publication of brochures which can render the information dated. He adds:

> It has been further put to the author that the brochure is primarily a sales document, and that to contain information that is negative about destinations defeats its purpose. However, it can be contended that the brochure is more than that. In many cases in the Small Claims Courts, it has been shown that a brochure is part of a legal contract. Clients certainly use the brochure as a reference document if only to confirm the wisdom of their choice of destination before they depart. It is a reminder of the removal of risk from the purchase decision.[56]

A few of the 'alternative' guidebooks do now contain specific sections which address some of the understandable worries of would-be tourists. For example, the 1992 *Rough Guide to Ireland* has the following to say about the security situation:

> If you are British or Irish it's likely that you'll have a strong response to the sight of British troops, tanks and weaponry on the streets in the North. Like the police, armed soldiers may stop and question you . . . Travellers from the Republic may experience more troublesome dealings with both the RUC and the army, as anyone with a Southern Irish accent will tell you. All you are obliged to tell the army is your name, address, date of birth and where you're going: the more open you are with them, of course, the less likely you are to have trouble; but in certain areas you may want to weigh against this the fact that appearing to be on good terms with the army will not endear you to the local population.[57]

The *Rough Guide* also alerts travellers to other daily features of life such as security checks on the roads ('tedious but nothing to worry about') and security zones ('areas where it is illegal to leave an unattended parked car'). No fewer than five pages of the guide are devoted to West Belfast ('as safe an urban area as any for the stranger to stroll around') with excellent descriptions of the Catholic Falls Road as well as the Protestant Shankill and Crumlin roads.[58]

There are thus two conflicting images of the North: that encapsulated in the first sentence of the 1992 NITB brochure of a 'land of blue mountains and forest parks, mazy lakes and windswept moors, white Atlantic sands, an inland sea' and that of a violent, war-torn society as portrayed by the media. Both sets of images serve the interests of their advocates

— either to help sell holidays or to help sell newspapers and TV programmes. There is some evidence to support the view that the NITB have tried to manipulate a variety of different images over the last twenty years as part of their marketing strategy to counteract the media coverage of the culture of violence. Nevertheless, the reviews and comments above would seem to suggest that more open acknowledgement of the troubles by the NITB in their promotional literature, coupled with reassurance that tourists under normal circumstances are unlikely to come to any harm, would assist their marketing endeavours. For nearly twenty years there has been an inverse relationship between the number of tourists visiting the North and the level of terrorist activity, although this connection now seems to be weakening for the reasons discussed earlier. Whilst it has usually proved premature to attempt to predict the future course of events in Northern Ireland, those involved in the tourist industry are probably more optimistic today about the future than at any time since the present troubles began.

NOTES AND REFERENCES

1   Unless otherwise stated, all the statistics and tables in this section are taken from the NITB *Visitors Reports* for 1988 and 1990. These reports also contain useful comments and analysis which have been drawn on in this section. The author would like to thank the staff of the NITB in Belfast for their unfailing courtesy and help in locating many of the sources on which this report is based. Some additional references, uncovered too late for discussion in the text, are also included in the following notes.

2   *Route 92*, shown on BBC 1, 11 May 1992. In fact, between 1960 and 1980 the Republic of Ireland also saw an overall decline in tourist numbers, and not just in Americans, which, 'while partly accounted for by rising real costs, this was also probably the result of association with "the troubles" of Northern Ireland'. This from Williams, A.M. and Shaw, G. (1990), *Tourism and Economic Development: Western European Experiences,* 2nd edition, Belhaven Press, London, p. 16.

3   *Tourism in Northern Ireland — A View to the Future* (1989), Northern Ireland Department of Economic Development, HMSO.

4   ibid., p. 6.

5   Moorhead, P. (1991), 'An Examination of the Relationship between Terrorism, the Media and Tourism with Reference to the Northern Ireland Tourism Product', unpublished MSc Thesis, University of Surrey.

6   ibid., p. 47.

7   NITB (1992), Corporate Plan, p. 36. A good example of such 'curiosity' tourism is to be found in P.J. O'Rourke's account of his visit to NI, aptly entitled 'The Piece of Ireland that Passeth all Understanding', included in his book *Holidays in Hell,* Picador, London, 1989, pp. 276-88. Payne estimates that about 2,000 'political tourists' visit West Belfast each year, which 'provides some interesting new locales for the mainly young, white, left-wing people who combine holidays

with politics'. Sinn Féin, the political wing of the Provisional IRA, will provide such visitors with their own map of that part of the city and will arrange accommodation with local families. The map shows them where to find British army barracks and observation posts, the Peace Line, Sinn Féin centres, cemetaries where the hunger strikers and other republican martyrs are buried, other places of political interest, and the location of the best wall murals. Payne concludes that this presentation of the troubles 'is either very clever or very cynical' D. Payne writing in *The European,* 27 February 1992, p. 14.

8   Ken Maginnis, writing in the *Belfast Newsletter,* 28 May 1992.

9   NITB (1992), *Corporate Plan,* p. 9.

10   Editorial column of the *Belfast Newsletter,* May 1992.

11   See note 1 above.

12   Wilson, T.M. (1993) (in press), 'Consumer Culture and European Integration at the Northern Ireland Border', in Van Raaij, W.F., and Bamossy, G.J., (eds.), *Cross Cultural Issues in Consumer Research,* Association for Consumer Research, Amsterdam. Reference to Fitzgerald, J.D., et al. (1988), *An Analysis of Cross-Border Shopping,* ESRI, Dublin.

13   Wilson, T.M. (1993), op. cit.

14   However, as this paper goes to press the withdrawal of the UK from the ERM, and subsequent *de facto* devaluation of sterling against the Irish punt by some 15 per cent looks set to generate another shopping boom for Northern Ireland border towns. The *Sunday Times* of 4 October 1992 recorded that 'some shopping centres in Ulster report an increase in trade of 30 per cent'.

15   Quoted in NITB (1948), *Annual Report 1.*

16   NITB (1958), *Annual Report 10,* pp. 14-5.

17   NITB (1971), *Annual Report 24.*

18   NITB (1972), *Annual Report 25,* p. 25.

19   NITB (1973), *Annual Report 26,* p. 10.

20   NITB (1974), *Annual Report 27,* p. 10.

21   NITB (1975), *Annual Report 28,* p. 12.

22   NITB (1976), *Annual Report 29,* p. 13.

23   NITB (1977), *Annual Report 30,* p. 12.

24   NITB (1980), *Tourist Facts.*

25   NITB (1981), *Annual Report 34,* p. 7.

26   Heeley (1989), quoted in Moorhead, P., op. cit., p. 140.

27   NITB (1985), *Annual Report 37,* p. 17.

28   Moorhead, P. (1991), op. cit., p. 142.

29   NITB (1986), *Annual Report 38,* p. 15.

30   NITB (1987), *Annual Report 39,* p. 8.

31   NITB (1989), *Annual Report 42,* p. 3.

32   NITB (1990), *Tourism Facts* lists the number of visitors to the top tourist attractions in descending order: Giant's Causeway (350,000), Ulster Museum (274,144), Belfast Zoo (209,204), Dundonald Old Mill (150,069), Ulster Folk and Transport Museum (146,604), Waterworld (121,742), Ulster American Folk Park (114, 039), Causeway Safari Park (111,213), Northern Ireland Aquarium (91,835), Portstewart Strand (90,081), Belleek Pottery (65,000), Carrickfergus Castle (54,070), Old Bushmills Distillery (52,625), Castle Ward (48,520), Bangor Heritage Centre (47,575), Tropicana (45,943), Carrick-a-rede Rope Bridge

(44,007), Belfast Castle (44,000), Streamvale, Open Farm (43,169), Armagh Planetarium (40,000), Marble Arch Caves (35,000), Butterfly House (32,488), Orchard Gallery (32,000), Shane's Castle (32,000), Mount Stewart House (30,434).

Forest parks, country parks and gardens are listed separately. The top ten in 1990 were Crawfordsburn Country Park (1,000,000), Botanic Gardens (350,000), Murlough Nature Reserve (300,000), Lady Dixon Park (300,000), Oxford Island Nature Reserve (257,412), Cave Hill Country Park (250,000), Scrabo Country Park (200,000), Belvoir Forest Park (175,000), Tollymore Forest Park (147,875), Silent Valley (121,600).

33 The following list is taken from the current (1992) NITB brochure *Land of the Causeway*. Under the heading 'other publications' it offers information on the following activities which can be obtained from the NITB: cruising; sailing; other water sports (e.g. water skiing, windsurfing, sub-aqua); coarse fishing; game fishing; sea fishing; farm study tours; motoring; golf; farm and country holidays; town and seaside holidays; rambling/Ulster Way; mountaineering; caving and pot-holing; youth holidays; pony trekking; riding (with tuition); bird watching; youth hostelling; geology; hang gliding; parascending; gliding; canoeing; caravan and camping holidays; Ulster heritage trails; genealogy; clan gatherings; holidays for senior citizens; homes and gardens; steam trains; hunting and shooting; archaeology and antiquities; fairs and festivals, National Trust; folk museums; bowling; cycling; gardening; coach tours; crafts and traditional industries tours.

34 Griffith-Jones, R. (1984), 'Northern Ireland — Putting the Record Straight', *Tourism Management,* 5:138-41.

35 Smyth, R. (1986), 'Public Policy for Tourism in Northern Ireland', *Tourism Management,* 7:120-6.

36 ibid., p. 122.

37 ibid., p. 125.

38 ibid., p. 125-6.

39 Leslie, D. (1991), 'Tourism and Northern Ireland — a Troubled Time', unpublished M.Phil. thesis, University of Ulster at Jordanstown, pp. 421-29.

40 Moorhead, P., op. cit., pp. 158-60. A different sort of proposal for the more effective marketing of hotels and holidays in NI is made by Leslie, D. and McAleenan, M. in 'Marketing Hotels, Tourism and Northern Ireland', *Tourism Management,* 1990, **11**: 6-11. They argue in favour of the establishment of a 'Northern Ireland Hoteliers Marketing Group'.

41 DED (1989), *A View to the Future,* op. cit., p. 22.

42 Milton, K. (1990), *Our Countryside, Our Concern — the Policy and Practice of Conservation in Northern Ireland,* a report for Northern Ireland Environment Link, p. 58.

43 Horwath Consulting (1991), *Review of the Quality and Supply of Tourist Accommodation in Northern Ireland,* p. 4, report commissioned by the Department of Economic Development and the Northern Ireland Tourist Board.

44 Pearce, D.G. (1990), 'Tourism in Ireland — Questions of Scale and Organization', *Tourism Management,* **11**:133-51.

45 O'Rourke, F. (1992), 'The Failure of Bord Fáilte', in *The Sunday Tribune,* 7 June. This article provoked a major debate in the Republic of Ireland press.

See, for example, O'Rourke's subsequent response to his critics 'The Tourist Controversy' in *The Sunday Tribune,* 5 July 1992, and G. Melia's article 'Attracting Big-Spend Tourists is the Key' in *The Sunday Tribune,* 12 July 1992.

46 Shaw, G., Greenwood, J., and Williams, A.M. (1990), 'The United Kingdom: Market Responses and Public Policy', in Williams, A.M., and Shaw, G., (eds.), *Tourism and Economic Development — Western Europe Experiences,* 2nd edition, Belhaven Press, London.

47 See notes 32 and 33 above.

48 Houston, S. (1984), 'Images of Ulster', unpublished undergraduate dissertation, The Queen's University of Belfast.

49 ibid., p. 12.

50 ibid., p. 13.

51 Moorhead, P., op. cit., p. 80.

52 NITB (1992), *The Land of the Causeway.*

53 Moorhead, P., op. cit., p. 138.

54 ibid., p. 159.

55 ibid., p. 138. The relationship between political violence and tourism generally has been reviewed by Richter, L.K. and Waugh, W.L. in 'Terrorism and Tourism as Logical Companions', *Tourism Management,* 1986, **7**: 230-8. They convincingly argue that tourists make attractive targets for terrorists for a whole variety of reasons. However, their remark that in NI the 'tourist areas are secure' (p. 231) is misleading. It is worth repeating here that whilst tourists themselves have never been deliberately targeted, the tourist infrastructure has been the subject of IRA attack as part of its policy of economic terrorism. Furthermore, their generalisation that 'when problems arise, the only response the industry knows is to market more vigorously' (p. 232) clearly does not apply to the situation in NI in the early 1970s.

56 Ryan, C. (1991), *Tourism, Terrorism and Violence — the Risks of Wider World Travel,* Conflict Studies no. 244, Research Institute for the Study of Conflict and Terrorism, p. 24.

57 (1992), *Rough Guide to Ireland,* p. 26.

58 ibid., p. 437-444.

8

Gifts of Tongues: Foreign Languages and Tourism Policy in Ireland

Juliette Péchenart and Anne Tangy

Foreword

Is the Irish tourism workforce well equipped to deal with the increased number of Continental European tourists coming to Ireland? This article will attempt to answer that question. Firstly it examines the change in tourism trends in Ireland over the last ten years. Then it examines the language policy of the state and gives an overview of languages in tourism policy. The last part of the article details the work carried out by CERT, the state training agency for tourism, and it concludes with a look at the future.

Change in Tourism Trends

TRENDS IN THE ORIGIN OF FOREIGN VISITORS

In 1991 more than three million overseas visitors came to Ireland. The tourism market in Ireland has traditionally been dominated by anglophone tourists, mainly from the United States and Britain. In recent years, however, there has been a significant increase in the number of visitors from mainland Europe.

Since the early 1980s, the number of mainland Europe visitors to

Ireland has risen by 165 per cent from 319,000 to 841,000 with a concurrent increase in expenditure. In 1981, mainland Europe visitors spent IR£55.4 m. in Ireland. This is estimated to have increased to IR£355 m. in 1991 (see Table 8.1).

Markets which have increased substantially in the last decade include France — up by 143 per cent, Germany — up by 124 per cent and Italy — up by a dramatic 470 per cent. This means that for almost one-third of our visitors now, English is a foreign language. And the figure looks set to rise.

TRENDS IN TYPES OF HOLIDAYS

This growth can be explained by several factors:

— The presence of Bord Fáilte, the Irish Tourist Board, in countries such as France and Germany for the past twenty years and Italy for the past ten years has largely contributed to the promotion of Ireland as an attractive and interesting holiday destination. It has increased awareness of Ireland through advertising, publication of informative literature, participation in travel fairs etc.

Table 8.1   Tourism from principal markets to Ireland 1981–91

		1981	1987	1990	1991 (preliminary)	1990–91 +/−%
Britain	000s	1,008	1,236	1,785	1,751	− 1.9
	IR£m.	110.5	213.6	213.6	350.0	5.3
N. America	000s	278	398	443	347	−21.5
	IR£m.	68.4	158.5	166.4	152	− 8.6
M. Europe	000s	319	390	744	841	13.1
	IR£m.	55.4	105.6	249.2	355	42.5
France	000s	92	113	198	223	13
	IR£m.	14.8	23.1	66.5	81.2	23
Germany	000s	90	103	178	201	13
	IR£m.	17.2	33.8	55.1	67.5	23
Italy	000s	n.a.	17	73	97	33
	IR£m.		4.9	23.5	33.9	43
Tot. Overseas	000s	1,680	2,098	3,096	3,060	− 1
	IR£m.	251.5	504.3	795.8	903	13.5

Source: Central Marketing Department, Bord Fáilte.

— The improvement and diversification of tourist facilities in Ireland through the European Regional Development Fund and other various incentive grant schemes.

— The increased concern for a cleaner environment, the 'emotional' appeal of Ireland in terms of its cultural and romantic heritage and perceived distinctive way of life — the scenery, atmosphere of tranquillity and the friendliness of the Irish people.

— The move away from the more traditional sun-destination and a greater demand for activity and special interest holidays such as fishing, cycling, golfing and horse-riding or the more passive activities such as visits to historical places, stately homes, gardens, national and forest parks.

CROSS-CULTURAL AND LINGUISTIC CONTACT IN THE TOURISM INDUSTRY

Tourism is very much a labour intensive industry and it involves a high level of cross-cultural and linguistic contact in all its sectors be they transport and travel, accommodation and catering or the more recent sectors of leisure/recreation facilities.

If Ireland wants to compete successfully in international markets, it must ensure a high quality of service. That service can only be enhanced if the Irish can communicate effectively with their customers.

It is now widely accepted in the export field that hosts must be prepared to speak their customers' language if they do not want to lose business. The Irish tourist industry must recognise that, as more and more visitors from other European countries come to this country, it cannot rely on the foreigner's ability to speak English.

Language, Policy in Ireland and Practice

'The Irish traveller arriving at Copenhagen or Amsterdam airport can engage the baggage handler in English conversation with the same confidence as his or her business or personal contact later in the day' says Professor Eda Sagarra in her preface to Mary Ruane's *Access to Foreign Languages*.[1]

Could the same be said of the Italian, German or French-speaking traveller/tourist arriving at Dublin airport?

This section examines the provision for foreign languages in postprimary education in Ireland. It then compares it with the situation in other European countries. It concludes by drawing the implications for tourism training in Ireland.

A review of the contributions to the special issue of *Teangeolas*, the journal of the Linguistics Institute of Ireland, on 'Languages and Language Policy in Ireland' (summer 1990), points to the conclusion that Ireland does not have a clear and coherent language policy.

As stated in the editorial, 'The subject of a national language policy has barely been touched upon in Ireland'.[2] Or as Helen O Murchú puts it,

> On this basis, it would appear that we have no lack of policy *statements* on the languages currently offered, *or not offered*, in our educational system; that some courses of action have been defined; but that we still do not have a *coherent language policy*, encompassing all the linguistic possibilities of our actual and potential situation . . . There are also *parallel* policies on the different languages taught at present. What is lacking is a coherent planning framework with some attempt at least at mutually complementary decision-making process.[3]

R.L. Davis echoes Helen O Murchú when he says 'While government was visibly committed to European social initiatives in general, the specific task of elaborating a coherent national language policy, with clearly defined goals and practically achievable objectives, has not been seriously addressed.'[4]

But what does actually happen in post-primary Irish schools as far as the provision and uptake of foreign languages are concerned? By foreign languages, we mean any language apart from the two national languages, Irish and English.

The striking fact is that in Irish schools foreign languages are not core subjects. They are not required subjects for school recognition purposes and whether at junior or senior cycle, foreign languages are not compulsory subjects for examination purposes. Figure 8.1 illustrates the Irish school system.

At present a student can go through second level education in Ireland without ever having been exposed to any foreign language. However, if a pupil decides to take up a foreign language, which are the foreign languages included in the curricula of Irish schools? At present, French, German, Italian and Spanish are the languages taught. As the following figures show, French is clearly the most taught foreign language while the rates for German and even more for Spanish and Italian are very low. Over the last few years, German has been strongly promoted and it has shown a definite increase.

The factors that will influence a pupil deciding to take or not to take a foreign language are grouped, as shown by Mary Ruane, in external factors such as gender differences, social composition of the schools (feepaying/non-feepaying schools), type of school (secondary, vocational, community/comprehensive), size and age of school, regional location or internal factors such as grouping practices (ability), type of curriculum offered, length of cycle.

It would be impossible in such a short article to study all these factors in detail but some conclusions can be drawn:

— more girls study foreign languages than boys;

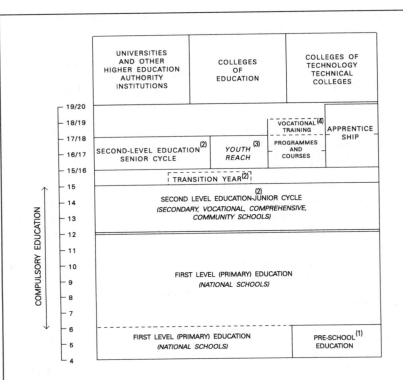

1   There is no national system of pre-school education in Ireland. However primary
    (National) schools may accept pupils on or after their fourth birthday. Existing pre-
    school services are mainly private and not part of the formal education system.
    The average age for starting schools is five years.

2   Second-level schools cover lower and upper secondary education — Junior and
    Senior Cycles. The four main types — Secondary, Vocational, Comprehensive and
    Community — all now offer a comprehensive curriculum combining academic and
    vocational subjects. The Transition Year, a one-year interdisciplinary programme
    is offered in a limited number of schools. The Junior Cycle leads to the new Junior
    Certificate providing access to the Senior Cycle.

    At Senior Cycle the main courses are the 2-year Leaving Certificate leading to higher
    education or employment, and the Vocational Preparation and Training
    Programmes which prepare for working life.

3   Youthreach is an education and training programme available to young people who
    have left school with no formal qualification. It lasts 2 years (A Foundation year
    and a Progression year).

    It is run jointly by the education authorities (Vocational Education Committees
    — VEC) and the Vocational Training and Employment Authority (FAS).

4   Training courses of various lengths are provided by FAS for unemployed young
    people: Skills Foundation, Community Youth Training, Local Training Initiatives.

*Figure 8.1   The Irish School System (Source: Commission of the European
           Communities)*

Table 8.2   Percentage of pupils taking different subjects at Intermediate/Group Certificate, 1986-7

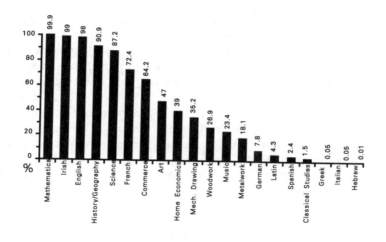

Source: Ruane, M. (1990), *Access to foreign languages*, RIA, Dublin

Table 8.3   Percentage of pupils taking different subjects at Leaving Certificate, 1986-7

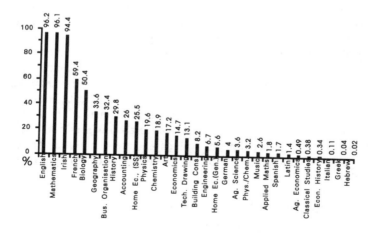

Source: Ruane, M. (1990), *Access to foreign languages*, RIA, Dublin

— foreign languages have by tradition been offered in secondary schools and feepaying schools are more likely to offer two or three foreign languages;

—until the early 1960s, foreign languages were not taught in vocational schools.

To conclude, let us go back to the Italian, German or French-speaking traveller/tourist arriving at Dublin Airport. It is unlikely that the baggage handler encountered will master these three foreign languages.[6] 'Our' French-speaking tourist will be lucky if he or she can exchange a few words in French as this might be the only foreign language the baggage handler has ever been taught.

This confirms the findings of the *Eurobarometer* of December 1987 that showed that 80 per cent of Irish people cannot speak a modern European language other than their own, that 17 per cent can speak one other language and that 3 per cent can speak two.[5]

This does not mean that Irish people are in fact poor linguists. Some of them have simply never had any access to foreign languages during their time at school.

However, the future holds some promise as the National Council for Curriculum and Assessment, established in December 1987, 'is currently considering the whole question of mandatory subjects at junior cycle level and the designation of a modern European language as a mandatory subject for all 12-15-year-old pupils in Irish schools.'[6] At senior cycle level, a number of significant initiatives have been taken as regards foreign languages. Modern language modules are included in Vocational Preparation and Training courses (VPT courses). The new Vocational Leaving Certificate programme includes a modern European language as a compulsory component.[7]

A more comprehensive study of all EC countries would show that all of them except Ireland have one compulsory foreign language as part of the secondary education curriculum. This has obvious implications for the training of young people in the hotel, catering and tourism industry. Pupils coming on these tourism-related courses have very mixed levels as far as foreign languages are concerned. Some have never studied a foreign language at all, others stopped at the Junior Certificate while others studied a foreign language (usually French) at Leaving Certificate level.

This fact obviously does not facilitate the implementation of language training on tourism courses. The fact that English is the mother tongue of the majority of Irish people as well as an inter-state language of the EC is one other major obstacle to the development of foreign languages on tourism-related courses.

Tourism Policy and Languages

PERFORMANCE OF IRISH TOURISM

Tourism is a major growth area of the Irish economy, responsible for almost 7 per cent of the national wealth. It supported the equivalent of 80,000 full-time jobs during 1990.[8] The government's target of doubling tourism numbers from overseas from 2.1m. to 4.2m. over the 1988–92 period with an increase of IR£500m. and a consequent increase of 25,000 jobs will require an annual compound growth rate of 15 per cent — three times that forecast for world trends in tourism (see article by Deegan and Dineen in this volume).[9]

HOW CAN WE ACHIEVE OUR TARGETS?

According to Bord Fáilte's preliminary figures for 1991, of the three main markets for Irish tourism — Britain, North America and mainland Europe — the only market which increased in 1991 was the mainland European market (see Table 8.1). There is, and has always been, increasing competition for Irish interests in these markets from long-haul exotic destinations. Together with the price factor, which is a dominant factor affecting Ireland's overall competitiveness, if Ireland wants to improve or even maintain its position as a popular tourist destination it will have to offer visitors a service as good as, if not better, than, that provided in other countries.

To keep attracting visitors from abroad it is important to find out what they want and need and one of the needs which has come up persistently in the various surveys done over the past decade is the need for improved language skills and facilities.

WHAT DO THE VISITORS SAY?

'We find much trouble in learning what things are. Sometimes the girls cannot explain it', said a French visitor about Irish restaurants back in 1984.[10]

In the recently published report on visitors to tourist attractions, prepared for the Heritage Attractions Consortium by Tourism Development International, 51 per cent of visitors surveyed would like to see the provision of more information and translation. The survey suggests that 'the facility to cater for Continental European visitors in their own language would add greatly to their appreciation of heritage attractions'.[11] Indeed, respondents, when asked to suggest improvements on the sites, most frequently called for more detailed information and for the material to be translated into the main overseas languages. When it is considered that most of the interviewing staff for these surveys are not multilingual, the question arises as to what could have been the comments of all those visitors whose English was not good enough to be interviewed.

WHAT DOES THE INDUSTRY SAY?

In the CERT 1986 report on the attitudes to in-company training in the hotel and catering industry, hotel and restaurant managers expressed a need for in-company or external European languages courses.

Again, in the CERT 1991 report on employment in the non-food/

non-accommodation sectors of the tourism industry in Ireland, the need for language training appears as even more crucial. Forty-five per cent of the forty surveyed sectors mentioned language training as part of their training needs. When the training needs were looked at in terms of priority and regions, languages were given second, third and fourth priority in the North West, South East, Mid West and South West regions respectively.

In a skill needs survey of Killarney prepared by CERT in 1991 for the EC Commission employees asked for their preferences for further training gave language training as first priority. It seems evident that there is a growing awareness of language needs and facilities in this country, apart from the non-English-speaking visitors as well as from the industry.

WHAT DOES EUROPE SAY?

The Irish economy in the 1990s has been forced to meet the challenge of European integration. The key words are mobility of labour, a trained skilled workforce and standardisation of qualifications. CEDEFOP (European Centre for the Development of Vocational Training), which deals with vocational training and standardisation of qualifications, has introduced comparability at Community level in respect of a number of occupations. In the tourism sector, the following ten occupations all include foreign languages as part of the job description: receptionist, porter, waiter/waitress, barman/barmaid, wine waiter/waitress, retail travel agency clerk, tourist information officer, animateur assistant, courier/tour escort, conference assistant.

The HOTREC (Confederation of National Hotel and Restaurant Associations in the European Community) in its White Paper on the 1992 challenge for the hotel, restaurant and café industry devotes a whole section to the theme of languages for the tourism industry. It stresses that 'front line and management staff need to speak more than one language' and that 'proper communication between guests and staff of hotels and restaurants is a necessity to give the guest a feeling of comfort and hospitality'.[12]

HOTREC recommends that the EC should encourage the tourism, hotel, restaurant and café industries to train their staff in languages and that the EC funding programmes should be attuned to language training of the present labour force.

It encourages the national associations to develop bonus systems for employees who are proficient in more than one language and the industry to support employees to participate in exchange programmes such as the HOTREC European Placement Programme.

'The language barrier can hinder the cultural enrichment of visitors from both inside and outside Europe', says the EC Commission in its *Community Action Plan to Assist Tourism* published in 1991.[13] It recommends that museums and cultural sites provide information material and documentation in a number of languages including minority languages as these services can prove inadequate if available only in the language of the host country.

The community supports pilot international programmes such as Petra, Comett, Eurotecnet, Erasmus, Euroform and, of course, Lingua, which all imply to a varying degree an element of language training.

In the report prepared by the IMHI (Institut de Management Hôtelier International), on *The Impact of EC Legislation on the Hotel, Catering and Tourism Industry*, the importance of language skills is emphasised once again.[14] Indeed, it appears that, in anticipation of the Single Market, language training is the most popular form of training. It seems clear that the tourism industry demands language skills but it is also evident that language skills are spread unevenly throughout Europe and that some countries are better prepared to offer these than others. Ireland is lagging far behind together with the UK, Spain, Italy and Greece. Overall, 70 per cent of adults in the EC speak no language other than their own and fewer than 10 per cent speak more than one other language.

WHAT DOES IRELAND SAY?

Ireland has been slow to recognise the importance of using the customer's own language as part of a quality service and indeed, too many people in the tourism industry still rely on the — wrong — assumption that all foreigners can speak English.

So what does the Irish government do in order to encourage a wider knowledge of foreign languages in the tourism industry?

There is no direct mention of language skills as part of a tourism policy in the government White Paper on tourism policy published in 1985. However, it is interesting to note that one of the listed attractions of Ireland as a tourism destination is the widespread use of the English language in the case of 'our two biggest markets, Britain and North America'.[15] Surely this could be seen as a weakness in the case of what has now become the second biggest market for Ireland, i.e. mainland Europe? And indeed, in the report prepared by Price Waterhouse for the government, *Improving the Performance of Irish Tourism* published in 1987, deficiencies are noted in the standards of key elements of the product and insufficient skills in areas of management, marketing and foreign languages are identified.

'The Irish brand of friendliness which is extended so readily to English-speaking visitors from the US and Britain is not visible to the French tourist and this leads to barriers to holiday enjoyment' says the report.[16]

This view is supported by Bord Fáilte in its report, *Development for Growth* published in 1989, in the following statement: 'The longer scale and wider range of activities now planned for will demand the development of additional skill areas particularly in leisure management, languages and advanced skills.'[17]

In its recommendations on product development the government included the following as part of a plan to improve European language skills and to increase knowledge of requirements of tourists in the Irish key markets:

— the introduction of European orientation and language programmes for trainee managers and other staff including training in overseas language schools and placement in Continental tourism operations;

— the introduction of intensive language courses focused on the needs of different staff functions in the tourism sector;

— the introduction by Bord Fáilte with the Youth Employment Agency or CERT of a European Orientation Programme for Trainee Managers in the tourism sector; [18]

— the introduction of intensive language courses for front-of-house staff for the commercial sector and for staff in the regional tourism offices.

IRISH INITIATIVES

The numerous reports which have been published in the past few years, at both European and national level, on the theme of tourism, the various surveys done in Ireland of overseas visitors and of the industry, have all stressed the need for improved language skills and facilities in the context of improving the performance of tourism. While the issue is still being overlooked by too many people in the industry it could no longer be ignored by CERT, the state tourism training agency, which has recently launched its languages for tourism scheme. It is hoped, through this scheme, to train up to 8,000 members of the tourism workforce by 1995 in basic and advanced language skills.

A Corporate Strategy for Language Training in the Irish Tourism Industry

INTRODUCTION

A language training scheme is now in place in Ireland's tourism industry, designed to train frontline staff in European languages. For the first time, language courses have been designed specifically for Irish tourism personnel and training is applied to practical work situations. Already over 2,700 tourism personnel and students have followed courses in European languages which were tailor-made for the industry. The scheme was set up and designed by CERT.

INSTITUTIONAL CIRCUMSTANCES

CERT, as the state training agency for tourism in Ireland, is responsible, on behalf of government, for co-ordinating the recruitment, training, education and placement of staff at all levels of the industry. CERT's concern, within the rapidly developing and highly competitive tourism market, is with the standards of product and service which are on offer, and the training at all levels which is required to meet the highest international requirements in this respect.

IMPORTANCE OF LANGUAGES FOR TOURISM

According to CERT, the development of foreign language skills within the training of young people and the career development of workers in the tourism industry is important to:

— give young people and existing workers in the industry the language skills necessary in order to communicate effectively with visiting tourists;

— enable young tourism workers to meet agreed qualifications and criteria as specified by the Community Hotel and Restaurant Committee;

— enable young people to avail of employment mobility within the tourism industry of the Community;

— facilitate cultural understanding and the appreciation of diverse cultural needs within the Community;

— assist the Irish tourism industry to compete on equal terms with other touristic destinations within the Community through the development of a bi-/multi-lingual workforce.[19]

A CORPORATE STRATEGY

In recognition of the importance of language training within the context of tourism in Ireland, CERT commissioned a preliminary research study into the area. Entitled *A Strategy for the Development of Foreign Languages in the Hotel, Catering and Tourism Industry',* the report was prepared by the School of Applied Languages, Dublin City University and presented in August 1989. The report reviewed the language training situation in the industry, identified key training needs, and made preliminary recommendations with respect to appropriate strategies in order to meet these needs.

The CERT consultative approach to curricula development is reflected in the ongoing work of language development. Language consultants, college teachers, CERT technical advisers and members of the industry are working together to ensure that the training programmes devised are both linguistically and professionally appropriate to the industry.

On the one hand, one could say that CERT, by reacting to the changing trends in tourism and growing demands for language skills rather than anticipating them, has delayed the process and it will take a number of years to develop a bi-/multi-lingual workforce in this country; meanwhile our continental traveller is still likely to be facing communication problems with the Irish baggage handler. On the other hand, the fact that CERT's approach to language training is a long-term, comprehensive, coherent and systematic approach means that there is now a language policy for tourism in Ireland with ongoing work in the areas of syllabus and material development, assessment, certification and teacher training.

Philosophy of CERT Approach

ANALYSIS OF LANGUAGE PROVISION AND TRAINING NEEDS

The conscious decision by CERT to develop a systematic approach to language training rather than a short-term haphazard approach meant that essential steps needed to be taken. Language provision had to be researched, training needs had to be analysed and programmes to be designed before any course could be delivered.

A review of language provision in the Irish tourism industry was thus undertaken in 1989 and it was found that:

— there was an absence of compulsory foreign languages on CERT courses;
— foreign languages on CERT courses had very low status;
— there was very uneven language provision as regards levels of linguistic ability, duration of courses and forms of assessment;
— there was no foreign language syllabus with defined aims and objectives;
— there was a lack of appropriate training materials;
— French predominated against other foreign languages;
— there was a diversity of the learning context. The five contexts in which training for the industry takes place are: second-level education (VPT courses in hotel, catering and tourism); hotel and catering training colleges; unemployed training programmes; staff working in the industry; foreign placement programmes.

Language needs were analysed with the five groups mentioned above through interviews and questionnaires and the following issues were discussed: content of language courses; practicalities and organisation of language training; and assessment and certification.

Content of language courses

It was found that French was by far the most popular language, followed by German, Italian and Spanish.

The greatest need was felt to be that of people who have the most direct contact with the customer, i.e. porters, receptionists, waiters/waitresses, bar staff and management, the emphasis being placed on those who have not had any training in a foreign language. The need was less acute for those with a school qualification in a language. It was felt that the emphasis should be placed on language for practical communication and there was a strong perception of the need for oral competence. There was a need for a standard syllabus defined in terms of aims and objectives, for communicative, job-related tasks, and for cultural competence.

Practicalities and organisation of language training
There was consensus among the three interest groups (teachers, trainees and employees) that learning should start as early as possible, and certainly as soon as a person starts training for the industry.

The teachers felt that there was a need to increase the number of hours allocated to language training and to integrate language learning into other skill areas. They also felt that the learners would have to be streamed according to their level of competence. The need for in-service training and access to periods spent abroad was also mentioned. People already working in the industry identified some factors contributing to the difficulty of organising language training among workers such as the seasonal nature of employment, the demanding nature of the work and the fact that the businesses concerned are very dispersed. It was recommended that: language learning be in-house; employees be allowed time off to attend classes, and an emphasis be placed on self-learning packages.

Assessment and certification
The industry reacted very positively to a transparent and coherent system of certification which would be task-based and job-related. Language teachers made a strong recommendation for a formal, compulsory language component to be added to the existing nationally-recognised CERT qualifications.

RECOMMENDATIONS AND CONCLUSIONS

The general recommendations and conclusions which arose from the research work carried out by the consultants are summarised below:
— the approach to language teaching/learning should be communicative;
— sociolinguistic competence was considered of paramount importance;
— class size should be limited to 15–20 people;
— specification is needed for modules leading to five defined levels of competence;
— self-instruction materials should be developed;
— exchanges and other links with foreign countries leading to credit transfer should be developed;
— assessment should be task-based, related to work situations and should emphasise oral competence;

— CERT should have a crucial role in syllabus development, assessment and certification, materials development and teachers' in-service training.

DEVELOPMENT OF A NON-LANGUAGE-SPECIFIC SYLLABUS

The second phase of the project focused on the devising of a modern languages syllabus for the industry. Formulated in terms of behavioural aims and objectives, that syllabus was to form the basis for devising particular courses to suit the needs of learners of particular languages, at particular levels and in particular sectors of the tourism industry.

The content of the syllabus was tailored to meet the needs of the tourism industry and had, therefore, a much more specific focus than a more general school syllabus.

Four general aims were identified:

— to provide the learner with the language required to communicate with a foreign guest;

— to provide the learner with the language required to be able to carry out the tasks related specifically to his/her area of work;

— to provide the learner with the language required in order for him or her to be able to relate socially with a foreign visitor in Ireland;

— to provide the learner with the language required in order for him or her to be able to travel to and work in the foreign country and socialise there.

The complete syllabus consists of two areas of language tasks, receptive tasks (listening and reading skills) and productive tasks (speaking and writing skills). There is also a cultural component which lists examples of topic areas to be covered and details of 'micro-syllabi'. The latter are, in effect, a subset of the general syllabus and list the various language tasks that should be concentrated on according to the level of competence and specific job occupation of workers in the industry, e.g. receptionists, bar staff, waiters/waitresses, etc.

FURTHER DEVELOPMENTS

CERT has built on the preliminary research and development work and has linked all its strategies to the recommendations of the initial report.

The project has moved very rapidly and in the course of two years a full programme of basic language training for tourism, spanning the four major European languages (French, German, Italian and Spanish), has been offered and advanced courses for each language developed.

Language training is now a compulsory requirement for national certification and all new recruits to the industry follow up to 120 hours of this subject. Part-time ten-week courses are also provided to personnel already working in tourism.

The courses offered at the moment will not produce fluency — that is not realistic, nor is it the main intention. They offer survival language skills. They arm people with the essentials needed to understand European customers and to communicate at basic level in their language. Thus, they challenge the commonly held view that unless something resembling total fluency is attained, a foreign language cannot be of use.

Due to partnership arrangements under various EC programmes, including Petra and Lingua, many of the trainees attending CERT courses in hotel and catering colleges have been afforded the opportunity to spend some weeks in the relevant country and some teachers have also had access to training courses abroad.

To aid language training, CERT has also developed an audio-pack which is now used as an integral element of its French courses. Produced on two audio-tapes with a companion workbook, the pack is also available to hotel, catering and tourism businesses as a self-learning course in practical French.

The pack is based on the syllabus for the basic French course and is unusual in the tourism arena worldwide in the sense that most of the language materials for tourism published to date have been geared towards personnel who have already reached an advanced stage of language proficiency.

One of the barriers that had to be broken down in getting the language scheme off the ground was the initial reluctance among many of the students to learn foreign languages. They were wary of the course and could not see the relevance of an 'academic' subject on a vocational course. This reluctance, however, quickly disappeared once they realised that the classes were enjoyable, and very relevant to their work and that grammar was picked up almost in passing. This approach to training has been a major factor in making the courses successful.

IRELAND A PIONEER?

The available body of international knowledge on language teaching and planning does not contain extensive research into the language problems associated with the tourism industry. The kind of research CERT initiated appears to be quite innovative in that it addresses the language needs of a specific group and in the manner in which it approaches the issues.

Although most of the other European countries have a compulsory language component in a variety of certificates and diplomas for this industry, the fact remains that a systematic approach to the industry's needs is only now beginning to be adopted.

Most of the research work which has been carried out worldwide has not been followed up by work on the production of syllabi and materials to the extent that one might have expected. Thus, the present movement can actually afford the Irish tourism industry the opportunity to play a pioneering role in developments in this area.

The Future

With the start of the new Lingua programme, one of the most recent of the EC educational projects, there are real possibilities of an even brighter future for the development of language skills in the tourism industry. Lingua is a five year project, running from 1990 to 1994.

> It was adopted on 28 July 1989 by the Council of Ministers of the European Community to promote foreign language competence in the European Community. Its principal objective is to assist Member States with the qualitative and quantitative improvement of foreign language teaching and training, by providing grants in support of mobility schemes and innovative projects in the initial and in-service training of foreign language teachers, language learning in vocational and higher education and the setting up of strategies for language training in economic life.[20]

Lingua is concerned with one particular means towards this end, the learning of foreign languages. As tourism is one of the priority sectors in the Lingua programme, CERT decided in 1992 to initiate a three-year transnational research project in the area of languages for tourism.

The project aims to respond to the rapid growth throughout Europe of cultural and activity-based tourism through the development of syllabi and training materials in French, German, Italian, Greek and English as foreign languages, for people working in that particular sector of the industry (e.g. tourist information officer, leisure assistant, tour escort, conference assistant, etc.).

The fact that Ireland, one of the smallest and least advantaged countries of the EC is leading this project together with major countries such as France, Germany and Italy emphasises the pioneer role of Ireland in the area of language policy for tourism.

The great hope for Irish tourism is still continental Europe. However, trends could change yet again. With tourism on the verge of becoming the biggest industry worldwide, tourist markets for Ireland could change in the next century and the small number of Japanese golfers who have been coming to this country for the past few years could increase more rapidly than one might expect. In that context, and with the expertise gained in continental languages, Ireland could be in a very strong position to anticipate rather than to respond to future needs and one could envisage the development of cultural/language modules for non-European languages such as Japanese.

In a fiercely competitive market, the Irish tourism industry cannot afford to lag behind in the quality of service being offered to visitors elsewhere. As was recently heard on national radio: 'There is no quicker way to a Frenchman's pocket than wishing him "Céad míle fáilte" *en français*.'[21]

NOTES AND REFERENCES

1 Eda Sagarra (1990), 'Foreword', in Mary Ruane (1990), *Access to Foreign Languages*, Royal Irish Academy, Dublin.
2 Editorial (1990), *Teangeolas*, No. 27, p.10.
3 Helen O Murchú (1990), 'A Language Policy for Irish Schools', *Teangeolas*, No. 27, p.15.
4 R.L. Davis (1990), 'Don't Disturb the Ancestors', *Teangeolas*, No. 27, p.21.
5 December 1987, *Eurobarometer*, 28, Commission of the European Communities, Brussels, p. A26.
6 Albert O Ceallaigh (1991), 'Current Provision and Future Developments: First and Second Level Education', unpublished paper, 'Ireland, Language and 1992 Conference', Killybegs, 6 April, p.5.
7 ibid., p.5.
8 Irish Tourist Industry Confederation (1991), *Tourism: Its Impact on the Economy (1985-90)*, Irish Tourist Industry Confederation, Dublin, p. 5.
9 Bord Fáilte (1989), *Tourism in the Irish Economy*, Bord Fáilte, Dublin, p.15.
10 Bord Fáilte (1978), *Thought for Food. A Report on the Attitudes of Tourists to Eating in Ireland*, Bord Fáilte, Dublin, p. 58.
11 Tourism Development International (1990), *Visitors to Tourist Attractions in Ireland in 1991*, Heritage Attractions Consortium, p. 32.
12 HOTREC (1989), White Paper, The 1992 Challenge for the Hotel, Restaurant and Café Industry, Paris, p. 106.
13 Commission of the European Communities (1991), *Community Action Plan to Assist Tourism*, Brussels, p. 26.
14 HOTREC (1989), op. cit.
15 (1985), White Paper, *Tourism Policy*, Stationery Office, Dublin, p. 26.
16 Price Waterhouse (1987), *Improving the Performance of Irish Tourism*, Stationery Office Dublin, p. 174.
17 Bord Fáilte (1989), *Development for Growth*, Bord Fáilte, Dublin, p. 65.
18 This is a similar programme to the one introduced by the Confederation of Irish Industry with the Bank of Ireland where a three-month placement by a graduate in an Irish company is followed by three months in a language centre in France, Germany or Italy and completed by a six-month placement in a relevant commercial undertaking in a continental country.
19 Anne Gibney, Juliette Péchenart and William Richardson (1990), 'A Strategy for the Development of Foreign Languages in the Hotel, Catering and Tourism Industry', *Proceedings of the 1990 ENCODE Conference*, University of Antwerp, Antwerp, p. 140.

20   Commission of the European Communities (1992), *Applicants Guide —*
LINGUA, Brussels, p.2.
21   'Morning Ireland' (1992), RTE Radio 1, 18 May.

PART V

Tourist
Services
and
Practices

9

The Construction of Heritage

David Brett

The purpose of this chapter is to investigate the notion of 'heritage' and to study the uses made of it; and in particular, the creation of historical theme-parks and reconstructions.[1] Large numbers of jobs are to be found in something described as a 'heritage industry' and this activity is being serviced by courses in 'heritage studies' and 'heritage management'. The concept appears in tourist promotions all over Ireland, in government publications and categories, budget spending heads and daily conversation. It bids fair to being a major preoccupation of local authorities. In areas of poor employment prospects heritage attracts funding and provides welcome opportunities for advancement. This is not a small matter in any country, but in Ireland, with high general unemployment and areas of acute deprivation, the promotion of local history through special exhibitions and parks is an important part of the tourist economy; itself an essential part of the national economy. The future, we may say, is in heritage . . .

The link with tourism is integral to the whole topic of heritage, both as concept and as policy. There are some parts of the world that largely impinge upon the global consciousness through being the site of tourism. In such parts there is a tension between the realities experienced by the natives and by the visitors; this tension may be internalised by the native in the form of a split consciousness of self, a 'for-self' and a 'for-others', between which an authentic self-understanding can fall.

Heritage is also, as we shall note, linked with various forms of regionalism and a general self-consciousness about distinct cultural traditions which is presently being constructed into a political ideology for a 'new' European dispensation. As such, heritage can be seen to serve interests. This is a matter of particular and tragic sensitivity for the inhabitants of Ireland who do not have an agreed national history around which an unproblematic heritage can be constructed. Indeed, we are obstructed with pseudo-histories.

A critical approach to the notion of heritage in relation to tourism and to historical study needs to be undertaken in order to inform policy, management, promotion and our mutual education. At a deeper level, it would make clearer the difficulties attending political and cultural life in Ireland today.

Given the pervasive uses of heritage it is not surprising that a certain amount of theoretical and critical literature has begun to condense around the theme. Typical of these are *The Heritage Industry; Britain in a Climate of Decay* by Robert Hewison (London, 1987), and Patrick Wright's more discursive *On Living in an Old Country* (London, 1985). At the time of writing, the firm of Routledge has begun to issue a series of studies on heritage topics. There has also been the development of a new and historically critical museology which seeks to investigate the development of museums and similar institutions and their role in the creation and ordering of knowledge.

Colin Sorensen has written of

> an almost universal . . . preoccupation with 'the past'. This is not so much an interest in history, which one might understand as an awareness of the process of cause and effect in some sort of chronological sequence, but much more an urgent wish to achieve an immediate confrontation with a moment in time, a re-entry into a vanished circumstance . . . [in which] . . . 'real', physical, audible and (especially popular) smellable realities of a distant 'then' become a present and convincing 'now'.[2]

I shall return later to this passage, and to the idea of an 'immediate confrontation'. But it is not simply the past that is brought forward into the present, but ourselves that are transported back into the past. This is perfectly expressed in the following extract.

> Sail away to the New World on the Brig *Union* and meet us at work in our kitchens and farms.
>
> Stroll around the grounds of the Ulster-American Folk Park and enjoy a few hours of living history. Visit the authentically-furnished thatched cottages of rural Ulster and the log cabins of frontier America and you will be sure of a warm welcome from our costumed interpreters as they busy themselves at their everyday tasks. Turf fires, the aroma of baked

bread and clicking of the spinning wheel all contribute to the special atmosphere of bygone days. You will learn a great deal about the lives of the thousands of men, women and children who left in the eighteenth and nineteenth centuries to seek their fortunes in the New World of America.

You can even travel with them on board the emigrant ship and experience the sounds, smells and dreadful conditions of life at sea.
Ulster-American Folk Park leaflet 1992.

In writing like this the language of tourism is being transferred from travel in space to travel in time. But in analysing it we have to avoid a facile irony and try to see why this is such a potent concept. And we must also recognise how much serious scholarship has gone into the creation of this and other parks. The Ulster-American Park is, moreover, an attractive place to visit, deservedly popular, as are many other such creations. The task is to question 'living history' and the idea that it can be 'immediately' confronted.

The existing and growing literature on heritage is useful for our purposes, but is too anglocentric to be a reliable guide in Ireland. Hewison, for example, locates this new museology within a climate and culture of 'decline'. His examples, all English, are chosen to reinforce rather than investigate his hypothesis; and indeed it is very easy to go along with the general direction of his argument. But as a serious theory with wider application it is inadequate, in fact, there is good evidence to the contrary. The earliest examples of simulated histories seem to have occurred in the context of national or local self-aggrandisement. In the 1900 Paris Exposition, as part of a celebration of the city's history, an entire quartier of an 'Old Paris' was created and peopled by salaried inhabitants in medieval costume. Some of the earliest heritage parks of which I am aware are the restored colonial and Independence houses and villages that are quite common in the United States. The role of the Rockerfeller family in the creation of 'Williamsburg', or of Henry Ford in the recreation of his own home workshop and those of Edison and the Wright brothers are almost paradigm cases in the construction of heritage, yet these are essentially didactic and celebratory rather than nostalgic. Other American instances make memorial of the Civil War and do not hide the tragic realities; still others make special features of religious or ethnic groups. The Ulster-American Folk Park is certainly of this kind. Though this is something that requires closer research I do not think that the construction of heritage under these premises could be ascribed to 'decline'.

Indeed, in England this does not seem to have been the originating impulse either. The first English example of living recreation is probably that of the Castle Museum, York, which in the early 1950s created a street and a square of period shops and workplaces; this came about at the same time as an attempt to tidy up a scruffy old town and to modernise it with slum clearances and ringroads. It is only during the past fifteen years that the toytown model has spread outward into the town around the museum and come to bear down upon and to create a new ('old') civic reality. Central York is now dominated by the tourist economy and increasingly resembles its own museum; it is possible to walk through the sixteenth-century alleys around the Minster and to think you are, indeed, within the walls of an exhibition, so antiquarian has the ambience become. For someone who spent much of his early life in the unredeemed city, this is a dismal experience. In this instance we seem to be dealing with a process that began with one set of values and ended with another.

Different again are the massive programmes of restoration undertaken throughout continental Europe after the war, to reconstruct whole city centres as they had been before universal destruction. In such we find new forms of architecture which, from without, appear ancient but are constructed with modern technology and services within. The efforts made to reconstruct old Frankfurt, Warsaw, Leningrad stand as monuments of national and civic determination; in these cases re-creation is not to create a 'living history', but to assert the continuity between the past and the living present.

To consider and critically assess the concept of heritage both in its wider and in its specifically Irish context I think we must pass beyond the decline explanation. Instead, we need to reconsider the 'universal preoccupation' of which Sorensen writes. To trace out the differences between history and the recreated 'then' of heritage.

History, like art and like sport, is not a fixed entity but an activity. History is the story we are constantly telling ourselves to explain to ourselves just how we came to be where we think we are. History, truly considered, is a verb, not an abstract noun. We history. From which it follows that history is not given, but made. The story that we tell ourselves is a form of self-definition and is therefore, and unavoidably, an ethical enterprise. This is why close scholarship is important; it bears a similar relationship to the intellectual life as humility does to the spiritual; it reminds us that we may be in error everywhere. The consequences of fantasy may be lethal. This is also why popular, non-technical historical writing is a serious activity that is very difficult to do well. In so far as heritage attempts to present a popular history in this way, it too must be taken seriously; and we should consider it as one of the forms that a popular history might take today.

The principles on which history is written, told and presented are, of course, not neutral. The present dispute between a fact-based and a process-oriented curriculum is a case in point: the recent British government has been trying to promote the first at the expense of the second and to bring back into British schools a view of history that some see as a history of the state rather than a history of the people. The teaching of history in Northern Irish schools is a notorious example of exclusions. Those who have heard the guide's account of the history of Kilmainham Gaol may well be aware of a certain coyness. The re-writing and re-telling of history, far from being a peculiarity of totalitarian régimes, is the privilege of every ruling group. And openly or covertly, counter-histories are created from the same or extended data to serve different ends; in more or less free societies these counter-histories have the role of an intellectual opposition which may, before long, assume power. Good teaching makes us aware that there are always several histories and teaches us how to distinguish between them.

When we come to museums, exhibitions and theme-parks we have a right to expect the same. But objects and places do not easily speak for themselves; some way must be found to enable the visitor to grasp what is seen in such a way that an informed freedom of interpretation is possible. Objects are not words; a seventeenth-century pile denotes nothing unless it is placed in such an order of other objects that we can infer its significance. Even then we will have to be told something of — say — infantry formations and the use of mounted arquebusiers etc. Evidence of several sorts is required before an array of objects can be understood; in effect, they must be placed in a narrative. This narrative (even if it is 'merely' a chronicle) is always interpretive and explanatory. That is further to say that it has been mediated.

Our encounter with the objects from the past is mediated by the circumstances in which we encounter them — special buildings, conventions of display, principles of ordering, systems of catalogues etc. Luke Dodd has recently expressed this very clearly: 'Objects do not have an intrinsic meaning which transcends history and context, and a museum is not a neutral space which allows this "intrinsic" meaning to be displayed. A visit to a museum is a highly mediated experience in which the "past" is used as a catalyst — museum displays tell us as much about our attitude to the past as they do about any particular period of the past.'[3] This is even more the case in special or thematic exhibitions.

A recent and relevant example was the exhibition 'Kings in Conflict' (Fig. 9.1) arranged by the Ulster Museum in 1990, in an attempt to give an even-handed account of the background to the Battle of the Boyne 300 years before. Like many such exhibitions it was organised according to a principle of circulation; one went with the flow of time along a corridor, passing maps, prints, portraits, weapons etc. At the beginning of the corridor were exhibits that showed the backgrounds of the main participants and something of the political and military history immediately preceding the conflict. Moving into the year of 1690 the corridor was opened out to include tableaux. The first was a sound and light display of the Boyne battlefield with contemporary accounts read over a soundtrack, with snatches of film and a model countryside; the second was a treaty discussion between the contending parties in which dummies were made to speak, with moving lips and eyes. The range of material displayed was wide and interesting.

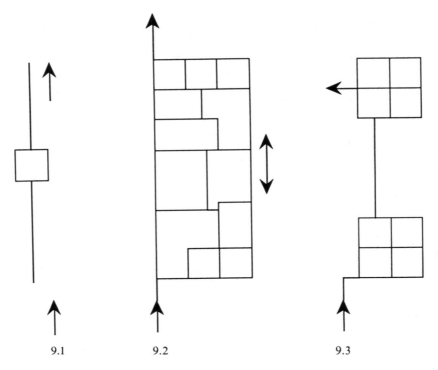

9.1   9.2   9.3

Figure 9.1   *Simplified plan of directive and non-directive circulation in the Kings in Conflict exhibition*

Figure 9.2   *Simplified plan of directive and non-directive circulation in Northern Ireland Folk Park, Cultra*

Figure 9.3   *Simplified plan of directive and non-directive circulation in the Ulster-American Folk Park, Omagh*

However, the narrative/corridor form the exhibition took structured the material in such a way that it was difficult to construct one's own interpretation. It was awkward to reverse direction and return 'upstream' to check on earlier exhibits; the visitor was borne along and directed. It was not possible to make one's own way through the maze of evidence because there was only one way — forward.

The purpose of this example is not to criticise 'Kings in Conflict', but to make a general comment on the kinds of historical understandings which are communicable in this essentially narrative form. The form works against other kinds of readings unless the visitor is very well aware of both the content and the bias given to it by the ordering. This example also brings out the question of topology; the relations of spaces to one another and the circulation patterns possible between them are factors which, apparently neutral, actually guide our understanding.

Of course, many exhibitions make no attempt at freedom of interpretation, and are frankly propagandistic. Others are directive in less stated ways. Notorious cases of this have been the arrangement of the rooms in the Museum of Modern Art, New York, which embodied a particular view of the course of modern painting. The recent re-arrangement of the Tate Gallery, London, was made to assert a different orthodoxy. One of the accidental advantages of the Irish Museum of Modern Art at Kilmainham is that the highly compartmentalised architecture makes it difficult to 'tell a story' in the continuously flowing way that one can employ in buildings specially designed for display.

The objection in the cases I have cited is not primarily to their particular orderings, since there is no way a collection can be displayed without some order, but to the premises of the ordering being made insufficiently plain. If they were made plain, we would be free to make our own critical interventions.

This is especially problematic in the Ulster-American Folk Park because the hidden premise is sectarian. This is not neutrally Ulster-American in a geographic sense, but Ulster-Presbyterian-American as a statement of a distinct cultural tradition. As it stands at present, it is possible to pass through the experience of the park without ever being made aware of this. The history with which it deals is pre-eminently that of the voluntaristic movements inspired in large part by political and religious idealism. There is small sense of the wretchedness that made the mass emigrations of the nineteenth century a matter of human survival and which were, of course, extensively Catholic and driven by economic necessity. This is a partial and, to say the least, uncritical view of Ulster. There is no objection to a partial view provided it is presented as such, openly. But what happens in this instance is that the partiality is inscribed in the very form of the experience, in its topology. Thus it cannot be disentangled from the content.

The park is sited in a broad and beautiful valley some miles north of Omagh. Here, several acres of rough ground have been laid out with a walk which emerges from a visitors' centre (which includes a static exhibition and the customary tableaux) and leads in a numbered sequence round a series of Ulster cottages and other reassembled buildings before taking us, by way of a port and quayside, through the hold of a ship (complete with sound effects and smells) into a Pennsylvania complete with maple trees and carpentered wooden houses. On the way we meet 'inhabitants' engaged in household tasks, offering oatcakes and scones made according to old recipes, and telling harrowing stories of their voyage. The exhibits are all interesting and some are moving.

A meeting house presents us with an image of ecclesiastical and local democracy in action; austere, orderly and egalitarian beyond anything existing today. There is an attention to detail throughout the outdoor exhibits which is admirable and also unpretentious. There is sometimes a sharp sense of having surprised another form of society in an unguarded moment, which goes some way to persuade us that this is indeed an 'authentic' experience. There is no doubt that this museum is greatly enjoyed by visitors. It contains, however, an element of compulsion; to see it in full we must follow the correct procedure.

In this it is different from its sister organisation, the Northern Ireland Folk Park at Cultra, Co. Down. A comparison of their respective plans reveals this quite clearly. In the first case (Fig. 9.2), though there is a natural flow to the progress of the paths, and signs encourage one route rather than another, it is quite possible to wander in other directions and to take the buildings and other exhibits in the order found. There is no one necessary order. At Omagh (Fig. 9.3), however, the visitors must pass through the strait gate of the emigrant ship. They move from an 'Ulster' — stone built, whitewashed and densely wooded — into an 'America' that is cleared and planted with rectilinear and carpentered houses. To do so, they have to progress through a town street and a quayside filled with strange sights and sounds into a constricted ship's hold containing tableaux of suffering and there hear tales of misery.

The subsequent emergence into the light of the 'Pennsylvanian' countryside from the enclosed almost subterranean world of the ship is a considerable *coup-de-theâtre* whose place in the narrative structure is that which in an initiation ceremony would be represented by the removal of the blindfold. We have been reborn into another level of existence. The narrative form is that of a ritual. The role played by the eating of 'authentic' oat cakes in the new habitation is exactly that of the ritual meal; it confirms membership of the new society.

This progress can be shown most easily through a 'story-board' (see Figs. 9.4a-l). It is precisely the ritual element in the park that prevents it from delivering a genuinely historical experience. Ritual exists to affirm or reveal given truths, but history investigates and attempts to construct explanations. Amongst those revealed is a system of binaries through which 'Ulster' and 'America' are defined; thus 'Ulster': 'America'; stone: wood; thatch: shingle; shaggy: smooth; grazed: planted; dense: cleared; 'natural': 'rational' etc. The two parts of the park are presented as the difference to each other's norm.

Such a system clearly bears little relation to the reality of settlement in the New World and reflects at the first level a retrospective concept of the difference between the two lands (with an Enlightenment gloss upon it), and at the second level, distantly but perhaps no less certainly, a reflection of the early Presbyterian concept of Ireland as a 'new-found land', to be cleared and planted and made rational. In the creation of the park, 'Ulster' has been imagined as the 'Ireland' that still exists in the mind of many Northerners and most British. In this aspect, the narrative structure

Figure 9.4a   We go to a thatched forge . . .

Figure 9.4b   . . . a cottage in the woods . . .

Figure 9.4c   . . . the meeting house . . .

Figure 9.4d   . . . down a shady lane . . .

Figure 9.4e . . . into the street . . .

Figure 9.4f . . . and pass by an arch . . .

Figure 9.4g . . . into the hold of a ship . . .

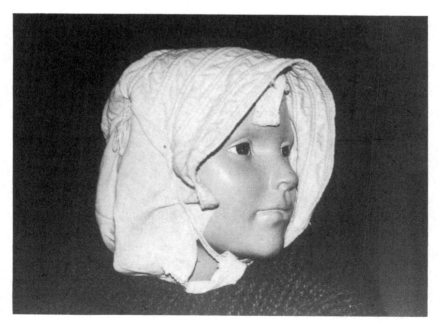

Figure 9.4h . . . meeting strange faces . . .

Figure 9.4i   . . . thence by a narrow place . . .

Figure 9.4j   . . . into cleared land . . .

Figure 9.4k ... of neat houses ...

Figure 9.4l ... and rectilinear gardens ...

Figure 9.5   In 'Pennsylvania'

of the park enacts the deep logical structure of the whole project of the
Enlightenment and modernisation, but it does so through a ritual form
whose premises are symbolic and unconscious and therefore ahistorical.

In the course of this process, rational interpretation has to be abandoned and 'immediate confrontation' preferred. This is most vividly illustrated by the way in which the reassembled buildings of 'Pennsylvania'
are experienced. As the visitor emerges he or she is confronted with some
beautiful, simple wooden houses. These are utterly unlike those in 'Ulster'.
Adzed and neatly trimmed slabs of timber (certainly not 'logs') are jointed
into one another and faced with neat shingles or grooved planks. The
aesthetic is tense, geometric and highly organised. Nothing we have seen
in 'Ulster' has prepared us for this, except perhaps the meeting-house roof.

These houses present us with a genuine historical problem. There is
very little precedent for this method of timber construction in British or
Irish vernacular architecture, which typically used timber for a frame which
was then filled with brick or lath and plaster walling, or faced with boards.
The houses, in 'Ulster-America', however, are massive carpentry of a highly
individual kind. There are certain affinities with Alpine and Scandinavian
housing in the manner of construction, but not of style. Are we looking
at housing types devised by shipwrights? Were the first builders Anglo-
Dutch ships' carpenters? Looked at from a strictly technological view, these

houses presuppose a timber industry of some scale, with saw-pits, possibly partly mechanised, and readily available good quality tools. If these are 'Ulster-American' houses, are they the unexplained outcome of the Irish timber trade? We recall that the Ulster plantations were as much the outcome of an insatiable demand for timber as for any other demand, since Ulster represented the last large scale resource of oakwoods in the islands. Or, more likely, are we looking at a translation of the frame and clapboard houses of east Anglia into a distinctly American idiom under the stimulus of limitless raw material and a technological spirit? To penetrate this problem is to get into the heart of a long and difficult set of questions about the relations between culture, technology and the natural environment.

We do not expect the park to resolve these points but, because the sudden confrontation with this architecture occurs at the climax of the narrative, we ought, if we are doing history, to show that this is, at least, an issue. Otherwise the new architecture is a mysterious 'given'. To make the whole problem more complex still, it is probably the case that the settlers were inscribing their utopian ambitions into their domestic building, and that the geometrical simplicity of their barns and houses connoted the four-square Heavenly City and the Temple itself whose earthly archetype was Solomon's Temple.

> And he built the walls of the house within with boards of cedar, both the floor of the house and the walls of the ceiling; and covered them on the inside with wood, and covered the floor of the house with planks of fir.
>
> 1 Kings 6:15

This element gives the whole dramatic structure an additional layer of meaning; the commitment, the voyage, and the successful arrival become not only figures for initiation and rebirth, but also for the pilgrim's progress 'from this world to that which is to come . . . wherein is discovered the manner of his setting out, his dangerous journey; and safe arrival at the desired country.' Bunyan's account of his pilgrim's journey was frequently printed with an imaginary road map which lead the reader out through the Wicket Gate to Vanity Fair and Doubting Castle to the Celestial City. Such maps resemble the maps of theme-parks.

This resemblance is not at all fortuitous, since both are related to the philosophical gardens and parks of the eighteenth century which presented concepts of public life and privacy, culture and nature, through carefully managed vistas and monuments. These domains had, frequently, a set of prescribed walks or carriage drives which enabled the relations between the parts of the whole to be seen allegorically; and included idealised cottages, hermits' cells, temples and ruins.

The philosophical garden, the pilgrim maps, the 'progress' and the park all have a common ancestor in the allegorical landscapes of the mind and of religious imagery, and the narrative structures of their respective journeys are based upon a profound archetype. Far from being unmediated, the park embodies, and manipulates, a network of associations.

The degree to which this manipulation is intentional is not easy to ascertain. Documents relating to the inception and development of the park are not available, and it is my guess that they would reveal very little. I hypothesise that the narrative structure grew out of a single 'good idea' that was then developed, on the one side, for the purposes of pleasure, and on the other for historical scholarship, without the two ever being brought together for critical analysis. Nor is it easy to see just what kind of critical analysis could or might have been employed at the time, there being no theory of heritage. What has happened — as quite often occurs in the world of popular entertainment and popular history — is that in the unconsidered ruck of bringing off a considerable feat, the unconscious imagery of the whole undertaking has remained unconscious.

No such question appears to exist in the folk park at Cultra, whose fundamental narrative admits of different 'readings', however similar its actual contents may be.

We might now ask the question: what would a theory of heritage be like and how might it develop a method of critical analysis? As a start, I would like to propose three headings under which any heritage park might be analysed: a) narrative structure/topology; b) simulation, and c) visualisation.

a) Narrative structure/topology

There is now an extensive theory of narrative, especially as applied to literature and film. The degree to which this may be useful when applied to heritage can only be discovered when we test it. My own contribution, above, is not offered as a model, being too cursory an essay. We should, however, be wary of attempts to impose terms formed for text and image analysis onto spatial experiences. The sort of narrative structure most appropriate might be similar to that employed by architects when they discuss problems of circulation. How spaces and places succeed one another, how they are entered and left, and the patterns formed by their relating qualities are all capable of yielding meaning. I believe I have shown that the comparative topology of parks can yield some insight into their intentions.

What this might mean at the everyday level could be brought out by asking such innocent questions as 'Why am I being led in this direction?' or 'Which is the more important of these features?' or (often an important query!) 'Why is this entrance made so narrow?'

b) Simulation

What all heritage manifestations have in common is that they employ the device of accurate replication. This may be in the form of a shop-front and street and even a whole town, or it may be in the form of dummy figures (sometimes animated), or of real persons dressing up in period clothes and simulating the life of that period, even down to details of speech and food. It also includes simulation assisted by taste and smell and sound-track. The use of taste and smell (as observed by Sorensen) seems to be important because of the highly evocative and 'primitive' character of these senses. In the hierarchy of the senses which is inscribed in Euro-American culture, taste and smell stand for the 'nature' that is to be controlled and ordered by sight; an intrusion of smell, especially, is an intrusion of the uncontrollable. It appears in heritage situations as an attempt to establish the 'natural' (i.e. successfully simulated) character of the display. Taste, too, fixes the place in memory so that it comes to be re-experienced as the memory of a real, rather than simulated, experience. The gritty texture and harsh taste of seventeenth-century oatcakes is the most vivid memory I have of 'Pennsylvania'.

The study of replication and the simulacrum takes us into many areas. The one that is most immediately relevant is that of the waxworks museum, the horror-show, and to the very specialised crafts that make such spectacles possible. A significant addition to these skills are the electronic crafts that make so many new developments possible.[4]

Here we are concerned with the concept of the authentic and the relation between real and fake. We are in a difficult area 'where scientific values may soon become indistinguishable from aesthetic ones, and where there is every likelihood that the aesthetic may dominate any scientific intention.'[5] But as Pat Cook points out, 'Too strong an insistence on a particular understanding of "reality" and "authenticity" may only serve to conceal other inauthenticities, or suppress other possible realities.'[6] In other words, our critique of the simulacrum must be balanced by a corresponding critique of the concept of the real that is being simulated.

c) Visualisation

The topic of simulation is closely allied to the topic of the mode of visualisation. The demand is that we see 'Pennsylvania', the 'Treaty negotiations', a Stone-Age village or the like 'through our own eyes', immediately. The 'living history' is activated by visual witnessing. Thus an intense attention must be paid to getting the details right. This is both the source of the hard detailed work the best of these exhibitions contains, and the source of intellectual corruption. In this respect, heritage bears a similar relation to history as photography was once held to bear towards painting — a sort of popular replacement whose validity is founded on a positivistic concern for 'accuracy', 'fact' and therefore 'Truth'.

The three topics converge in heritage as they first converged in the mass entertainment of the early nineteenth century. This is the point where the connection between visualisation and the commodification of experience was made most decisively. In particular we can point to the panoramas and dioramas that accompanied the Great Exhibition of 1851. *The Times* of 21 August of that year advertised a number of these spectacles which included vistas of the European capitals, the Niagara Falls, and all the sights that might be seen on an overland visit to India by way of the Pyramids, culminating in the Taj Mahal. Other favourite subjects were the battles of Waterloo and Trafalgar. These displays (which were, of course, early ancestors of the cinema as well) were either static or created by unrolling huge scrolled or revolving paintings; in other cases they were miniaturised into small scale tableaux viewed through peep-holes or lenses.

The diorama theatres were an early form of vicarious tourism which existed by courtesy of mass cheap travel and holiday rail-fares. When vicarious tourism becomes actual movement — either through the Grand Tour or through the package tour — then local differences become simulated and commodified as 'local customs', travel becomes a form of narrative delivered through Baedecker's guide books, and new visual experience becomes 'sight-seeing'. A special rhetoric is created to bind all these together as one experience — that of the tourist promotion. The effect upon real local differences, upon the consciousness of the visited, has already been suggested; if the values of tourism are internalised we experience a division of consciousness, which raises in acute form the question of what our customs and characters really are (see article by O'Connor in this volume).[7]

The heritage experience is an extension of the same process into time rather than space, by offering us a 'sight-seeing' into our own or others' presumed pasts.

Nor are the voyeuristic connotations of sight-seeing irrelevant. The combination of the simulated tableau, the narrative and visuality all come together in obscene entertainment. Within a few years of the invention of the daguerrotype it was being used for pornographic purposes; simulation (even historical simulation) is an ancient part of the brothel's repertoire.

My suggestions here are not whimsical, but bear on essential features of contemporary visual experience. Feminism has accustomed us to consider the objectification processes associated with the gaze and the scopophiliac character of gender/power relations. It may be that this is a secondary consequence of the overall power of visual objectification which sight-seeing in all its ramifications (topographical, historical or erotic) induces. I mean by this, that the power of objectification, which is prior to commodification, is immensely enhanced by all those panorama-like visual media which now constitute the central ground of all visual culture. This extends its empire over sexuality through the photograph, over human geography through tourism, and over the market through pictorial advertising. The heritage industry represents a further extension of the power of the manipulated spectacle over history.

Considered like this, heritage is an assault upon our power of self-definition, a part of the more general commodification of experience. As such, the industry should be resisted, satirised and exposed without mercy. On the other hand, as a form of popular history, heritage needs to be treated with some critical and constructive seriousness. Ways should be found to make it responsive to the free and informed intelligence. It may be possible to create a coherent and useful body of critical theory which would make the problematics of the spectacle fully visible.

And this returns us to the beginnings of my argument. Heritage has become part of government policy, a feature in the economy and an element in education. It has become a formative concept. If we are not critical it will become a normative practice creating a de-problematised pseudo-history. This constitutes a loss of self — a 'for-others' consciousness which reduces the subjects to participants in their own spectacle. Such a transaction takes place in what Edward Said describes as 'a discourse that . . . is produced and exists in an uneven exchange with various kinds of power . . .'[8]

This is why, universally, but especially in Ireland, the concept of heritage must be considered by critical theory. Pseudo-histories we can happily do without. To be a willing participant in an uneven exchange is to rob your own pocket. Popular history is a necessity, but it has to be a history that is open to inspection, openly mediated. The forms this history may take include exhibitions and parks, but ways must be found to involve each one of us in the activities of self-definition.

NOTES AND REFERENCES

1   This chapter derives from an article of the same name by myself in *Circa* No. 53, Sept./Oct. 1990, and from subsequent articles on similar themes by Pat Cook and Luke Dodd (see notes 3 and 4 below), to whose insights I am indebted.

2   Sorensen, C. (1989), 'Theme Parks and Time Machines', in Vergo, P. (ed.), *The New Museology,* Reaktion Books, London.

3   Dodd, L. (1991), 'Sleeping with the Past', *Circa*, No. 59, Sept./Oct.:29.

4   The Disney Corporation has now taken over the role of Madame Tussaud. The Disney enterprises are an especially curious case, since the 'Disneylands' are simulacra of fictions.

5   Cook, P. (1991), 'The Real Thing; Archaeology and Popular Culture', *Circa*, No. 56, March/April:26.

6   ibid., p. 28.

7   For a discussion of this process in an African context, see 'The Invention of Tradition in Colonial Africa' by Terence Ranger in Hobsbawn, E. and Ranger, T. (1983) (eds.), *The Invention of Tradition,* Cambridge University Press, Cambridge.

8   Said, Edward (1978), *Orientalism,* Routledge Kegan Paul, London, p. 12.

10

City of Culture: Dublin and the Discovery of Urban Heritage

Colm Lincoln

The designation of Dublin as 'European City of Culture' in 1991 presented the city with an exciting challenge, offering the chance to the city authorities, as well as those who market its tourist image, to project a favourable image of the city. Instead, the occasion was to highlight a number of less comforting realities. Dublin is a city which has suffered from negative stereotyping. If the city has grown into a sprawling metropolis, it has as an entity failed to find adequate political expression. And yet — as the very act of seeking the City of Culture title suggests — there may at last be a faltering recognition of the importance of urban Ireland; a recognition which is echoed in the tourist domain by the discovery of Dublin as a heritage product. Welcome as this discovery may be — after the many years in which urban heritage has hardly featured on the agenda — it is only a beginning. Heritage is just an aspect (though an extremely potent one) of what should be a wider agenda — the maintenance of identity and continuity in the urban community.

At the outset, it must have seemed that Dublin's designation as European City of Culture ostensibly offered a chance of papering over those uncertainties which are all so symptomatic of its uncertain status in Irish life. However, well before the year got underway, it became evident that the occasion could turn out to be a mixed blessing: in the words of Ian Lumley, spokesman for the Dublin City branch of An Taisce. 'Are we really fit to stand up to such scrutiny?'[1] It began to look as if we were not. In a major feature the *Observer* noted that while Dublin could stand alongside Venice, Amsterdam and Bath as a supreme example 'of the city as a corporate work of art' it was unlikely to be true a decade from now 'if the national and local government's disregard for the historic fabric of the city continues'.[2] Others echoed this bleak prognosis. The London *Independent* published a report illustrated with a sequence of damning photographs captioned 'Going . . . Going . . . Gone!'. In the accompanying article (under the heading 'Call this a city of culture?') the architectural historian, Dan Cruickshank, bluntly asserted that 'no European city has done more in recent years to destroy its architectural heritage'.[3]

While the corporation's spokesman blamed 'the negative radio, television and published criticism abroad'[4] or the pernicious influence of Frank McDonald, environment correspondent of *The Irish Times,* others seem to have been less convinced. In a plaintive letter from Helsinki, the chief architect of the Finnish Ministry of the Environment told how it had been 'my dream to see this city' and when at last the opportunity arose on the occasion of an international conference in Dublin in September 1991, 'I tried to find all the streets and places I had only seen in the books'. The result?

> It is difficult to express my disappointment and sad feelings as I saw the horrifying state of buildings and the streetscape. I have been travelling around a lot, but I don't think I have anywhere else seen so many beautiful buildings — and right in the centre — left empty, left in the hands of vandals and weather. It looked like Dublin's historic core was left to rot. In the great cities of Europe walking along the river 'inhaling the spirit of the city' is usually the very best souvenir one can take with one when leaving . . . it certainly was not so in Dublin.[5]

In an assessment of Dublin's year as European City of Culture *The Irish Times* saw it as a 'missed opportunity'. The main problem was not just a lack of money, 'though its budget was pitifully small: it was lack of planning'. As the paper noted:

> There was never any evidence that anyone at Government level had a strong vision as to why Dublin should be City of Culture in 1991. We seem to have gone for the title simply because it was there, and seemed prestigious. Once we had it, there were scandalous delays in appointing an organising body, and further delays in financing it. Under these circumstances, the organisers can take some pride in real achievements; the Government cannot.[6]

One of those real achievements was *The Dublin Arts Report,* which was compiled at the behest of the Dublin City of Culture organisers, with the support of the agencies responsible for the development of the arts in the Dublin area: Dublin Corporation, Dublin County Council and the Arts Council. The report, which was compiled by a working group of all the agencies concerned (though based on extensive research by Martin Drury), was challenging critical of the policies pursued by the very same agencies. 'Dublin contains the greatest concentration in Ireland of the problems associated with unemployment and social deprivation', it noted. 'Hundreds of thousands of young people are growing up in a social context that is determined by unemployment and in communities with few recreational facilities, and almost none that could be classified as cultural.' The Arts Council, we are told, 'has no policy in Dublin . . . its funding of the arts in Dublin is a matter of totalling expenditure on a range of organisations and events rather than of reflecting a conscious and coherent policy.' The report radically reappraised the role of 'high art' in cultural policy and the way in which existing resources were allocated in both city and county given the demography of the population. However, the problem as outlined in the report was not just a shortage of resources but, more crucially, 'the absence of policy-led planning'. This absence, according to the report, 'is endemic in the arts and represents the single greatest impediment to progress in Irish life'.[7]

Dublin as Negative Stereotype

The absence of policy-led planning is not unique to the arts nor, indeed, to Dublin, either in its guise as the greatest urban entity on the island, or in its role as Irish capital. Indeed, the reality is that Dublin has rarely featured in recent history as a place meriting special attention. Its role as capital has seldom counted as a matter of any material consequence, still less, as a 'locus' of Irish culture in which people should have pride. Dublin has enjoyed an ambiguous relationship with the country of which it is capital and the urban culture which it represents has seldom been viewed as something of which Irish people should be proud. 'Dear dirty Dublin' (to use Lady Morgan's phrase) was a case apart in the nineteenth century for in that 'great age of cities' the Irish capital was in decline, its case not helped by the fact that the political goals of the Irish Parliamentary Party were determined by nationalist objectives and rural needs. Louis MacNeice's thesis that Dublin was the Augustan capital of a Gaelic nation has had a long currency, feeding on the resentments nurtured in the days when Dublin rule meant British rule. From Thomas Davis onwards, the emotional thrust of Irish nationalism has been anti-urban, inclined to see the real Ireland as exclusively rural and peopled by a peasantry who in essence were not only Gaelic-speaking but Catholic as well. If Joyce can be credited with inventing Dublin 'with meticulosity bordering on the insane' both he and his invention have been held in equal suspicion for as many years. Lady Gregory was probably closer to the mainstream view when she wrote, 'My imagination is full of Ireland when I no longer see it, and it is always the worse for every sight of Dublin'.[8]

The image of Dublin as a down-at-heel capital, parasitically feeding off the rest of the nation, has been recast in recent years, with the roles

being reassigned to the real people (still rural) versus 'Dublin 4'. The Dublin
4 concept was brilliantly deployed by John Healy, who used it with
devastating effect as a stick to beat the coalition government of Garret
FitzGerald. As with many of his creations, Healy 'deliberately and wil-
fully adapted language and reality to the purpose of creating a greater truth'.
To quote John Waters, the Dublin 4 metaphor 'was recognised by people
from a wide range of backgrounds as crystallizing something on the political
landscape not in tune with themselves.'[9] According to Maurice Manning,
'What Healy meant by Dublin 4 was a part of the country which was cut
off from the natural springs of the country.' Luke Gibbons sees 'Dublin
4' and 'rural Ireland' as mutually reinforcing stereotypes, one depending
on the other for affirmation. The fact that UCD (which since the 1960s
has been identified with a revisionist approach to Irish nationalism) and
RTE (which is seen as an effective conduit for UCD views) are both located
within the actual Dublin 4 postal address was of relevance, confirming the
aptness of the metaphor as signifying 'a place which is at pains to redefine
itself outside of traditional models of Irishness'.[10]

What, of course, these traditional models of Irishness have not allowed
for is the reality of bourgeois Ireland and, in its Dublin 4 guise, those
elements of bourgeois culture which are to be found in the media and the
professions and who, fortunately or otherwise, are believed to exert a strong
influence on public forms of expression. One of the most interesting
features of this caricature is that it has not been solely determined by external characterisation but that it has also developed in response to that
group's own view of itself as a frustrated ruling élite. This aspect of the
Dublin 4 phenomenon can be traced back to the early years of this century, to the period when the new Catholic professional class was preparing to come into its own, with the anticipated arrival of Home Rule. It
was to this up-and-coming élite that Conor Cruise O'Brien's grandparents
belonged: 'My grandmother intended, quite consciously I believe, to preside
over the birth of a new ruling class: those who would rule when Home
Rule was won.'[11] But then it all unravelled in 1916 and after when — to
use an image coined by Brian Farrell — 'the Christian Brothers men took
over from the Clongowes boys'.[12]

The result has given us the other side of the Dublin 4 phenomenon
— to quote Fintan O'Toole — 'an anti-establishment establishment . . .
with a deep seated sense of itself as a class of outsiders'. And, of course,
there is its antithesis 'our other establishment — the country-and-western
alliance' which 'also manages (even though it has run the country for the
last 70 years) to think of itself as made up of outsiders, persecuted by smart
Dublin 4 types and their media sidekicks'. The consequence, if this interpretation is correct, is that 'we end up with two sets of people who have
immense power but yet manage, through their complementary myths of
persecution and marginalisation, to avoid responsibility for the state of

the place'.[13] Indeed, the very Taoiseach who suffered most from the devastating use of the Dublin 4 metaphor seemed to say as much at the Dublin Crisis Conference in 1986. He frankly, if unwisely, told the gathering, 'I'm conscious of the fact that, though I'm Taoiseach of this country, I find it very hard often to see what course of action is open to me to achieve an objective in the kind of area you're concerned about through the systems and mechanisms that exist — whether it is central or local government, the level of the officials, the councillors or the community at large.' As Anthony Cronin (admittedly, hardly a camp-follower of Garret Fitz-Gerald's) told his readers, 'there you have it. Even Garret himself has no power to prevent the further destruction of the city in which he lives. Haroun Al Raschid comes among the people — well, at least among the concerned liberals — listens to their complaints, speaks sympathetic words and goes away again. But nothing happens.'[14] In fairness, it must be said that Garret FitzGerald's government did make efforts to initiate a Dublin policy, but the validity of the Dublin 4 image, as a negative stereotype, had been sustained.

Certainly Dublin has not profited from this double-edged stereotype. If, in the four decades after independence, the population of the Dublin area increased consistently as it fared well in relation to manufacturing and service type employment, since the 1970s the position has been the reverse. In the period between 1971 and 1989 the Dublin sub-region (Dublin county borough, Dublin County and Dun Laoghaire) recorded a total loss in industrial employment of 32 per cent. Even in services, where Dublin has for long been the dominant employer, the growth rate since 1971 has fallen behind other areas in the Republic. Its share of the national total of manufacturing firms also declined during the same period, from 31 per cent to 25 per cent. In the 1970s, at a time when every other region in the state was experiencing significant employment growth, the opposite occurred in Dublin. The situation worsened in the 1980s. In 1989 there were almost 25,000 fewer jobs in manufacturing industry than there had been in 1980.

The reasons for this dramatic decline are twofold. In part it reflects a worldwide trend where, contrary to previous experience, the attractions of the main urban concentrations have declined, due to a combination of high land prices, shortage of space and problems of congestion. However, it is not only the market which has acted as a brake on industrial development in the case of Dublin but also the government for, since the early 1950s, a range of government policy measures has encouraged new development to locate, if at all possible, outside the Dublin region.

These measures included the establishment of 'designated areas' in the 12 western counties with higher levels of manufacturing grant aid, the setting-up of Gaeltarra Eireann (now Udarás na Gaeltachta), Shannon

Free Airport Development Company (now Shannon Development), and county development teams in the western counties. Furthermore, the IDA was given the task of fostering 'the national objective of regional industrial development' and of achieving the 'maximum spread of development'. The 'advance factory' programme was also heavily weighted in favour of areas outside Dublin. Thus, by 1985 the IDA (together with SFADCO and Udarás na Gaeltachta) had constructed or purchased an estimated 21 million square feet of industrial property of which 80 per cent was located outside the east region.[15]

While new industry was being encouraged to locate elsewhere, the Dublin region continued to remain heavily dependent on traditional industries and it was these that were most at risk in the increasingly competitive environment arising out of European Community membership in 1973. If the most badly hit industries were in food and drink, textiles and footwear, paper and printing, all sectors of indigenous industry were adversely affected. Most of these indigenous industries on which Dublin depended closed down, therefore, at a time when government inducements were being given to the new growth industries to locate outside the Dublin region. If membership of the EC was good for rural Ireland its immediate impact was the opposite in the case of Dublin but, instead of trying to compensate for this imbalance, government policy was effectively to tilt the imbalance even further.

Dublin as Sprawling Metropolis

The city has undergone a major transformation in the years since independence. As recently as 1926 over half of the metropolitan population lived in the area encircled by the canals. Since then the total population has more than doubled to over one million, whereas the population of the area within the canals has declined from over 250,000 to 100,000. Whereas the population of the inner city was half of the total for the metropolitan area in 1926 it constituted less than one-eleventh by 1981. 'Up to around 1966, change was generally gradual and incremental' but since then Dublin's rapid suburban expansion has consumed approximately 1,000 acres of agricultural land each year. 'From a small, compact and high-density city, Dublin has been transformed into a large, sprawling and decentralising metropolis.'[16]

The small compact city of the 1920s was distinguished, if that is the word, by some of the worst slums in Europe. In 1911 almost a quarter of the population (23 per cent) lived in one-room tenements, a statistic which singled out Dublin from all the other cities in these islands, the next worst being Glasgow which, for all its infamy, had only 13 per cent of its population living in one-room tenements. It was the collapse of two houses in Church Street, killing three adults and five children, in September 1913 which gave rise to one of the most important enquiries into working class housing conditions in the city; the published record is amongst the most harrowing documents in the history of modern Dublin.[17]

In the circumstances it is not surprising that the most lengthy and sustained programme in which the corporation has played a leading role is slum clearance. It is an experience which has had its impact on the city administration, accounting, perhaps, for its pathological view of old buildings as decaying bodies which, if not demolished, may collapse and kill an unsuspecting public. When the assistant city and county manager was asked to explain at a public meeting in April 1988 why there was so much dilapidation in the inner city, his answer was that most of the area's building stock was more than seventy years old and therefore, 'well past its prime':[18] a view which would have raised eyebrows if expressed elsewhere in Europe.

Though the corporation initially favoured some rehousing within the city — in particular so that the poorer workers could be close to potential sources of employment — they were subjected to much abuse on this score by garden city advocates who contrasted the benefits of open spaces in the suburbs to the horrors of reconditioned flats in the city 'with their open halls unprotected the night long from the evil things of the street'.[19] The Tammany Hall-like reputation of many councillors did not help the case for rebuilding in the city, as was seen from the reaction to a play by Oliver St John Gogarty and Joseph O'Connor in the Abbey in 1918.[20] If the play presented 'an amazing tableau of civic corruption and piffling charity' it had only to be compared to newspaper accounts of a recent meeting in the City Hall 'which reduced the satire of *Blight* to a mere statement of plain facts'.[21] The plot centred on the rising fortunes of Stanislaus Tully who, through good fortune, is able to buy out the tenement house in which he lives. With slum property in his pocket, a seat on the corporation was essential for speculation, 'so where before he blamed the corporation, he now blames England as being the root of all evil . . . when his sister from her sick bed applauds this patriotic sentiment, he shocks her with his frankness: "Isn't it better to have the boys blaming England than blaming me?"'[22] The play was 'a tract for the times, where we may observe how beautifully patriotism, ignorance and respectability, play into the hands of those whose economic advantage is served by the prosperous slum industry'. 'The first performance of *Blight* was something of an event, and mustered an audience such as has not been seen at the Abbey theatre since the high and far off days of the Playboy riot . . . The intellectuals agreed that the play was a great success, and the box office receipts subsequently registered a confirmation of the verdict.'[23] With publicity like this neither the inner city nor its advocates seemed to have much in their favour.

When it came to the major housing programmes of the 1930s, the suburbs continued to win out despite the city manager having 'rather hastily' enunciated a two-to-one policy in favour of inner-city flats in 1934; that hasty change in policy having been prompted by the fact that the poorest families could not afford to rent houses in the new estates.[24] However, a combination of finance — a three-bedroom suburban cottage (£474) was way less costly to build than an inner-city three-room flat (£720)[25] — and a lack of confidence in the very idea of living in the city ensured that the exodus from the city to the suburbs was to be a continuing motif (and that the most impoverished were the last to be rehoused). Many of those who moved out from the inner city did so with misgivings; involuntary explorers 'cast adrift without map or compass, deprived of familiar co-ordinates, "thrust as Jim Larkin put it in 1939, into areas to which they are not acclimatised"'.[26] Dominic Behan has described it as being a case of 'To Hell or to Kimmage'.[27] Crumlin was the most unpopular of the new estates and 400 of its 2,000 tenants applied to be retransferred back into the city. The corporation's allocations officer believed that 'if we were to circularise the Crumlin tenants, and ask how many of them would like to go back into the city, we would get a thousand applications'.[28] In general it was 'the poorer people who want to get back'; indeed, 140 families were so dispirited that they actually vacated their new homes in Crumlin.[29]

In the period after the Second World War major housing schemes were developed at West Cabra, Ballyfermot and Finglas and, from the late 1950s, at Artane and Coolock. The 1960s were unusual in that this was the only decade in which flats accounted for a quarter of the total provision. Apart from the Ballymun project — seven 14-storey towers named after the leaders of the 1916 Rebellion — there were major flat schemes in the inner city at Dominick Street, Marrowbone Lane and Basin Lane. It was only in 1975 'under ministerial pressure and in response to community demands' that the corporation at last initiated a policy of house building in the inner city as well as in the suburbs.[30]

The development plans of the last two decades have drawn their inspiration from the advisory plan and final report prepared in 1967 by Myles Wright for the Dublin region; this included the city as well as the neighbouring counties of Dublin, Meath, Kildare and Wicklow. Whereas Wright recommended expansion in four new 'fingers' stretching westward from the city — at Tallaght, Clondalkin, Lucan and Blanchardstown — the County Dublin Development Plan reduced the number to three: Tallaght, Blanchardstown and Clondalkin. Lucan and Clondalkin, two villages with identifiable centres, were incongruously forced together 'because the local authorities, in a series of discreet deals, had bought up most of the land in between. Otherwise, what could and couldn't be built, where and when, was largely determined by the location of sewerage pipes.'[31]

In a cover story, called 'Dublin — the Town that Launched a Thousand

Plans', the magazine *Business & Finance* explained to its readers that the three satellite towns 'will be separate communities outside the built-up metropolitan area but the idea is that they should have a symbiotic relationship with the city'. Each, when finally completed, was expected to have a population of over 100,000 and would eventually become largely self-contained with possibly 80 per cent of the people working in the actual area. 'In this respect they differ from the English New Town concept where the town is a completely fresh unit removed from any city and thus all the social infrastructure has to be provided at the beginning. Tallaght and the rest will be built up gradually with their dependence on the city tapering off as they near their intended final form: schools and shops will be added as they become necessary.'[32] It was a thesis, or a variant of one, that had been heard before and one which suited a local administration as ever short of cash. For, in the new housing estates that had been built on the city's fringes back in the 1930s and 40s, it had also been assumed 'that for a long time to come the inhabitants would continue to look towards the city for their work, social contacts and daily needs. Hence there was no attempt to create a self-sufficient community by building shops and factories though it was necessary to provide new churches and schools'.[33]

In the circumstances it is not surprising to find that many Dubliners have an ambiguous relationship with their city; living in poorly serviced suburbs and dependent on a tenuous bus link to make the crucial connection with the centre of their metropolitan world. Its essence has been captured in a recent book of photographs by Tony O'Shea where one finds a world denuded of the symbolic places, the monumental buildings, by which we normally identify a city.[34] Instead we see people moving from one place to another; the reality of their Dublin captured in a series of photographs taken on buses. In the novels of Roddy Doyle there is an almost complete absence of description, for the characteristic of an outer suburb — such as the fictional Barrytown — is its lack of particularity; it is the people and their sense of community who constitute the place.[35]

The flight from the city to the suburbs was already a well-established trend in the case of the middle classes. Throughout the nineteenth century the centre city experienced a gradual filtration of the middle classes to the more fashionable suburban townships where, apart from any other attractions, they enjoyed the advantage of lower domestic rates (local taxes). The confessional affiliations which so affected Irish political life of the period only exacerbated the trend — from the mid-century Dublin city was under Catholic-Nationalist control whereas in the suburbs the independent townships were seen as beleaguered, if affluent, outposts of the old ascendancy. In the case of the north inner city the change was more rapid, though Mountjoy Square lingered on longer as an enclave of the upper middle classes.[36] In 1914 it could still boast of a knight and several clergymen along with the inevitable solicitors, two private hospitals and 'the Distressed Irish Ladies' Home'. However, by 1920 Sean O'Casey had arrived, installed for a few months in a tenement in No. 35 (since demolished) which became the setting for *The Shadow of a Gunman*.

With the terrible poverty that was so prevalent, especially in the north inner city, Georgian Dublin seemed doomed to decay and disappearance. A pioneering light in the founding of the first Georgian Society in 1909 was Sir Pentland Mahaffy who lived in No. 38 North Great George's Street. The society was founded to record what still existed of the Georgian city before it finally vanished and its legacy was the five volume *Georgian Society Records*. The society was not, however, dedicated to preservation and when a new Irish Georgian Society was founded for that purpose in the late 1950s it had much prejudice to overcome, in part due to the memory of Mahaffy's 'deliberately reactionary celebration of the Georgian style'.[37] In his famous 'belted earls' speech to the Dáil on the contested redevelopment of Hume Street, Kevin Boland doubtless reflected the feelings of many others when he effectively described the Georgian city as the expendable left-over of an arrogant and alien ruling class.[38] The Georgian society had limited collateral to call on and, instead, it was the rainbow coalition made up of groups such as An Taisce, the Dublin Housing Action Committee (who were incensed by the fact that structurally sound houses were being demolished while many people still lived in overcrowded accommodation) and the Dublin Living City Group (who were committed to the continuity of urban communities in the inner city) who carried more weight in the campaign against the loss of inner-city houses to the office sector.[39]

Apart from the continuing flight to the suburbs and the conversion of much of the south inner city into offices, the third most evident factor to have impacted on the physical fabric of the city has been the corporation's road plans. In a highly contested decision of 1980 the city council adopted the idea of creating an inner tangent. This was seen as a means of diverting traffic around the central business district, thereby allowing for the creation of traffic-free 'environmental cells' within that area (traffic-free, in that cross-city traffic would be greatly reduced within the cells). The plan involved the creation of two part-loops swinging to the west of the century city: an 'inner loop' running from Parnell Street to St Stephen's Green and an 'outer loop' running along a parallel axis further to the west. The plan was highly controversial for, irrespective of its theoretical premise, the tangent in reality — according to its critics — would allow more cars into the city, thereby adding to congestion.

The tangent and related road improvements — such as those on the western quays — were to result in the widening of no fewer than eighty-two streets and the demolition of hundreds of buildings. The cost to the city fabric has been enormous and the traffic benefits are not at all certain. However, according to a study carried out in the late 1980s by

independent consultants on behalf of the government and the European
Commission the road widening on the inner loop, 'is probably beyond a
point where anything useful could be gained in an environmental sense
by not completing the remaining sections'. While the consultants accepted
that it would serve an essential function in enabling 'environmental cells'
to be created in the central business district, they recommended that any
further work should be preceded by an environmental impact study and
that environmental improvements and redevelopment would be a priority
on existing sections of the route. The outer loop and spur roads to it were
considered by the consultants to be quite 'a different matter . . . . The
strategic argument for these routes, given a motorway ring to the west and
particularly a port access route are on the evidence available not compelling', especially given the 'considerable amount of property demolition
and environmental problems' involved.[40] The visual consequences are certainly all too evident in the city today.

   The consultants — a consortium consisting of economists Davy
Kelleher and McCarthy, town planners Reid McHugh and Partners and
accountants Stokes Kennedy Crowley — were bleak in their assessment
of the city. 'Side by side with prosperity and affluence are to be found
poverty, decay and dereliction in twilight areas adjoining the central
business district. The rapid growth of the city in peripheral areas has been
paralleled by decline at its core. Failure to resolve conflicting pressures and
demands, together with a lack of investment in physical and social infrastructure in the inner city, has contributed to the nature and extent of
the problem which now exists.'[41]

A Rudderless City

Who might have expected to resolve the conflicting pressures faced by
greater Dublin? Apart from the government, which controls the purse
strings (local councils have limited fund-raising authority) there is Dublin
Corporation and Dublin City Council for, despite the limited scope of their
powers, it is councillors who have the authority to adopt development plans
and, more notoriously, to overrule the planning and zoning policies which
they have already adopted. The reality, however, in a political culture in
which there has been no restriction on the 'cumul des mandats' is that
local councils have been treated as stepping stones on the way to real power
elsewhere, with the major political parties paying little real attention to
physical planning or the needs of local government. The removal of
domestic rates — as part of Fianna Fáil's electoral programme in the 1978
general election — was a body blow to the local taxation system and to
any real independence which local authorities may have enjoyed. With their
powers of raising direct funds restricted solely to rates on commercial property and charges for services the scope for any independent initiative on

the part of local authorities was emasculated and replaced by a degree of centralisation which runs counter to the regional thrust of EC policy.

'None can observe the practice of government in the Dublin area in the past sixty years without a sense of despair as to its quality, its ability to discharge its responsibilities . . . . In the last analysis is *anyone* in charge?' The words were spoken by a former director of the Institute of Public Administration, Tom Barrington, in an address to the Dublin Crisis Conference in 1986.[42] The failure to which he so plaintively referred has been exacerbated by the fact that the metropolitan area falls under the control of three separate local authorities: Dublin Corporation, Dublin County Council and the Borough of Dun Laoghaire. Various proposals have come and gone on a possible reorganisation of this local authority structure but they have had little impact; as a result the corporation has little political power to influence orderly development beyond its boundaries and, at times, seems to have equally little influence on its own officials. 'Under these circumstances, co-ordinated planning is', to say the least 'made difficult and there is no Dublin city voice which can speak for the entire built-up area.'[43]

Perhaps the only voice that can speak with any real authority for greater Dublin is that of the city manager. Since the introduction of the city manager system in 1930, the city has been under the tutelage of the manager who, since 1940, has also held administrative responsibility for Dublin County (Dun Laoghaire remains autonomous). The view of Frank Feely (manager at the time of Tom Barrington's plea) is not encouraging. In an interview in March 1987 he quoted approvingly from Jane Jacobs:

> When we deal with cities we are dealing with life at its most complex and intense. Because this is so, there is a basic aesthetic limitation on what can be done with cities. A city cannot be a work of art . . . The intricate order of cities — a manifestation of the freedom of countless numbers of people to make and carry out countless plans — is in many ways a great wonder. Emphasis on bits and pieces is of the essence. This is what a city is — bits and pieces that supplement each other and support each other.[44]

Frank Feely went on to quote Brendan Behan's maxim that 'a city is a place where you are least likely to be attacked by a wild sheep'. No doubt it raised a smile but some light relief was needed given the fatalism inherent in the 'bits and pieces' vision of what a city might be all about.

Ireland as Urban Reality

If Dublin the place — and Dublin the image — have taken a battering on numerous fronts there are signs, nonetheless, that a change may be taking place. On one level it is simply a question of demographics. With a young and mobile population — half of whom are under 25 — and over

a million people in the Dublin region alone, it is at last becoming evident
that urban Ireland is not merely a reality but, demographically, *the* reality
which constitutes contemporary Ireland. Not surprisingly, it is an urban
sensibility which imbues the literature of contemporary writers such as
Dermot Bolger and Roddy Doyle and, to different degrees, Aidan Mathews,
Joseph O'Connor and Michael O'Loughlin.

At government level one of the first signs of change was seen with
the announcement in March 1986 of a scheme of special tax incentives
for urban renewal in Dublin, Cork, Limerick, Waterford and Galway. The
Fine Gael/Labour Coalition was going to ensure that new life would be
brought back to these run-down areas, particularly 'at the core of the
nation's capital'. They were to become 'attractive areas in which to live
and work', to go shopping and spend leisure time. Whatever about the
specifics of the proposals, the very fact that urban renewal was on the
political agenda — and that a junior minister had the designation 'Minister
of State with responsibility for urban renewal' — suggested that there was
a change in the climate of political opinion.[45]

In the case of Dublin there were three designated areas, along the Gard-
iner Street axis (91 acres), on the quays (68 acres) and Henrietta Street (2.5
acres); in each, the limited period for which the package of tax incentives
was to apply was three years. Then, in a special category of its own, there
was the 27-acre Custom House Docks site, where a much more attractive
package of incentives was on offer — with 100 per cent capital allowances
as against 50 per cent in the other three areas — and where a special
development authority was given the task of preparing an overall planning scheme for the site. Developers were invited to make submissions for
the overall development of the site including an international financial services centre which had to be completed in a five-year period.[46]

The corporation was to become the 'development broker' for the other
three designated areas, bringing together landowners, developers and potential investors. However, the Minister for the Environment, John Boland,
was 'taken aback' by the low-key approach adopted by the corporation
and remarked, with evident regret, that there was 'much merit' in the suggestion that the venture should have been 'handled by a special development authority'.[47] So unimpressed was John Boland by the corporation's
lack of dynamism that he created a special authority, the Dublin Metropolitan Streets Commission, to promote actively another initiative to turn
the city's axis — the area running from O'Connell Street to Grafton Street
— 'into a showpiece of architectural sensitivity and environmental
awareness'. Seven commissioners were given £10 million and three years
in which 'to brighten the face of Dublin's heartland, making it once more
an area of style and character'.[48] However, after Fianna Fáil were returned
to power following the 1987 general election, the commission was quickly
terminated, its case not helped by the suspicion that amongst its

priorities was the possible rebuilding of Nelson's Pillar.[49]

While another coalition creation, the Dublin Transport Authority, was also aborted before it could give life to any real initiatives, Fianna Fáil took enthusiastically to the designated area idea; the existing areas were extended, as was the period for which the tax benefits applied. Fianna Fáil also came up with its own proposals: during the 1987 general election campaign Charles Haughey declared that the Temple Bar area — where CIE had been acquiring property as a site for a bus station — 'had to be preserved' as one of the most historic and attractive parts of the city.

Ironically, it was CIE's responsible attitude in letting out their property on short-term leases (as opposed to demolishing the buildings) which gave rise to the various restaurants, recording studios and galleries with which Temple Bar had become synonymous. If the Dublin City Association of An Taisce had proposed that it be conserved back in 1985,[50] it was Mr Haughey's declaration that he 'wouldn't let CIE near the place' which carried weight. The die was cast; the Dublin Corporation planners produced an 'action plan' and finally a special development company was established to take over CIE's holdings and to spearhead development in an area running all the way from Westmoreland Street to the Civic Offices. In his preface to a catalogue of the various competition entries in the architectural framework competition for the area, Mr Haughey referred to Temple Bar as a cultural quarter: 'The preservation and sensitive renewal of Temple Bar and its development as Dublin's Cultural Quarter will make it a prominent feature of our capital city in the years ahead, and give it a special place on the itinerary of visitors'.[51]

What is significant about many of these recent changes in official attitudes to the city is the degree to which they have been inspired by external prompts; dependent, in many cases, on a perception of what others are considered to believe to be of importance, both in relation to Ireland as a tourism product and Ireland as a supplicant in search of EC funds. The city and county manager, Frank Feely, while supporting the idea of an integrated development plan for Dublin being made to the EC Commission recognised that, in the final analysis, it was going to be subservient to other considerations. 'As we get our money out of the EEC in certain ways — from the Regional Fund, the Common Agricultural Policy, etc. the danger is, if you have an integrated programme for certain specified areas, in dealing with far more authorities and all that, in the heel of the hunt, you might not get as much money for the country.'[52] This, of course, has been the position traditionally held by central government; namely that EC funds are in themselves a good thing and should be maximised as a first priority; the precise use for which they are required being, in effect, of secondary importance.

The funds to which Frank Feely referred may have a significant impact on the city. Yet, despite a plethora of independent initiatives by various groups on how to tackle the city's manifest problems, there was little real consultation with either community groups or locally elected representatives on how the structural funds might best be used.[53]

According to Frank McDonald, when 'the Department of Finance belatedly realised that the EC Commission would be insisting on at least a veneer of consultation . . . it established an entirely new set of seven "sub regions" . . . consisting of officials drawn from government departments and the relevant local authorities to cobble together "plans" for each region' under the chairmanship of the Department of Finance (the nine existing regional development organisations being abolished). Despite the ostensible existence of 'advisory groups' — consisting largely of representatives of the employers, trade unions and farmers, along with a few local politicians — 'neither the Department of Finance nor the Government were interested in fresh imaginative solutions to Dublin's problems'. It was only after direct pressure was brought to bear on the EC Commission by former Lord Mayor Carmencita Hederman, among others, that the government-appointed consultants, who were to undertake a major study of Dublin in order to maximise the amount of potential aid, were allowed 'at the insistence of Brussels . . . to look beyond what was already on the table'.[54] However, while the report may have looked further afield, the menu was selected by government and so the bulk of the proposed funds (some £300 million), was earmarked for road construction with just £27 million for public transport, a balance which is curiously at odds with the thrust of the Commission's *Green Paper* on the urban environment.[55]

In the case of the designated areas the scheme which has received most attention from government — and the most favoured tax status — has been the Custom House Docks site, the Fianna Fáil government of the late 1980s seeing it as Dublin's answer to London's docklands. Despite the role envisaged for the other designated areas as catalysts of urban renewal no special authority was established to push for redevelopment as in the case of the two most favoured projects, the Custom House Docks site and Temple Bar. Indeed, public sector investment on upgrading the designated areas has been described as 'parsimonious'. In a paper presented by John Blackwell and Frank Convery, at a seminar on urban renewal in October 1991, it was said that the 'array of complementary policy instruments needed to maximise the potential of the [tax] incentives . . . appear to be too weak and too sporadically marshalled to be fully effective'.[56] According to figures presented by Ged Pierse at the same seminar some 700,000 square feet of new buildings have been developed in Dublin since the introduction of the urban renewal incentives in 1986; however, only 10 per cent has been in houses or apartments. Despite the fact that there was an oversupply of office space — with much of it unlet — there were still another 500,000 square feet of commercial developments in progress and Dublin Corportion had 'in addition received planning applications for a further 2.2m.

square feet of developments, again with the residential element well below 10 per cent'. While 'the failure of designated status to promote large-scale housing development in the inner city' was, according to Mr Pierse, 'a great disappointment' his own research showed how heavily the dice were loaded against housing developments for 'the combination of tax relief and remission of rates is more than five times greater for a commercial development that for an owner/occupier residential development'.[57] If, as Patrick Dempsey has claimed, 'the prevailing . . . intellectual climate' is that gentrification is seen 'as the long awaited solution to Dublin's most intractable problems',[58] it is a solution where the waiting looks set to continue. The problem may not be merely — as Dempsey suggests — that there are inherent flaws in gentrification (or in any other simplifed form of social engineering) but the failure to recognise that any solutions to Dublin's problems must encompass a strategy for the whole as well as the parts — suburbs and inner city.

Dublin as a Heritage Product

Tourism is a key factor in influencing a change in attitudes to the urban environment at least at official level. According to Michael Hough 'every town that has seen better days and can boast of a past has an eye to capitalising on its own historic specialty for tourist entertainment and dollars' though the result can be that genuine 'regional differences are stylised into the cute and kitschy tourist attraction'.[59] In the Irish case, there are — according to the chairman of Bord Fáilte — three particular strengths on which the tourism industry should build: a high quality environment for leisure activities, the vast reservoir of people of Irish descent and 'our cultural heritage'. 'There is potential to attract new visitors through Irish literature, theatre, architecture, archaeology, music, and so on. But it is not just a matter of telling potential visitors about our heritage — the need is to package and present the heritage in a form that makes it attractive to buy.'[60]

The impetus for this interest in heritage tourism came as part of an overall drive to double the numbers of tourists from overseas within the five year period 1989–93; in so doing it was hoped to create 25,000 new jobs (see article by Deegan and Dineen in this volume). Bord Fáilte's product development plan 'Development for Growth' identified history and culture as an area of major potential and the Operational Programme for Tourism 1989–93 allocated some 40 per cent of European Regional Development fund grant aid 'to this product area'. In 1990, Bord Fáilte commissioned a report, co-funded by the EC Commission, which audited 'visitor attractions and other aspects of Irish heritage and culture'. 'The concern that prompted the proposal of an "audit" was that the availability of ERDF funded assistance' would not optimise 'the Irish tourism product' if there was not a carefully targeted and prioritised range of development initiatives.[61] The report made a number of proposals on strategy; namely that there be a framework for the selection of themes for interpretation which would help international tourists to experience the 'real Ireland'. Those tourists who come to Ireland for reasons other than business or visiting friends and relations 'are essentially motivated by an expectation of distinctive destination . . . the history and culture of the country is the entrée to experiencing this distinctive Irish atmosphere'.[62]

While Dublin should enjoy an inbuilt tourist advantage given its role as capital the city as such seems to have made little impact as a place of 'distinctive destination'. Ironically — though revealingly — an American academic, Victor Luftig, has expressed concern over 'Joyce's prestige as a Dublin writer' and the fact that Joyce was being harnessed to serve 'only to a Dublin-centred past'. We are told that if we visit the Irish Tourist Board offices on Madison Avenue the brochures 'will direct you to Dublin' the city of 'Sheridan, Joyce, Shaw, Wilde, Synge, Yeats and O'Casey — "Dubliners who have made their mark on world literature and drama"'. Even on a short holiday, where only three days of a six-day Aer Lingus 'shopping spree' are given to Ireland (Scotland taking up the other three) and where Dublin is fitted in on a single day, along with stops at Bunratty Cottage and the Blarney Woollen Mills, the reference to Dublin comes with the inevitable rider 'home of many great poets and writers'. Luftig sees all this as proof of the 'tendency to equate Irish culture with the culture of Dublin' and goes on to tell us that Joyce found inspiration in other parts of Ireland; indeed, that contemporary culture is alive and well and living beyond the Pale.[63] Unfortunately, Mr Luftig has missed the point for the fact that Dublin, literary references and all, can be squashed into a single day (along with Bunratty Cottage and the Blarney Woollen Mills) is hardly proof of the city's monopoly on the American tourist's attention but, rather, of its failure to generate any attention at all. Bunratty and points west are still the *real* Ireland with an imagery rooted in landscapes that *must* be seen whereas Dublin is everything and nothing, having failed to generate a tangible imagery which is in any real sense distinctive (see article by Nash in this volume).

To ensure that Irish tourism attractions will generate a sense of 'distinctive destination' the 1990 tourism consultancy study proposed that heritage attractions be developed along storylines which fit into five key themes — 'live landscapes', 'making a living', 'saints and religion', 'building a nation' and 'the spirit of Ireland' — the idea being that investment funds should not be wasted by duplicating the same themes. Up to thirty different storylines were indicated but more could be added and existing storylines divided into sub-groups, if necessary.[64] From the marketing point of view this could prove to be a useful tool if it prevents a duplication of investment, though this has to be weighed against the fact that there is a potentially unlimited degree to which anything can be classified, themed or storylined (see article by Brett in this volume). Presumably those tourists visiting the Book of Kells (storyline: 'saints and scholars') might also be interested in their surroundings; while the spectacular Long Room is a worthy cathedral for such a treasure, the Augustan splendours of Trinity tell us more about the scholars of the eighteenth century (and later) than the saints who produced the ninth-century manuscript of the Gospels. Perhaps Trinity could even help fill that fascinating gap — the storyline for 'Pagan Ireland' which apparently has no Dublin attraction to illustrate its message.

While 'over 40 per cent of the European Regional Development Fund for tourism development is earmarked for the history and culture product'[65] this is quite different to earmarking it for conservation, or for projects which are of importance because of their value in retaining or enhancing areas which constitute a vital part of the city's urban memory. As a report commissioned by Bord Fáilte on the development of heritage and cultural tourism has noted, 'historic importance is not in itself a justification for large-scale investment'.[66] In tourism terms heritage is just another commodity; an important one perhaps but a commodity which is valued in terms other than those relating to cultural or social significance.

This is quite a distinct and different focus from the way heritage tourism has developed in other European countries. In France — and French and Italian tourists are crucial to the increase in Irish tourist numbers — a survey by the Ministry of Culture and the Secretariat of State for Tourism discovered that more French adults prefer to spend time visiting old neighbourhoods than going to the cinema. Heritage was an issue on which there was common agreement; 77 per cent of French people considered it the duty of the public authorities to protect national monuments. Indeed, despite the considerable resources spent on architectural heritage in France, only 26 per cent of the public thought that the amount was sufficient. From Bord Fáilte's point of view what was of interest was that 67 per cent of the public associated heritage with tourism.[67]

Heritage and, in particular, the conservation of the urban heritage has enjoyed a favoured place in French cultural life for some time. The Commission des Monuments Historiques was created in 1837, and today there are some 40,000 classified monuments. In the intervening period there has been a whole evolution in the way 'monuments' are conceived of. From an initial concern with classical remains and the religious architecture of the Middle Ages, the heritage concept has expanded to include all forms of building construction, from formal to popular architecture and extending from a concern with specific buildings to include the site in which they are located and, eventually, not just neighbourhoods but entire towns and, on occasion, groups of towns.[68]

If France has had legislation on *secteurs sauvegardés* since 1962, the concept is still novel to the Irish administration as is the very idea of 'listing' which only made a tentative entry into the planning process with the passing of the Local Government (Planning and Development) Act, 1963. In some respects the legislative concern with conservation started off on the same trajectory as elsewhere, commencing with a concern over ancient monuments. The first legislation came about as a by-product of the Irish Church Act of 1869 which disestablished the Church of Ireland. Money was set aside for former ecclesiastical buildings which deserved to be maintained as national monuments because of their 'architectural character or antiquity'. While this categorisation was gradually extended, the National Monument Act of 1930 'which has provided the basis for the protection of archaeological sites, monuments and artefacts for the past fifty years' was still very much archaeological in spirit and 'buildings of more recent periods remained unprotected and their cause was not supported in any widespread or concerted way'.[69]

In the case of Dublin, eighteenth- and nineteenth-century buildings were afforded no legal protection until the adoption of the city's first development plan in 1971, though that protection often proved to be illusory in the face of pressure for commercial redevelopment and road widening. Studies by An Taisce have shown that many buildings have been demolished or irreparably damaged despite being listed. The narrow focus in which listing has taken place is illustrated by the fact that as late as 1980 the corporation had 'so far failed to take any step to list even a single interior'.[70] And yet — as Alistair Rowan has noted — 'the independent character of Dublin's street architecture leaves its greatest legacy in the variety and richness of the eighteenth-century domestic interiors', seen in the work of the joiners and blacksmiths and, of course, the legacy of plasterers 'who endowed the city with its greatest claim to European significance'. Other capitals 'have fine examples of this peculiarly eighteenth-century art', yet in Dublin 'the proliferation of elaborate plasterwork in house after house, figurative and abstract, opulently confined or exuberantly free, gives to the city a character that must make it, even for interior work alone, one of the most important urban environments in Europe'.[71]

Ironically, it may be the very Irishness of Dublin's architecture which has contributed to its downfall. 'A glance at the facades of some of the major streets and squares . . . will show one of the most persistent of Irish characteristics, the dislike of uniformity.' Even if there is a greater appearance of regularity in later Georgian planning 'regularity is never absolute. Symmetry and balance, which contribute so much to a sense of order and are almost a norm in the neo-Classical development of European cities are foreign to Dublin's urban scene.'[72] Thus when the Electricity Supply Board wanted to justify its demolition of sixteen structurally sound houses in 1961 and recruited the English architectural historian Sir John Summerson to support its case, he blithely dismissed Fitzwilliam Street as having 'no special architectural coherence; it is not a planned facade, nor an architectural entity . . . simply one damned house after another'.[73] The city architect, Daithi Hanly, not having the benefit of being foreign to Dublin's urban scene, saw the same 'damned houses' in quite a different light. In a report that was never circulated he argued that Lower Fitzwilliam Street was part of a magnificent unbroken facade built by Irish craftsmen, 'To break or interrupt this by the intrusion of a modern building, no matter how good on its own would spoil this unique street . . . this eighteenth-century townscape' which should be seen as part of 'a single civic entity directly related to our Irish civilisation'.[74]

The danger — despite the prospect of greater protection for historic buildings and areas tentatively proferred by the National Monuments Bill of 1986 — is that the city's architectural heritage will only be seen as worthy of protection in as far as it fits our perception of what incoming tourists might expect to find. Perhaps it is merely a question of using whatever visual image comes easiest to mind to sell a concept but the continuing references to Temple Bar as Dublin's Left Bank are dangerously suggestive of a tourism product which could have a short shelf life; certainly, the Parisian Left Bank's bohemian image has long passed its 'sell-by' date (destroyed, amongst other reasons, by its becoming little more than a tourist image). What may be of interest, if we have to look to France, is the popularity of its 'portes ouvertes' initiative, initiated by Jacques Lang in 1985, when national monuments not normally open to the public — most notably a whole series of government ministries (including Lang's own private office) — were opened to all-comers for a day and the event well publicised. In Dublin — a city noted for its interiors but where few of them are accessible to the public — it may be an idea worth exploring; certainly, the decision of Albert Reynolds to open the Cabinet offices on Saturdays suggests that the door is not necessarily closed to the idea of public accessibility.

If, as Bord Fáilte's research has suggested, tourists coming to Ireland 'are essentially motivated by an expectation of distinctive destination'[75] it is unlikely that this expectation will be realised if the focus is on presenting them with an image developed on the basis of what we think they might like Dublin to be. The city is not a theme-park nor, indeed, is it Bord Fáilte's suggestion that we sell our heritage 'for a bowl of soup made from imported ingredients'.[76] However, much of what is most distinctive about Dublin as a physical entity seems in danger of not surviving into the next century. If, as Alistair Rowan has suggested 'the independent character of Dublin's street architecure leaves its greatest legacy in the variety and richness of the eighteenth-century interiors',[77] few of those interiors have been adequately surveyed and listed for protection, and, unfortunately, much the same holds true for the streetscape as was seen with the demolition of houses in Eccles Street in 1988, despite the fact that it is one of the few architectural setpieces in the city with the portico and spire of St George's in centre stage as one looks southwards from the Mater Hospital.

Perhaps appropriately the various themes which coalesce to give an image of the city come together on the city quays: 'riverrun, past Eve and Adam's, from swerve of shore to bend of bay, brings us by a commodius vicus of recirculation'.[78] It is here that it all began, at the meeting of the Liffey and the bay. It is the quays which provide the most memorable aspect of the city's architecture, with the unassuming and the monumental ranked in an apparently random, if happy, disorder along the Liffeyside. Unfortunately, it is here too that we find the tangible evidence of the lack of any co-ordinated vision which is all too characteristic of the city's recent history. Here are some of the few inner city flat complexes built in the 1930s to accommodate the inhabitants of the slums, though more eloquent is the absence of any public housing until the arrival of corporation houses on City Quay in the late 1970s, the intervening years marked by a haemorrhaging of the inner city population to new suburbs on the city's fringes. The consequences can be seen in the steady closure of the inner city churches with, in the case of the quays, St Michael and John's becoming a Viking centre and St Audoen's the home to another heritage foundation.

Most evident of all are the works most directly associated with Dublin Corporation. If the civic offices are an unloved monument to officialdom — their overwhelming scale illustrating only too clearly the lurking authoritarianism inherent in the city's motto *Obedientia civium urbis felicitas* (the obedience of the citizens is the happiness of the city) — so too are those stretches of widened quays whose mutilation was methodically plotted out by the road engineers in the early 1980s.[79] If central government would see its monument as the Financial Services Centre — to quote Charles Haughey 'the golden city which is now to be the Bloomusalem in the Nova Hibernia of the future'[80] this has to be set against the unsettling nature of the developments in the designated areas upstream, the failure to tilt the tax advantages in favour of community housing policies and the continuing demolition of buildings which are crucial to the memory of Dublin's very real urban achievements.

Heritage, Memory and the Maintenance of Continuity

While — as far as conservation is concerned — the 1991 Finance Bill set the stage for a potentially interesting shift in direction, by tilting the balance of tax incentives in favour of refurbishing existing buildings (as opposed simply to favouring new construction) this crucial change was limited to the Temple Bar area; the 'cultural quarter' with which Mr Haughey had so publicly associated himself. Elsewhere in the designated areas the incentives have been for clearing and rebuilding; consequently, Dublin's year as European City of Culture was marked by the demolition of a structurally sound terrace of Georgian houses on Arran Quay (which formed an integral part of the setting for St Paul's Church) in order that it could be replaced by a development which could better capitalise on the area's designated status. Even in Temple Bar — where the architectural framework plan places great emphasis on the retention and refurbishment of its stock of historic buildings — there was disquiet over the fact that the first major refurbishment exercise failed to retain many of the buildings' original features, most notably replacing an original 1820s shipfront with a 'facsimile' which was 'stretched' to better incorporate a new layout.[81]

The unwitting loss of so much of the built environment is not something that should be lightly countenanced. We do need a tangible and enduring sense of the physical entity of which we are a part for, in the case of most of us, it is an inalienable part of our everyday life. Architecture — a room, a house, a street — is the means by which we map our world and, like language, it is dependent on memory. Quintilian (AD c. 35–95) drew up the classic rules of the mnemonic art by utilising an architectural system (the technique was to think of an imagined building whose numerous rooms were to be used to deposit an image of the idea to be remembered).[82] For the Greeks, memory — which they personified as Mnemosyne, mother of all the muses — was the patron of architecture for, of all the faculties, memory has most to do with architecture. 'What we used to say about the lessons in infant-school reading books can be said equally about the buildings and monuments, streets and squares, churches and factories which constitute our horizon of vision: we read them *into* ourselves.' As Seamus Heaney has described it, 'they take us in and we take them in, first as imprints on the retina, then as known dwellings, then as remembered forms. They begin to insist themselves into our consciousness as a kind of language which, like any language, embodies certain values and enforces certain ways of knowing reality.'[83]

The destruction of memory can take place on various levels, though the most evident is with the undermining of key elements of the built environment for it is that which still has the most profound and inescapable effect on us. Irrespective of whether buildings originated, in Seamus Heaney's words from 'the desire for beauty as the end of building' or, if 'their construction was a matter of urgency and utilitarian purpose' they nonetheless 'by virtue of their age and their naturalisation within landscapes and townscapes' can become 'objects with emotional, historical and cultural force'. They move from a first life where they fulfil 'secular purpose and an immediate social need to a second life where they fulfil a need that is psychological and spiritual . . . they provide a locus where human affections can attach themselves; they provide contours for the inner landscapes as well as the outer one'.[84]

Significantly, in attempting to map this inner landscape a small-town

Canadian community developed what the locals called a 'sacred struc-ture'.[85] Faced by economic decline, they wanted to exploit the historic and special character of their town for tourism, without falling victim to the frozen wax museum authenticity of the 'preserved historic town'. They suc-ceeded in identifying and preserving what they valued in the face of change by having a planning process that not merely took account of heritage buildings and places but which also focused on what people did and where they did it, identifying those daily informal rituals which would be irre-vocably disrupted by changes in land use. The real issue of preservation became not just the conservation of a heritage site but the maintenance of continuity and community life as an element of change. The focus on heritage as mere tourist product as opposed to heritage as part of the con-tinuing life of the community can destroy the continuity which is necessary to the life of any city.

If some of the more memorable physical images which constitute the city (such as the houses in Eccles Street) were destroyed as Dublin osten-sibly celebrated its millennium, the destruction — as we have seen — also continued in the year that Dublin became European City of Culture. Ironically, the very designation threatened to undermine the idea of the city even further for, to commemorate Dublin's ephemeral title, it was pro-posed that the city quays be renamed, the argument being that 'existing quay names, such as Wellington, Victoria and Sir John Rogerson were not particularly suggestive of Dublin'.[86] If, as Aldo Rossi has suggested, 'the city itself is the collective memory of its people . . . the *locus* of the col-lective memory',[87] and memory attaches itself not just to objects and places but also to names, this was a proposal that threatened to replace destruction by obliteration. For Dubliners these names are not merely sug-gestive of the city, they are Dublin — the means by which the city is known and orally constituted.

Oblivious to changes elsewhere in Europe — which had seen places such as St Petersburg revert to their original names — it was claimed that few Irish people 'would have any great interest in the old imperial legacy of Wellington or Essex'; indeed, that it was unlikely the Burgh Quay was 'named after Chris de Burgh'.[88] More pertinent was David Norris's remark that the idea of renaming the quays after writers whose names would be more 'suggestive of Dublin' — was in any event a dubious honour: 'Considering the dereliction in this part of the city it is not much of a com-pliment, especially when one considers that among the Corporation's plans is included a motorway and bridge which will obliterate [No.] 15 Usher's Island, the setting of Joyce's great story "The Dead".[89] The debate (as well as the proposal) eventually fizzled out — though not before the London *Times* had editorialised on the issue, seeing the rejection of the old street names (with all their vice-regal associations) as yet another example of Irish ambivalence 'about their British roots'. More accurate — and more

wounding — was the comment that 'the desecration of Georgian Dublin
. . . including the failure to protect . . . the quays' meant that 'to a conservationist, Dublin is now the City of European Philistinism'.[90]

Of all the works arising out of Dublin's reign as European City of
Culture few were as dispiriting as this discussion of what might be suggestive of the city or appropriate to our image of it. In effect the oral
memory of the city was to be reprogrammed, themed so that the names
would better respond to an external tourist image of Dublin. It was an
approach which, if realised, would mean that the returning emigrant would
no longer find — like the hero in one of Michael O'Loughlin's stories —
'its wrecked buildings and blasted centre'[91] — but wrecked buildings and
a themed centre, themed to prompt an image which would satisfy the requirements of Dublin as heritage product. For a city which has been the
birthplace of so many great writers it would have been an unfortunate
memorial, not alone to tolerate the continued destruction of some of the
more memorable elements of the city which those writers knew — and
maybe loved — but to deny the very names by which they would have known
it. It might, however, have been an appropriate memorial to a political
culture which has not alone failed to develop an image of the city — and
of its role in an urbanised Irish society — but whose very idea of fêting
Dublin's role as European City of Culture was to deny the very language
which can suggest how that culture came into being; having failed to develop
appreciation of the city's identity — be it oral or physical — we should
now 'theme' what heritage remained so that it might better equate to what
we imagine the tourists might expect to find.

As it turned out, the ironic reference to Chris de Burgh may have hit
the right note — though the wrong musician — for if any image of Dublin
entered the European consciousness in 1991 it was due to music: 1991 was
the year of U2's 'Achtung Baby' and, most powerfully of all, the year of
The Commitments or, at least, of the film version of Roddy Doyle's novel
with its depiction of a city which is characterised by its very lack of physical
distinctiveness. And, appropriately enough, it was with a concert by the
Galway-based band, the Saw Doctors, that Dublin's year as European City
of Culture ended. It could easily have been Ireland's capital that they had
in mind as they sang:

> i useta lover, i useta lover once
>   a long, long time ago
> it's gone, all my lovin is gone
> it's gone, all my lovin is gone . . .

NOTES AND REFERENCES

1   Letter from Ian Lumley in *The Irish Times,* 19 January 1989.
2   *The Observer,* 30 October 1989.
3   Dan Cruickshank, 'Call this a City of Culture?' in *The Independent,* 21 November 1990.
4   Letter from Noel Carrol in *The Irish Times.* A similar view was expressed by Senator Eoin Ryan, Chairman of the Corporation's Planning and Development Committee, in a letter to *The Irish Times,* 23 January 1991.
5   Letter from Kaija Santaholma in *The Irish Times,* 15 October 1991.
6   Editorial in *The Irish Times,* 15 October 1991.
7   *The Dublin Arts Report* (Dublin 1992). For a summary account see Brian Boyd 'Arts Report calls for Radical Change' in *The Irish Times,* 7 February 1992.
8   Lady Gregory, *Seventy Years,* quoted in Joseph V. O'Brien (1982), *Dear Dirty Dublin, A City in Distress, 1899-1916,* Berkeley and Los Angeles, p. 39.
9   John Waters, 'Dublin 4: Geographical Location or Cast of Mind' in *The Irish Times,* 1 February 1991.
10   ibid.
11   Conor Cruise O'Brien (1972), *States of Ireland,* London, pp. 62-3.
12   Brian Farrell (1971), *The Founding of Dáil Eireann, Parliament and Nation-Building,* Dublin, p. xix.
13   Fintan O'Toole, 'Myth that lets Dublin 4 Evade its Responsibility' in *The Irish Times,* 27 May 1992. For a more positive view of the importance of Dublin 4 liberal values see Michael McDowell, 'The Dublin 4 Insult' in the *Sunday Independent,* 31 May 1992.
14   Anthony Cronin, 'Powers and Planners' in *The Irish Times,* 25 November 1986.
15   P.J. Drudy and Orla McKeon of the Centre for Urban and Regional Studies at TCD, 'Dublin Loses Out in Drive for Jobs' in *The Irish Times,* 15 November 1991.
16   Michael J. Bannon (1986), 'The Regional Context' in Gerry Cahill and Loughlin Kealy (eds.), *Dublin City Quays: Projects by the School of Architecture UCD,* Dublin, p. 6. See also, National Economic and Social Council (1981), *Urbanisation: Problems of Growth and Decay in Dublin,* NESC No. 55, Dublin.
17   *Report of the Departmental Committee Appointed to Inquire into the Housing Conditions of the Working Classes in the City of Dublin,* (cd. 7273) H.C. 1914, xix, 61. See also *Evidence and Appendices* (cd. 7317) H.C. 1914, xix, 107.
18   Quoted in Frank McDonald (1989), *Saving the City. How to Halt the Destruction of Dublin,* Dublin, p. 19.
19   L. McKenna S.J. (1919), 'The Housing Problem in Dublin', *Studies,* **vii**, No. 30, June:281.
20   'Alpha and Omega' (1918), *Blight: an Exposition in Three Acts,* Dublin. The play was written by Oliver St John Gogarty and Joseph O'Connor.
21   'Alceste' reviewing *Blight* in *New Ireland,* **v**, No. 8, 29 December 1917.
22   Darrell Figgis reviewing *Blight* in *New Ireland,* **v**, No. 8, 29 December 1917.
23   'Alceste' op. cit. See also Ulick O'Connor (1964), *Oliver St. John Gogarty: a Poet and His Times,* London, pp. 150-6.
24   *Local Government (Dublin) Tribunal,* 1938, pp. 19-20.

25 *Dublin Housing Inquiry,* 1939-43, p. 120.
26 Fintan O'Toole (1988), 'Kick the Can', in Dermot Bolger (ed.), *Invisible Cities. The New Dubliners: A Journey Through Unofficial Dublin,* Dublin, p. 107.
27 Dominic Behan (1961), *Teems of Times and Happy Returns,* London, p. 122.
28 *Dublin Housing Inquiry,* 1939-43. Verbatim report of proceedings, par. 5003.
29 ibid., par. 5026. For an account of life in the Crumlin estate see Fintan O'Toole, op. cit., pp. 105-13.
30 Michael Bannon (1988), 'The Capital of the New State', in Art Cosgrove (ed.), *Dublin Through the Ages,* Dublin, p. 139.
31 Frank McDonald, op. cit., p. 79.
32 Finn Gallen, 'Dublin, Dublin, how does your City Grow?', *Business & Finance,* **10,** No. 18, 24 January 1974, p. 10.
33 I.P. Houghton (1970), 'The Urban-Rural Fringe of Dublin', in N. Stephens and R.E. Gausscock (eds.), *Irish Geographical Studies in Honour of E. Estyn-Evans,* Belfast, p. 365.
34 Tony O'Shea (photographs) and Colm Tóibín (text) (1990), *Dubliners,* London.
35 Roddy Doyle (1987), *The Commitments,* Dublin; (1990) *The Snapper,* London; (1991), *The Van,* London.
36 See B. Murnane, (1988) 'The Recreation of the Urban Historical Landscape: Mountjoy Ward Dublin circa 1901', in W.J. Smyth and K. Whelan (eds.), *Common Ground: Essays on the Historical Geography of Ireland,* Cork, pp. 189-207.
37 R.F. Foster (1988) *Modern Ireland 1600-1972,* London, p. 167. Mahaffy's essay 'Society in Georgian Dublin' which was published in Vol. III of the *Georgian Society Records* caused great indignation; for a brief account see Desmond Guinness's introduction to the 1969 reprint of the *Records,* p. viii.
38 *Dáil Debates,* 11 March 1970. For a retrospective analysis of the Hume Street débâcle see Deirdre Kelly, 'The Lost Battle of Hume Street' in *The Irish Times,* 17 June 1990.
39 See Desmond A. Gillmor (1972), 'The Changing Centre of Gravity of Office Establishments within Central Dublin, 1940 to 1970', *Irish Geography,* **VI,** 4:480-4. For an analysis of how the office market has developed see Andrew MacLaren, Morag MacLaren and Patrick Malone (1987), 'Property Cycles in Dublin: the Anatomy of Boom and Slump in the Industrial and Office Property Sectors', *The Economic and Social Review,* **18,** 4 (July): 237-56.
40 Davy Kelleher McCarthy, Reid McHugh and Partners, Stokes Kennedy Crowley (1989), 'Greater Dublin Area Development Programme Preparation Study', unpublished. Quoted in Frank McDonald, op. cit., p. 16.
41 ibid.
42 Quoted by Anthony Cronin in 'Powers and Planners' in *The Irish Times,* 25 November 1986.
43 Michael Bannon (1988), op. cit., p. 147.
44 Quoted by Frank Feely in an interview with Deirdre Purcell, 'Streets Ahead' in *The Sunday Tribune,* 8 March 1987.
45 See 'Urban Renewal: an *Irish Times* Special Report' in *The Irish Times,* 26 November 1986.
46 For a report on the Custom House Docks developer/architect competition see *Plan,* **18,** No. 11, November 1987:28-40.

47 Quoted in 'Getting Out There and Selling' in *The Irish Times* (special report), 26 November 1986.
48 In 'Fair City Awakening' an advertisement by the Department of the Environment in *The Irish Times,* 11 February 1987.
49 See reports in *The Irish Times* of 2, 4 and 30 April 1987. For an outline of the commission's proposals see Kathryn Meegan, 'Dublin Metropolitan Streets Commission', in the *Irish Architect,* No. 63 (September-October 1987), pp. 20-21. For proposals for a replacement of Nelson's Pillar see Shane O'Toole (ed.) (1988), *Collaboration: The Pillar Project,* Dublin.
50 (1985), *Dublin, The Temple Bar Area — A Policy for its Future,* Dublin, a report compiled by the Dublin City Association of An Taisce.
51 (1991), *Temple Bar Lives — A Record of the Architectural Framework Competition,* Dublin.
52 Deirdre Purcell, op. cit. (see note 44).
53 See Deirdre Kelly et al., (1986), *Dublin Crisis Conference — A Report* (Dublin Crisis Conference Committee); Dean Victor Griffin, et al., (1986), *Manifesto for the City,* Dublin Crisis Conference Comittee; Peter Pearson, et al. (1985), *Dublin — The Temple Bar Area,* An Taisce Dublin City Association; Una Sugrue, co-ordinator (1986), *Temple Bar Study,* Temple Bar Study Group; (1986), *Towards an Inner City Policy for Dublin,* Society of Chartered Surveyors in the Republic of Ireland; Gerry Cahill and Loughlin Kealy (eds.), op. cit.; John Blackwell and Frank J. Convery (eds.) (1988), *Revitalising Dublin — What Works?,* Resource and Environmental Policy Centre, University College Dublin; Dublin Chamber of Commerce (1989), *Strategy for Dublin: A Private Sector View',* a paper for consideration in relation to the National Programme of Community Interest for the Greater Dublin Area 1989-94, Dublin.
54 Frank McDonald (1989), op. cit., p. 158.
55 See Commission of the European Communities (1990), *Green Paper on The Urban Environment,* Brussels-Luxembourg, pp. 61-6.
56 See *The Irish Times,* 9 October 1991.
57 Quoted in an article by Con Power 'Finance Conference Challenges Designated Status System' in the *Evening Press,* 4 October 1991.
58 Patrick John Dempsey (1992), 'Gentrification or Urban Revival', *Studies,* **81,** No. 321 (Spring):75.
59 Michael Hough (1990), *Out of Place. Restoring Identity to the Regional Landscape,* London, p. 155.
60 Martin Dully (1989), 'Doubling Tourist Numbers on the Way', *Business & Finance,* (January): 35.
61 Ventures Consultancy Ltd. (1990), 'A Development and Interpretation Strategy for Heritage and Cultural Tourism in Ireland: Summary Report', published in *Developing Heritage Attractions: A Conference to plan the Development of Culture and Heritage-based Tourism Attractions in Ireland — October 30th, 31st 1990,* Bord Fáilte, Dublin, p. 40.
62 Seán Browne (1992), 'A Strategy to Interpret Ireland's History and Culture for Tourism', in *Heritage and Tourism: Second Conference on the Development of Heritage Attractions in Ireland — 28 & 29 January 1992,* Bord Fáilte, Dublin, p. 1.
63 Victor Luftig (1991-2), '"A Standard of Sophistication and Service": Joyce and the Tourism Trap', *The Irish Review,* No. 11, Winter: 64-70.

64   Seán Browne, op. cit., pp. 1-8 to 1-17.
65   Seán Browne, op. cit., pp. 1-2.
66   Ventures Consultancy Limited, op. cit., p. 45.
67   (1987), 'Le Patrimonie Superstar', *Le Point,* 785, 5 October:84-9.
68   For a discussion of the heritage concept see Francoise Choay (1992), *L'Allégorie du Patrimonie,* Editons du Seuil, Paris. See also Pierre Nora (ed.) (1984), *Les Lieux de Mémoire: 1 — La République,* Gallimard, Paris and (1986), *Les Lieux de Mémoire 2 — La Nation,* 3 vols, Gallimard, Paris.
69   Ken Mawhinney (1989), 'Environmental Conservation Concern and Action, 1920-70', Michael J. Bannon (ed.), *Planning: The Irish Experience 1920-88,* Dublin, p. 91.
70   Kevin B. Nowlan (1980), 'Conservation and Development', in Kevin B. Nowlan, Nicholas Robinson and Alistair Rowan (eds.), *Dublin's Future: The European Challenge. A Conservation Report for An Taisce,* Country Life, London, p. 10. A 1982 survey by An Taisce of the surviving 650 listed buildings in Dublin proposed a twelve point conservation policy through reasonable levels of residential use and the provision of adequate public funding, see *'Urbana' Dublin List 1 Buildings — a Conservation Report for An Taisce,* Dublin, 1982.
71   Alistair Rowan (1980), 'The Historic City', in Kevin B. Nowlan, Nicholas Robinson and Alistair Rowan, op. cit., p. 3.
72   ibid.
73   Quoted in the *Quarterly Bulletin of the Irish Georgian Society,* v, 1, Jan.-March 1962:3. See also K. Corrigan Kearns (1983), *Georgian Dublin: Ireland's Imperilled Architectural Heritage,* London, pp. 58-67.
74   Quoted in Frank McDonald (1985), *The Destruction of Dublin,* Dublin, p. 25.
75   Ventures Consultancy Ltd (1985), op. cit.
76   Matt McNulty, in Ventures Consultancy Ltd, op. cit., p. 91.
77   Alistair Rowan, op. cit..
78   James Joyce (1939), *Finnegans Wake,* London, opening lines.
79   See D. Culligan (1986), 'Road Widening and the Liffey Quays', in G. Cahill and L. Kealy (eds.), op. cit., pp. 19-26.
80   See 'The New Bloomusalem', in Ronan Sheehan (1988), *The Heart of the City,* Dingle, pp. 171-81.
81   See Frank McDonald, 'Concern over Dublin City Project' in *The Irish Times,* 26 March 1992.
82   See Daniel J. Boorstin (1986), 'The Lost Arts of Memory', in *The Discoverers,* Penguin, Harmondsworth, p. 481.
83   Seamus Heaney (1989), 'From Macenas to MacAlpine', in John Gracy (ed.), *150 Years of Architecture in Ireland, RIAI 1839-1989,* Dublin, p. 69.
84   Seamus Heaney, op. cit., pp. 70-1.
85   Michael Hough, op. cit., p. 172.
86   See 'Mitchell Proposes Renaming Quays' in *The Irish Times,* 22 March 1991.
87   Aldo Rossi, *The Architecture of the City,* Cambridge, Mass., p. 130.
88   See note 86.
89   David Norris (1991), 'Books, Bookies and U2', *Cara,* **24,** 3 (May-June): 27.
90   *The Times,* 23 March 1991. For a response from Gay Mitchell TD, see *The Times,* 6 April 1991.
91   Michael O'Loughlin (1989), *The Inside Story,* Dublin, p. 17.

11

Rural Tourism and Cultural Identity in the West of Ireland

Anne Byrne, Ricca Edmondson
and Kathleen Fahy

The tourists who drive among the smouldering hills and glittering bog lakes of Connemara are the subject of some contention among official and semi-official participants in the tourist scene. Though extracting money from these visitors is the basic objective of the tourist industry, the questions of how this should be done and what effects it can be expected to have are by no means simply answered. The background to this article is the contrast between a straightforward market-driven approach to tourism — tourism is simply about effective selling — and a more subtle form of 'soft' or 'rural' tourism. Asking how 'Connemara' has been presented to visitors in the past and in the present, we shall see that 'rural' tourism seems consonant with the ways Connemara has been perceived in the past and is thought of as presenting less destruction to the area than other forms of exposure to the industry. Moreover, when we ask who are the tourists who visit Connemara and what types of facility they favour, there is some evidence that they feel at home with a sophisticatedly gentle but at the same time competent approach — to the landscape and its contents.

But what evidence is there to suggest that 'rural tourism' is what the inhabitants of Connemara can easily provide? The economic consequences of tourism have been presented as a panacea for the problems of people who dwell in remote rural areas. Is it likely, in fact, that tourism will provide solutions to the economic problems of a marginal region such as Connemara? Is rural tourism especially promising in this respect? It is women in particular who often bear the brunt of the interaction between visitors and hosts, as well as of trying to manage households on low incomes; what are the prospects for the poorest women in Connemara of rescue by tourism? Lastly, how can we expect a tourism which concentrates on the 'natural' and the 'authentic' to affect the more vulnerable sections of communities in areas such as this? Are local people really well placed to sell the sort of 'authenticity' tourists want to buy?

Although we support a cautious development of rural tourism, in this paper we stress the fact that even this form of tourism is not a straightforward path which leaves communities untouched. It is not without social and political as well as economic implications and these need to be weighed openly rather than obscured. Government plans and reports have selected tourism 'as a major axis of economic development' because of its potential for 'substantial and sustainable job creation' (see article by Deegan and Dineen in this volume). The Operational Programme for Tourism, for example, is 'designed to prepare the tourism sector to compete successfully in the internal and certain external markets and to help stimulate economic growth needed to reduce unemployment and to raise per capita income toward average Community levels.'[1]

Within the framework of this optimistic scenario, it is sometimes asserted that a particular type of tourism — 'soft' or 'rural' tourism — can provide the best of both worlds, bringing economic advance without the depradations associated with earlier forms of mass tourism. According to Bernard Lane,

> Soft tourism is generally seen as being holistic in its approach, value rather than profit conscious, socially and environmentally considerate and cautious, relying on small and slow developments by local interests. Farm economies are strengthened and retained rather than replaced. Existing buildings are re-used rather than being replaced by new buildings. 'Low tech', low rise, car-free concepts are favoured. New kinds of experiences are sought — these visitors spend time on repeat visits to an area, looking for 'experiences' rather than 'sights', seeking memories, recreation and new insights rather than postcards, souvenirs, and excitement. Sunshine is not important — but heritage, in all its forms, is.[2]

In contrast to the view that rural tourism is necessarily non-intrusive, we examine some of the types of change rural tourism can be expected to bring, especially as they affect the poorer and most powerless sections of the community — many of them women. We argue that if rural tourism is to bring genuine progress, it must be associated with a much more proactive and community-oriented approach than is evident at present.

In this chapter, then, we shall trace the following points:
1. Tourism is promised as a panacea for the socioeconomic problems of

places such as Connemara. This is seen as a development issue. In this context, rural tourism is seen as (a) the economically most effective form of tourist development and (b) the form of tourism most effective in preserving cultural identity. We shall pursue each of these themes here.

2. Even though we support many of the objectives of rural tourism, we stress that the issues involved are more complex than many proponents of rural tourism make clear. It is not obvious that economic benefits will automatically ensue from the enterprise for the population as a whole; it is not clear exactly whose cultural identity is being projected or preserved.

3. As far as cultural identity is concerned, we show that the 'identity' which is projected is always affected by sociopolitical factors deriving from the observer's needs as well as from characteristics of the area in question. This is demonstrated by the history of the changing perceptions of visitors to Connemara (see article by Nash in this volume). Most of these images are not centrally concerned with the identity of the groups who are the focus of rural development.

4. In terms of the general strategy of rural development and the socioeconomic structure of the area, there is one section of the population in particular whose predicament is intended to be improved. This section consists of lower income households, where we single out the predicament of women. There is reason to doubt that a market-oriented, individualistic approach to rural tourism will assist marginalised groups in general and women in particular.

5. We have evidence to show that visitors to Connemara are looking for experiences compatible with the idea of rural tourism. However, the provision of these experiences is typically predicated on skills and possessions which those involved in rural tourism cannot be expected to acquire without assistance. That is, participation in rural tourism in fact demands cultural changes of many kinds from the operators concerned.

6. There are also reasons in principle for denying that rural tourism can ever leave cultural identities just as they were. This need not deter us from supporting rural tourism; but it is not as non-intrusive and non-political as it is claimed to be.

7. All these reasons lead us to conclude that the more vulnerable sections of the population will only benefit from a community oriented, holistic approach to rural tourism. A holistic approach is one which is not oriented exclusively to individuals' economic gain, but which places value on all aspects of the social development of the local community. In order for holistic development to occur, statutory, voluntary and private interests must embrace such an approach and must recognise that it will inevitably bring with it cultural as well as economic change.

Connemara as Visited: Romantic 'Authenticity'

Very many of the images which have been projected of Connemara in the past have been 'romantic'. A central theme has been the expectation that this outlying region of lakes and hills can somehow provide the visitor with insight into a natural and unspoilt form of existence, and can demonstrate a different way of living life. This is just what rural tourism celebrates. Writers such as Murphy and Wahab opine firmly that

> The genuine environment always attracts more tourists than the imitation.... the creation of 'artificial' environments, similar to that which the tourists have at home, does not promote tourism in the long term. Thus a destination area would be well advised to retain those elements which make it distinctive, and to present its cultural heritage in a way that would be both meaningful for themselves and convenient for the visitor.[3]

Here we shall briefly review some images of Connemara to show that the concept of the 'natural' is unlikely to have the same meaning for indigenous inhabitants as for visitors. 'Connemara' as perceived from one social vantage point or another is a construct which is assembled out of different components, depending partly on the requirements of the viewer.[4] Connemara has been seen as a magical peripheral area, a paradigmatic contrast to urbanised industrial life, or else as the repository of intrinsic Irishness; no version of these conceptions issues simply from features of the area alone, and all are shaped in part by the origins and predicaments of the groups which evolve them. Some persist to the present day, as in the characterisation of West County Galway in particular by O'Dowd and Lawlor as 'the heart of the nation', or 'the heart of a metaphorical kneeling monk who is Ireland'.[5] There is not, then, just one easily describable Connemara which can be presented to the visitor as part of a rural tourism package. Moreover, the different Connemaras perceived by visitors have different implications for their effects on the lives of the inhabitants of this geographical area. And, not least, there are some projections of Connemara as a haven for rural tourists which not all operators can convey unassisted.

Although Connemara has repeatedly been experienced as 'authentic', there is a long history of accounts which provide a composite and contested set of versions of this authenticity. The cultural and political developments of the Irish Revival, for example, affected views of the region by perceiving it as a physical location for unpolluted Irishness. It was a version of this ideal which made Pádraig Pearse choose his cottage in Ros Muc. Like the American Wild West, Luke Gibbons points out, Aran and the West of Ireland have been seen as a 'last frontier', a place of escape from 'the forces of centralisation' which at the same time point up true values of Irish life. As for the question of what these true values are, where Synge saw in the West an exalted and sensuous lawlessness, Canon Sheehan preferred to concentrate on the peasant's moral virtues, 'comfort without wealth, perfect physical health without passion, love without desire', in short, 'clean bodies, keen minds, pure hearts'.[6] The fact that it is possible for Synge and Sheehan to consider themselves observers of the same place but to produce such startlingly variant accounts of its culture warns us not to accept at face value any particular version of what Connemara 'is'.

Views of Connemara in the nineteenth century had centred on the contrast between the magnificence of the scenery of North Connemara and the smallness of human beings — a contrast encapsulated in the illustrations of W.H. Bartlett.[7] These are largely in tune with the later descriptions written in 1875 by the Catholic convert John Yates. He stresses the fact that the scenery is 'the grandest and yet perhaps the wildest and loneliest in the whole of Ireland'. He writes of the 'stern grandeur' of the Twelve Pins with its views of

> nature in some of her most rugged aspects — rugged, but toned down at the bases of the eternal hills with charming glimpses of rivers, streams, loughs, and islands crowded with the very brightest of green foliage, but never for a moment missing the sensation of loneliness, of want of life, of the solitariness which the hermits and sages of old so loved to dwell in.[8]

Where the nineteenth-century visitor had praised the grandiose aspects of nature, the early twentieth-century enthusiast treasured its solitude. Praeger finds 'something infinitely satisfying about those wide treeless, houseless undulations, clothed with heather and Purple Moor Grass, so filled with lakes and so intersected by the arms of the Atlantic that water entangled in a network of land becomes imperceptibly land entangled in a network of water ...'[9]

Visitors like this would nowadays be prized by proponents of rural tourism. Bartlett, Yates and Praeger idealise in the scenery of North Connemara all that is opposite to metropolitan life. Whether or not this perception coincides with the views of the inhabitants, travellers such as these would want if possible to leave the region undisturbed.

The nineteenth century also fostered a different type of tourist — one whose activities would also be compatible with the ideals of rural tourism today. The visitors, many of them English, who visited North Connemara for fishing, played a large role in opening up the area to a little more prosperity — but they also exerted considerable cultural influence on the region. To this day the natives of the North of the region are perceived by the inhabitants of South Connemara, whose landscape is less romantic and more inaccessible, as having adopted anglicised cultural expectations. It is still the case that North Connemara interior decors, exhibited for example in public house furnishing, are eloquent of 'country comfort' to an extent absent in much of South Connemara. The 'rural tourism' of a century ago has made lasting changes in local culture.

Women visitors to Connemara in the late nineteenth century included

Somerville and Ross and Jane Barlow.[10,11] Both *Through Connemara in a Governess Cart* (1893) and Barlow's sardonically titled *Irish Idylls* (1893) treat Connemara in a way which — despite the affectionate irony of Somerville and Ross — emphasise its emotional accessibility to those prepared to deglamourise it. In view of the fact that virtually every other presentation of Connemara had in some way emphasised its wild, exotic or even barbaric qualities (both these texts appeared little more than a decade after the Maamtrasna murders[12]), these authors' rejections of romanticisation take on not only originality but, also particularly in Barlow's case, some political significance.

Somerville and Ross write of trying to push through the roads of Tully on market day, and being scarcely able to penetrate the crowds (apart from some holiday cottages, much of this area is virtually deserted today); they describe the daily difficulties of getting on with cattle, dogs and donkeys. Barlow shows intense solidarity with the perennial problems of life in a region which, despite its great beauty, is harsh to those who live in it all the year round. She chronicles the unending strategies required from householders, women in particular, attempting to survive with their families in conditions of such poverty that a wooden floor was a thing unheard of. Far from presenting them as strangers to herself or her readers she identifies with her subjects, writing of what 'we' do to get by and how 'we' support each other in quotidian struggles to secure continuing life in the face of almost insurmountable obstacles. Her account of Connemara is politically pointed in that its effect is to demystify accepted attitudes to the area. In doing so, she points to hardships of rural living which are not very amenable for conversion into tourist objects — though many of these deprivations persist to the present day.

Tourism as a 'Development Panacea': Rural Development and Tourism

Rural development comprises a set of strategies intended to improve the well-being of those who not only live in rural areas but also depend on the rural environment to provide them with a livelihood. Attention to rural development has been provoked by the increasing 'flight from the land' throughout rural Europe, where smallholders can no longer eke a sustainable living from traditional farm enterprises and agricultural diversification is limited. While until recently there have been few local initiatives, rural interventions on a national and EC level have been apparent since the publication of the *Future of Rural Europe* by the EC in 1988. These include projects funded by the third EC anti-poverty programme, one of which is located in North-West Connemara. Such rural development programmes are described as attempts to develop alternatives in rural communities so that people can continue to live in rural areas and sustain a living from the natural resources at their disposal.

Rural development, as most generally understood, involves an attempt to improve the economic, social and cultural wellbeing of those who live in rural areas as well as providing infrastructural support. Tackling poverty is often an essential goal in development strategies, as poverty is conceived to be a result of the unequal distribution of economic, political and social power structures.[13] Why then does economic development alone seem to be a priority in many rural initiatives that are taking place? While the state-funded Combat Poverty Agency recognises that building a strong, local economic base is the best antidote to unemployment in rural areas, the agency also recognises that there is much other ground work to be done before such a strategy can be successful.[14] This work includes building a network of community groups, training community leaders, encouraging local participation in activities, fostering good relations among various partners and forging links between the statutory, business and voluntary sectors. The third EC anti-poverty programme is designed to bring together

> local communities with all the agencies which have the resources and power to tackle the different aspects of poverty and social exclusion. This pooling of resources and expertise is intended to lead to a much more intensive, co-ordinated and multi-disciplinary assault on poverty.[15]

But who benefits from these programmes? What are the assumptions underpinning the strategies adopted to improve the quality of rural life? Examination of the allocation of funds under the LEADER programme, for instance, indicates that, since recipients were obliged to provide matching funds, only those with significant resources could benefit under the scheme. Often, people with no other common purpose join together simply to raise funds. This is an example of resource-led rather than development-led response. This calls into question the strategy of helping those who are better off in preference to those who are most disadvantaged in the community. Are the poor being included in development, economic or otherwise?

Many tourism initiatives represent only economic development; these do not include socio-cultural development in a wider sense. Despite good aspirations, in concrete cases economic development is a priority. Nonetheless, there is a plethora of interest groups, community groups, private enterprise associations and state agencies committed in principle to the management and development of rural tourism in Ireland. These include such established organisations as the Irish Countrywomen's Association, Fáilte Tuaithe, Irish Farmhouse Holidays, the Irish Farmers' Association and newer organisations such as the National Rural Tourism Co-operative, together with state agencies such as Bord Fáilte, Teagasc, FÁS, the Office of Public Works and voluntary associations of locally based tourism groups.

Many of these groups are not in a position to market as well as to develop tourism, to analyse the more subtle consequences of rural tourism, or to establish exactly what is the nature of the tourism product. In very recent times Bord Fáilte has begun to evince an interest in countryside tourism; it provides a range of services to tourists which include information and advice about touring, accommodation, dining and leisure pursuits. More importantly for our work, as far the operator is concerned Bord Fáilte also has a referral system for approved accommodation listed in a handbook. Accommodation which has been 'Bord Fáilte approved' must meet certain standards of space, hygiene, bathroom facilities and room numbers. Bord Fáilte-approved guest houses have a higher publicity profile than non-approved houses. While the referral system may be advantageous to many operators, there is an unknown number of non-approved guest houses and self-catering units operating in every region. Bord Fáilte claims that non-approved facilities predominate in many rural areas, particularly North-West Connemara.

Rural tourism is also being pursued by a number of governmental and voluntary agencies as a strategy to cope with the increasing economic crisis on small farms and the lack of agricultural development opportunities for small holders. Teagasc (the Farm Research and Development Agency), FÁS (the Development and Training Authority), and other agencies have begun to respond to the problems associated with developing tourism in marginal regions. In North-West Connemara, FORUM, sponsored by the third EC anti-poverty programme, represents one such development agency which is made up of statutory, voluntary, community and private interests devoted to developing locally based activities to improve the lives of the most disadvantaged in the region. With the support of Teagasc, FORUM ran an eight-week tourism course which attracted a good deal of interest from local participants, a majority of whom were women.

Against this background, the position of rural women has received some consideration in recent times. It is often stated that women living in marginal agricultural communities are affected by a combination of factors which has led to the reduction of their farm role and limited their capacity to create alternatives to improve the quality of their lives.[16] These factors, identified as 'problems', are variously listed as physical isolation from others, continual societal expectations to be the prime caregiver, no opportunity for employment off the farm, lack of income, lack of representation in decision-making bodies at community level and little or no opportunity for further training or adult education.[17,18] Some writers are enthusiastic about the potential of rural tourism for alleviating these problems, especially for women. Not only do visitors bring additional income to rural areas, but it is claimed by Lane that real friendships are made between visitor and host, breaking down the isolation of rural women and offering new ideas and challenges to the traditional roles of women in rural society.[19] Undoubtedly tourism creates part-time work opportunities for some rural women and is enthusiastically embraced by Lane, who advises that 'economic success brings confidence and an independent identity for many women: this new confidence may bring further developments into other business fields later'.[20]

In North-West Connemara there are a number of tourism groups in operation, some of which have been in existence for a number of years, others more recently established. These groups are composed of local people actively involved in the tourist industry and have a number of diverse objectives which include the improvement and promotion of tourism resources and facilities in local areas and increasing employment. Activities range from producing information brochures, advertising accommodation in both 'approved' and 'unapproved' lodgings, setting up beach and litter patrols, becoming involved in tidy towns competitions, staffing tourist information points and lobbying the county council to improve local roads, water and sewage systems. We may note, however, that many of these activities are directly beneficial to individual entrepreneurs, with only indirect benefits to the community. It is also questionable whether these groups identify with the region as a whole or whether they are more concerned with promoting their own interests within each locality. Quinn and Keane have shown that 'traditional rivalry between parishes' was an impediment to development of a number of agri-tourism pilot projects.[21] While there is a surge in interest in tourism in rural areas, then, it is not yet clear in how much detail long-term consequences for lower-income households or for local cultural identity have been taken into account.

Low-income Households and Tourism

A SOCIO-ECONOMIC PROFILE OF THE AREA

We have indicated a little of the history of different perceptions of Connemara's cultural identity, each of which separates out for emphasis those features which are most salient to the visitor — various searches for quintessential Irishness, the yearning to escape the grind of the industrial world, the provision of comfortable fishing, or the negotiation of everyday life by women. How can Connemara be described in the 1990s? In order to describe the daily life of the indigenous inhabitant, we draw on the findings of a detailed baseline study of the region carried out under the aegis of FORUM, the third EC anti-poverty programme.[22]

North-West Connemara spans a large area of territory, with local populations concentrated around Clifden, the main town, and Renvyle, a coastal area. There are vast tracts of mountain and hinterland which are largely depopulated. According to the 1986 census of the population, there were 7,061 persons (3,418 females and 3,643 males) living in 2,026 households. The population has decreased by half in the period between 1926 and 1986 and there are strong indications that the main cause of population loss is migration. From the census data it can also be seen that the area has far fewer couples with children than the national average, and far more childless couples, or couples with adult children still living as a part of the household. Households of couples with young or school-age children comprise 37 per cent of households — as compared to 50 per cent of households in Ireland as a whole. The census data also shows that there are differences between districts — some areas have the highest proportions of families with young children, while other districts have high proportions of adult children living at home. There is also a higher proportion of elderly people in the area than the national average and in some districts there are four to five times the national average of elderly men living alone. As will become clear below, the presence of children in a household seems to be a major impetus to participation in tourism among lower-income households.

The majority of people are dependent on agriculture as their main form of livelihood, but the largely poor quality of farm land in North-West Connemara only supports the raising of drystock cattle and sheep. Agriculture in North-West Connemara is a marginal and declining activity, many holdings consisting of thirty acres or less. Three-quarters of the land in the region is held in commonage and is not suitable for traditional agricultural development. Most smallholders survive through dependence on sheep and cattle headage payments, social welfare monies and sporadic income from farm activity. It is estimated by local agricultural advisors working in the region that state transfers account for 70 per cent of farm income.[23] Findings from the baseline study carried out in the area indicate that nearly three-quarters of all farmers are dependent on social welfare payments as their main source of income.

Those who are not full-time farmers are dependent on manual labour and services for employment. There are few white-collar positions available in the region. The unemployment rate is also markedly higher than in Ireland as a whole. In a rural economy such as that in North-West Connemara, however, it is often difficult to classify people as being either 'employed' or 'unemployed'. Most people adopt a wide range of economic strategies designed to make ends meet. These include waged work, small-scale farming and fishing, bed and breakfasts and other small-scale businesses. Income sources thus include wages, social welfare payments, headage payments, and profits from trade. What is evident from the analysis of occupational structure in the region is the extreme lack of economic diversity, not only in agriculture but in all other enterprises as well. This is typical of many rural areas throughout the Republic of Ireland and is at the core of the challenge of socioeconomic development in such regions.

In an analysis of the 1986 census data, indicators of deprivation were identified for the region as a whole. These included an 'ageing' factor, an 'economic deprivation' factor, and an 'isolation' factor. The ageing factor links an ageing population with small farm size, economic deprivation is linked with high rates of unemployment and adult population loss, while the isolation factor links poor access to cars with areas in which there are large numbers of elderly people living alone. This analysis showed that on every key variable, the study region was in a much worse position than the rest of Ireland. However, it is evident that there are also pockets of prosperity and relative wealth, in which people have taken advantage of the essential commercial enterprises and services required in any area. This is the context in which tourism development is taking place.

To assess the potential for development in this community and to find out the impact of poor living conditions on people's lives, 121 heads of low-income households were interviewed in the summer of 1990. The main findings are further indicators of the extent of disadvantage in the region and highlight the many areas in which development needs to take place. Some of the general findings have been extracted from the baseline study and are summarised in brief below.

Housing, transport, and infrastructure
The housing stock of the area contains quite a large volume of substandard privately-owned accommodation and lacks many basic amenities that most people have taken for granted in the late twentieth century. Almost half of all households stated that extensive repair work needed to be carried out to their accommodation.

There are many complaints about the transport service in the area with only one-fifth of households using the service on a regular basis. People are forced to rely on the expensive option of owning and running cars on poorly maintained roads. Given the isolation of many people from services, it is significant that almost one third of households do not own a car and are dependent on the public transport system. Poor infrastructure is identified by the population as one of the major impediments to improving the quality of life in the area.

Education
In households with primary school children, one in three stated that one or more children have reading, writing or learning difficulties. Most have no access to special attention at school to help them overcome this learning disadvantage.

In addition to learning difficulties, there is a very high rate of early-school leaving, particularly among boys, while in the past twelve years only 12 per cent of students in North-West Connemara have transferred to a third level course.

The lack of relevance of the education system to local employment opportunities is marked and the need to earn an income is cited as one of the main reasons why young people leave school early.

There has been little provision in the area for adult or continuing education which would enable adults to retrain and equip themselves to face new economic circumstances.

Employment and social welfare

A social welfare system based on means tests can thwart people's attempts to break out of the poverty trap. Many people do not engage in activities or enterprises that could make their lives more economically secure for fear of losing social welfare benefits.

One third of all households have an unemployed main earner and most of these are households with children. Families in these circumstances tend to have more than four children, and many are experiencing severe financial problems.

While the provision of jobs is perceived by local people as a solution to unemployment, large industries are not likely to locate in North-West Connemara due to poor infrastructure and the lack of a skilled, trained industrial workforce.

Many respondents feel that the development of tourism is a key activity which can supplement household income or offer new sources of employment in the area. A few women are contributing substantially to household income by running a bed and breakfast business from the family home. This is an entry point for some local women to the tourism enterprise but needs to be further explored to include more low-income households.

Ways to increase the involvement of low-income households in the tourist industry need to be considered, if tourism and the expansion of leisure facilities are used as devices to support local economic development.

Involvement in local activities

There is a high level of involvement by households — over half — in community activities and events. However, only a very few involve themselves in administration or fundraising activities. Many women have little access to transport and are responsible for caring for others, and are thus impeded from becoming further involved.

There is a lack of leisure and meeting facilities for young people. Most organisations are for older people and for men rather than women.

Poverty

More households are dependent on unemployment payments than on any other source as their main income. Level of payments are low and many families are living a marginal lifestyle. Average weekly income is below the recommended adult minimum of £60.

Most households rely on child benefit payments to supplement other income sources. This money is used to pay bills, buy food and household items.

While almost half of all households are currently in debt, one-fifth have fallen behind with repayments. Most households say that they are worse off now than they were five years ago. One-fifth say that they have had to borrow or seek credit from friends, family and the local shop to provide for day-to-day needs.

Almost a quarter of the people here consider that they are poor. Most of these are dependent on social welfare with large families. However, the remainder also said that they were barely making ends meet. Any crisis or emergency requiring a financial outlay would put many of these families in debt.

Most of the women interviewed are fulfilling traditional roles in the home, doing domestic work, caring for children and elderly dependents. A few are engaged in farming activities, while others have part-time employment in the services sector and tourism industry. It is women who bear most of the daily burden of trying to manage on low incomes; they described specific problems in relation to loneliness, transport difficulties, poor health, inability to generate income, unemployment, lack of support with child care, and lack of participation in the wider community in which they lived. Younger women are inclined to emigrate on leaving school rather than stay in the area. Few wish to lead the same lives as their mothers.

There is scant opportunity for women to generate additional income or to engage in small business activities. The few who have managed to set up small businesses did so from the family home with the help of family members. But overall women have little access to income of their own and a few are forced to rely on weekly assistance from the community welfare officer or local charity organisations.

It seems clearly unreasonable to expect many people in this economic predicament to develop tourist enterprises unaided. It may be therefore that purely market-led tourism, whether it is a 'rural' version of tourism or not, excludes from participation those who lack resources, both material and cultural. Nonetheless, in a region in which pluri-activity is the dominant survival strategy, a small number of lower-income households have managed to enter this area, and we shall look at these families next.

LOW-INCOME HOUSEHOLDS IN TOURISM

We now turn to that group of low-income households which are minimally, at least, involved in tourism. In what ways are they characteristic or uncharacteristic of rural low-income households? It would seem unlikely that low-income households facing economic difficulties and hardship would have the capacity or resources to become directly involved in tourism. Involvement can take place at many levels, from participation through the service sector in the hotel and restaurant industry, to owning and operating an enterprise such as a bed and breakfast business or craftshop. The sample described in the baseline study provides an opportunity to examine the capacity of low-income households to benefit from tourism in rural areas. What is the level of involvement? Are there certain types of households which participate directly in the tourism business? What are the characteristics of such households? How are they different from those who are not involved? What are the characteristics of households where members are employed in the service end of the tourism industry? Do such households have the capacity to develop small business activity and thus become more directly involved in tourism?

Of the 121 households examined in the baseline study, twenty-one are involved in the tourism sector. Of these, members of thirteen households are associated with the hotel industry, working as waitresses, cleaners, kitchen assistants, receptionists and chefs. Eleven married women and two married men represent these households. (The wives of the two men run their own bed and breakfast businesses.) All of these jobs are held on a part-time seasonal basis. While chefs and receptionists are comparatively well paid, the average take-home pay for a cleaner is about £2.30 per hour. One additional household moves out of the family home into temporary accommodation in order to rent their home to tourists for the summer period, while another has chalets to let. The remaining eight households have ventured to set up their own businesses in the form of bed and breakfast enterprises.

It is to this latter group that we shall pay particular attention, and though the numbers are small, they are engaged in a development which is not normally associated with low-income households with scarce resources and little spare capital. In addition, while the service sector does provide part-time opportunities for households to earn much needed additional income during the tourist season, it is also a sector which is associated with poor working conditions, long hours and low rates of pay. It is difficult to assess whether this level of participation in the tourist industry is a precursor to further entrepreneurial development or whether it merely provides opportunities for some members of low-income households to engage in labour-intensive activity for minimal returns. Working as a waitress during the summer months does provide an injection of cash into a household short of capital. Whether it is an effective ingredient required to assist other members to set up their own business, though, is highly debatable. It seems more realistic to assume that additional income earned in this manner is a haphazard benefit of tourism. Working part-time in the service sector is subject to the whim of seasonal variations, and is at best exploitative, especially for women. By examining the characteristics of the eight households whose members have managed to generate their own income and thus alleviate some of the stress of not having enough to maintain themselves, we shall attempt to provide some insights into the arguments highlighted above. As the sub-sample is small, we cannot claim representativeness, but we can indicate trends and patterns which differentiate these particular households from their neighbours.

The eight households are based in the Roundstone, Clifden and Renvyle regions, which are arguably the most visited areas of North-West Connemara. Being on the tourist route is an obvious asset when trying to set up a tourist-related business. The composition of all households in the larger sample is described in Table 11.1 below, and it is notable that only two types of low-income households participated in the bed and breakfast enterprise. These were two households consisting of retired couples with no children or dependants living at home and six households consisting of younger couples with children. The number of children ranged from six to two, with an age range of 3–21 years. Six of the women and men are under 45 years of age, with the remainder over 60 years old.

What other characteristics have these households? Four own their properties outright, while the other four have mortgages to repay. The retired couples are included in the former category, which is more typical of the pattern of ownership in the region. Within the larger sample of 121 households, those with mortgages represent only 17 per cent of the total. Owning one's own home would also seem to be another important factor contributing to the success of the bed and breakfast enterprise. When we look at those households who are employees of hotels and shops during the tourist season, most live in either rented accommodation or county council housing.

All of the sub-sample are happy with their accommodation and in

Table 11.1 Structure of Household Sample (N = 121)

Category	Number	Proportion %
Person living alone	14	12
Couple living alone	6	5
Couple with children	76	63
Couple/children and others	11	9
Lone parent/children/others	11	9
Other related adults	3	2
Total	121	100

Source: Byrne, A. et al. (1001) *North-West Connemara: A Baseline Study of Poverty,* FORUM, Letterfrack, Galway.

many instances the building has been refurbished or newly furnished in anticipation of the forthcoming tourist season. This differentiates them from the larger sample, in which 31 per cent are not satisfied with the physical state of their homes, many of which are in need of extensive repair. Seven out of eight households own their own car but few are happy with the level of service and provision of public transport.

As regards educational qualifications, people in six households had advanced training prior to setting up their own business. This training included nursing, secretarial work and hotel work, most of which was acquired in England or the US; it was not usually specifically oriented to tourism. Within the overall sample, by contrast, few have had training beyond primary school level. Also, in terms of current occupations, both partners in each of the eight households are generating income. All of the women are in charge of the bed and breakfast operation, while their spouses are part-time salesmen, fishermen, mechanics, shopkeepers or chefs. It is notable that none of the spouses are involved in the hotel industry as cleaners, waiters or kitchen assistants. However, while five of these households also receive social welfare payments, two households receive old age pensions, two receive top-up payments in addition to income received from part-time work and one receives unemployment assistance for three months of the year. While the sub-sample are similar to the sample as a whole in having to engage in a number of activities in order to generate household income, they are exceptional in that in each case one of the heads of household, most typically the male, has a source of regular income from work as an employee or as self-employed. In the sample as a whole, out of 121 households one-third of the main household earners are unemployed, most of them for one year or more. It would seem that a regular source of earned income may be a prerequisite for poor households setting up their own business.

When we ask about the circumstances which motivated the women to turn their homes into guest houses, it appears that the retired couples sought an occupation and interest in retirement, but all others are motivated through financial necessity. Losing a job, no job opportunities, having to repay huge debts, and needing to raise capital to refurbish the family home are all cited as reasons for embarking on this venture.

All of the women are running the bed and breakfast business themselves, with the assistance of their husbands and family. None employs other people, all depend on family members to serve and assist at meal times, to tidy rooms, to do the laundry and to cook evening meals. Five of the households have been in the business for three years or less, while one women has twelve years' experience. Most are very happy with the additional income earned from the enterprise, which ranges from £500 to £2,000 a month while the season lasts. The typical season extends from June to September, with July and August the busiest months.

We asked the women what skills they feel are important when setting up a business in their own homes. 'Good housekeeping skills', 'the ability to generate warmth and hospitality to guests', 'good hygiene', 'ability to keep on your toes at all times', 'having a sense of humour', and 'being able to cook' are listed as priorities. There is little mention of business-oriented skills such as marketing, developing new markets, balancing income and expenditure; rather, the emphasis is on points of contact between guest and operator. Plans to expand businesses are minimal, one or two women mentioned that they would like to build on extra rooms but cannot afford the cost; others are considering providing evening meals for guests. Most of the women suggested that if local entertainment and leisure facilities were improved, then visitors would remain for longer periods in the region, particularly in bad weather, which would in turn benefit their business. While there is a widespread perception that the development of tourism is the basis for the future survival of the region, many women are concentrating all of their energies on maintaining the businesses and consider the development of the tourist industry to be the responsibility of others. None of the eight households is registered with Bord Fáilte due, they say, to a combination of reasons which include the cost of registration and inspection, a fear that their premises would not meet the required standards, a wariness about having to pay income tax and a general fear of losing welfare and health benefits if they became 'official'.

In order to understand the barriers to development in rural areas, we need to be aware of the economic context in which people attempt to make ends meet. These eight households are in many respects the exceptions rather than the rule for low-income households. On the one hand, they demonstrate that participation in tourism can be achieved even from non-optimal starting points. On the other, they strongly suggest that, for those who do not have even the benefits of this group, participation in a new form of socioeconomic activity requires some type of community-based support. Without this, those whose economic situation is closest to entrepreneurship are likely to benefit from tourism to the exclusion of weaker sections of the society.

Contemporary Tourists: Views and Expectations

We have indicated reasons for distrusting a less than holistic approach to rural tourism; what reasons are there for believing that tourists require rural tourism at all? The information we have on tourists' preferences in Connemara suggests that such an approach would indeed be appropriate. In the summer of 1991, data was collected from 350 tourists passing through a number of villages in North Connemara.[24] Over two-thirds of these were under the age of forty. Almost half were middle-class professionals, and nearly one-fifth were students. Nearly three-quarters had cars with which to view the area; younger people used public transport, cycled or hitch-hiked. Sufficient numbers were staying in the area for a period of days to make it appear worthwhile to develop local amenities. We did notice, however, that those who stayed longest tended to stay with relatives. People who needed to seek accommodation tended to prefer bed and breakfasts if over twenty-five, and to camp or use hostels if younger.

In the main, people said they were satisfied with accommodation facilities, although 21 per cent of the sample, young Europeans in particular, felt that accommodation was expensive. Despite the fact that just over half of the respondents stated that eating facilities in the area were 'good', when asked to suggest improvements in what the area offered, the same facilities came in for considerable criticism. More home-produced goods, light meals, more various meals, including vegetarian fare, would all have been desirable.

The main activities engaged in by tourists were walking, touring, nature pursuits such as bird-watching or botany, and visiting islands and historic sites. Horse-riding, golf, and water sports were less popular — in 1991 July and much of August were wet — but fishing was undertaken by a considerable number. Many respondents said they wanted more access to outdoor sports; about half visited islands and historic sites but these, together with boat trips, were aspects of the area about which visitors knew least. Kylemore Abbey was thought of as 'the' historic site of the area, and knowledge of other sites was extremely limited. Bord Fáilte would like to see the development of similar sites. Most people had heard about North-West Connemara from friends or from guidebooks. Only 6 per cent had consulted a travel agent and only 2 per cent used Bord Fáilte; English visitors especially reported no information about the area from any travel agents. Europeans appeared to be the best users of information services and travel agents. A large number, 42 per cent of the visitors interviewed, stated that they had not seen any Irish tourist brochures for the region.

Many (60 per cent) had been to Connemara before, but of these most were Irish or English. Nearly three-quarters of the Europeans were on their first visit. When asked about their main reason for visiting the area, 90 per cent said it was primarily for the scenery and environment, especially mountains and lakes. At the same time, 25 per cent appreciated 'the people and relaxed atmosphere', walking, listening to traditional music, visiting pubs and dancing, as well as visiting relatives or friends. Visitors commented on this 'unspoiled area which lets us totally unwind' and commended 'the beautiful scenery' as well as 'the atmosphere, music, people in pubs', together with 'the serenity of the place and the laid-back attitude of locals'. These aspects of the area came well to the fore of more traditional, 'heritage'-based aspects, and in general people did not seem to expect extensive tourist facilities. Most interviewees, for example, did not wish for any improvements in the area of recreational facilities, either in the daytime or in the evening. The most dissatisfaction was expressed in relation to children and young people, for whom there was little provision, and there were also complaints about amplified music in pubs, inferior standards of service in hotels, restaurants and pubs, and about garishness apparent in such places as Clifden. Here, items such as loud speakers outside pubs and gaudy tourist shops were singled out for criticism in an especially busy August. These comments appear to signal the tastes of the typical rural tourism customer.

As far as basic amenities were concerned, over 50 per cent of visitors felt that road conditions were bad; potholes were ubiquitous, signposting inadequate, and the roads too narrow to walk along in safety. All these features could be improved within the ambits of rural tourism. Admittedly, 40 per cent complained about the weather. Families with children indicated that some provision for indoor activities would be gratefully received. Weather was, however, the reason — together with work commitments — why 65 per cent of respondents indicated that they would not visit Connemara in the off-season.

We have here an outline which appears highly indicative of possibilities for developing a 'soft' tourism in Connemara — even if not all operators are aware of this possibility at present. The visitors who felt that they would be able to return in the off-season tended to be Irish professionals aged between twenty-six and forty, who stayed in bed and breakfast accommodation or self-catering facilities (some of which, it is worth noting, are owned by local co-operatives). Over 60 per cent of this group claimed to be perfectly content with Connemara as it is; those who were not objected to the weather, the condition of the roads, and the lack of indoor facilities. They stressed repeatedly that any development of tourism in the region must be compatible with its great scenic and environmental importance. When asked for ideas about future development of the region, many visitors simply said, 'No development'.

This does not imply that the tourist industry in Connemara is already perfectly adjusted to rural tourism. It appears, in fact, that there is a gulf between the perspective of the visitor and the interests of some operators. Tourist brochures, moreover, are not widely read, and nor are they particularly informative or sensitive to what 'rural' tourists are likely to want to know. Such Bord Fáilte promotion as occurs does stress the natural beauties of the region and its pleasant atmosphere. 'The first time that you go to Ireland, you go for the beauty of the place. The second time you go for the people.'[25] But while marketing strategies romanticise the landscape and the 'traditional' nature of Irish society, this does not necessarily translate into the day-to-day activities of operators in the region.

Rural Tourism and Rural Authenticity

In the past, tourism and its effects were often conceived in terms of the depredations caused by mass tourism and the cultural homogenisation this was assumed to bring. Tourism in itself was expected to destroy cultural identity. It can be maintained nowadays that the era of mass tourism is past and that tourism tends to be more fragmented and specialised.[26] The visitors to the West of Ireland described above do seem to be looking either for 'unspoilt' scenery, or for particular activities, such as golfing or hillwalking, or for particular ways of life, which they would wish to see preserved. This does not mean, though, that rural tourism will not attack cultural identity. It is true that other agents of social homogenisation (television, for example, or fashions in domestic architecture) may be quicker and more potent bearers of change. But there are further threats to local authenticity which may be posed by the influx of large numbers of people unfamiliar with an area. These threats are subtle, and possibly unavoidable, however 'soft' the tourism involved. They are connected with the nature of tourists' perceptions of places and societies, and with what happens when indigenous occupants try to persuade visitors that they are perceiving an authentic environment. Tourists seeking 'otherness' may change the nature of the place they are visiting, and indigenous inhabitants are changed by participation in tourist-oriented communication (see article by O'Connor in this volume).

THE QUEST FOR 'LIMINALITY' AND ITS EFFECTS

Following the views of Turner, it has been suggested that the tourist, particularly the 'soft' tourist, is quintessentially in search of 'liminal' experiences, experiences which take him or her completely out of everyday existence into another, somehow revelatory, world.[27] This appears to be consistent with many of the images of Connemara projected in the past two centuries, and with some of the implications of 'rural' tourism: the traveller is invited to escape the mundane or even corrupt quality of city life and exchange it for the purity of the countryside.

We suggest that the 'liminal' experiences associated with rural tourism are those in which the visitor to a different cultural world comes to experience the functioning of human life as exotic in a way which is not disconnected from his or her daily life but in some way casts light on it. Instead of feeling trapped in everday sameness, the tourist can experience the fact that it is possible for the world to be different. In this new world, the tourist himself or herself feels transformed — though still needing the security of primitive comforts. Hence the emphasis of tourists on familiar arrangements for personal hygiene, causing homes which formerly had no bathroom suddenly to sport half a dozen, in the expectation of bed and breakfast visitors. Matters of hygiene seem to be too intimately bound up with what visitors feel essential in their own personalities for them to relinquish their bathrooms in new social circumstances. For people who know a local culture well, malfunctioning lavatories may not matter so much, as long as they are the only things out of order in an otherwise familiar world. For the visitor seeking liminal change, there is a greater subjective threat from the chaos involved in abandoning intimate habits.

Rural locations are now increasing in popularity among visitors and may be expected to continue to do so as the world becomes more urbanised. But there are several reasons why even those seeking exposure to new cultures will not be able to avoid altering them, however unintentionally. Some of the features which make the culture and atmosphere of one place different from those of another may well not be perceptible to its inhabitants, and therefore cannot be consciously preserved by them. For example, one highly salient, but little-analysed, distinguishing feature of local cultural identity consists in local forms of reasoning. What appears as a reasonable action in terms of one cultural identity (attending weekday Masses, or having six children) may appear histrionic or almost depraved in another. Not only this, but the underpinnings of thought itself, the unspoken assumptions which license speakers to move from one argumentative step to another, differ somewhat between cultures.[28,29] The social position of a speaker is not an intrinsic part of an argument in industrialised Europe, but status is important in areas such as the West of Ireland. Rural cultures acknowledge the human dimension to communication by counting it relevant to the contents of an argument about education whether, for example, the speaker is a schoolteacher or not, whereas urban cultures prefer purportedly 'objective' criteria and count the speaker's position as strictly irrelevant. Such local features of communication contribute to the characteristic ambiences of localities — even though seldom consciously noticed to do so — and they play a large part in bringing newcomers into the different worlds of experience they are seeking.

We suggest that this blend of familiar and unfamiliar worlds of thought edges travellers into behaving in ways new to them. This adds up to much of the fascination and the *frisson* which people seeking liminality find in the destinations they prefer. But the traditional aspects of local identities contained in their special 'thought worlds' are vulnerable to the weight of the tourist 'gaze'. In terms of industrial culture, traditional ways of thought appear not to make sense, and hosts may be tempted to adapt to visitors' expectations about what is intelligible and what is not; the visitors, after all, come from more politically and economically powerful cultures. When indigenous inhabitants of places like the West of Ireland gradually abandon local criteria regulating forms of reasonable thought and feeling, they will have become much more similar to people everywhere else.

THE ARGUMENTATIVE USE OF SETTINGS IN TOURISM
There is a further feature of tourism which rural tourism claims to escape but cannot, and which also affects the cultural identity of those visited.

Tourism must use settings, interior and exterior, to persuade visitors of something — here, that some form of authentic living actually has been maintained. Authenticity itself no longer simply occurs but must be 'staged'.[30,31] In this sense, touristic settings function as arguments in themselves. But in order to take effect as an argument, a feature of a setting has to be widely comprehensible. If the public which is intended to interpret it is composed of both indigenous and foreign members, the argumentative signs used have to straddle very different semiotic vocabularies. Many of the streets of Galway, in the process of being refurbished now, communicate 'authenticity' by using signs of past-ness rather than restorations of artefacts which really existed in the past. Streets are being cobbled as a sign that the past is being deferred to, rather than to restore their original state (quite possibly mud). Since such signs need to be generally legible in order to function as signs, Galway uses the same sorts of symbol of the past as other towns in Western Europe — lamp-posts and wastebins which are recognisably but vaguely old-fashioned, irrespective of what the 'original' lamp-posts and wastebins looked like.

Tourist semiotics, then, not only puts indigenous populations on the defensive in presentations of their cultural identity, it also forces them to use a new language of signs. This adopted language must be highly visual — it must communicate quickly to people who have no time for the extensive interaction needed to learn local cultural vocabularies. In a culture such as that of the West of Ireland, where social semiotics have relied in the past on building up gradual networks of indirectly expressed relations, new signs have to be adopted; and, old signs take on new meanings. Thus it is that the minutiae of cultures must change in the face of tourism.

There are therefore two main ways in which visitors to the West of Ireland tend to perceive its 'identity'. The first way relies on any one of a number of projections onto Connemara from outside; here the majority of versions do not take much realistic account of the lives of less advantaged people in the region. The second way of perceiving identity is, we suggest, responsible for a great deal of what 'soft' tourists are seeking in terms of experience — but it is hard even to make conscious and to describe, let alone to defend and preserve, particularly by people who are less socially powerful than their visitors. This does not mean that we should necessarily reject touristic or other opportunities for low-income groups to gain more prosperity. We are merely arguing that rural tourism cannot simply be seen as that unique touristic form which leaves cultural identity unaffected.

Conclusion

Those who are already directly involved in tourism enterprises benefit from the further development of the tourist industry. There is a great distance between those with few resources, not engaged in tourism development, and those with resources who are involved. Our own conviction is that community developments which actively involve all sections of a society are those most likely to offer genuine cultural and socioeconomic development in Connemara. People from low-income households, in particular women, are unlikely to benefit from a development of tourism based on market demands alone.

We have tried to establish both that all forms of tourism bring with them cultural change, and that the projection of cultural identity is by no means a simple matter of showing what already exists. Such a projection is certain to erode much that is indigenous and precious to an area, and is therefore an option with great costs: we must be sure that it is worthwhile. If the lower-income households intended to be assisted by tourism are excluded both from the economic activity involved and from participation in much of what evolves as the area's 'official' identity, one which links into traditions of perceiving the area which are not based on the lives of lower-income groups, this amounts to a development failure. We can only see the incorporation of such households in rural tourism if it evolves on an integrated community basis. If tourism is touted as a solution to rural development problems, therefore, it is reasonable to analyse both the social and the cultural costs of this solution, and how all sections of the community are being enabled to participate in it.

NOTES AND REFERENCES

1   Department of Tourism and Transport (1985), *Ireland — Operational Programme for Tourism 1989-93*. Stationery Office, Dublin, p. 5.
2   Lane, B. (1988), *What is Rural Tourism?*, Conference Proceedings, Countryside Recreation Conference, Bristol, p. 61.
3   Murphy, P. (1985), *Tourism: A Community Approach,* Methuen, New York, p. 145. Murphy is quoting from Wahab, S. (1975), *Tourism Management*, Tourism International Press, London, p. 49. In this paper we are pointing to some difficulties with the concepts of the natural and authentic endorsed by these authors; others are touched on in some of the articles in *Hosts and Guests: the Anthropology of Tourism*, (ed.) V.L. Smith (1978), Blackwell, Oxford.
4   Compare in particular, for an exposition of the ways in which views of a place can be composed mainly in relation to needs within the perceiver's culture, Said, E. (1978), *Orientalism: Western Conceptions of the Orient*, Routledge and Kegan Paul, London.
5   Nolan, W. (1992), Review of P. O'Dowd and B. Lawlor, 'Galway is the Heart of the West', *Journal of the Galway Archaeological and Historical Society*, **46**:214-5.

6   This contrast between Synge and Sheehan is taken from Gibbons, L. (1984), 'Synge, Country and Western', in Curtin et al., (eds.), *Culture and Ideology in Ireland*, Galway University Press, Galway.

7   Bartlett's works were immensely popular in the nineteenth century and are still in evidence in antique shops and in the homes of the educated middle classes in the West of Ireland today. An example is reproduced in Kilroy, P. (1989), *The Story of Connemara*, Gill and Macmillan, Dublin.

8   Dunleavy, J. (1991), 'John Yates, A Traveller in Connemara, 1875', *Journal of the Galway Archaeological and Historical Society*, **43**:128-38; this quotation is taken from p. 130.

9   Praeger, R. L. (1980), *The Way That I Went — An Irishman in Ireland*, Allen Figgis, Dublin, p. 160.

10 Somerville, E., and Ross, V. (1990, first published 1893), *Through Connemara in a Governess Cart*, Virago, London.

11 Barlow, J. (1893), *Irish Idylls*, Hodder and Stoughton, London. This work, full of analytical intelligence as well as sympathy, deserves to be better known.

12 Waldron, J. (1992), *The Maam Trasna Murders*, Edmund Burke, Dublin. The murder of five members of a single family in North Co. Galway in 1882 caused horror throughout the country at the time; the matter was never satisfactorily understood and it is now believed that one of those hanged in Galway for the crime was an innocent man, Myles Joyce. The episode also illustrates the huge sociocultural distance between the Irish-speaking peasants of a harsh, remote region and those who were charged with trying to establish what had occurred and why.

13 Varley, T. (1988), *Rural Development and Combatting Poverty — the Rural Projects of the Second European Combat Poverty Programme 1985-9 in Historical and Comparative Context*, Centre for Community Development Studies, Social Sciences Research Centre, University College, Galway.

14 Combat Poverty Agency (1989), *A Framework for Community Participation in Integrated Development*, Combat Poverty Agency, Dublin.

15 FORUM (1992), *Plan of Work 1992-4 — A Rural Development Partnership in North-West Connemara*, FORUM, Letterfrack, p. 5.

16 Byrne, A. (1991), 'Working With Rural Women, North and South: Report on Work in Progress between Rural Women's Research Group, Women's Studies Centre University College Galway and Rural Action Project Northern Ireland', *Phoebe: An Interdisciplinary Journal of Feminist Scholarship, Theory and Aesthetics*, **3**,1:7.

17 Lane, B. (1989), 'Rural Tourism and Rural Women: Issues and Ideas from England', paper delivered at the Seminar on Rural Tourism as an Alternative Employment for Women, Avila, Spain, 1989, p. 3.

18 Owens, M. (1992), 'Women in Rural Development', *University College Galway Women's Studies Centre Review*, **1**:17.

19 Lane, B. (1989), op. cit., p. 4.

20 ibid.

21 Quinn, J. and Keane, M. (1991), 'Community Tourism in Rural Ireland', in Varley, T., Boylan, T. and, Cuddy, M. (eds.), *Rural Crisis: Perspectives on Irish Rural Development*, Centre for Community Development Studies, Social Sciences Research Centre, University College, Galway. See also the excellent

study by M. Keane and J. Quinn (1990), *Rural Development and Rural Tourism*, Social Sciences Research Centre, University College, Galway, p. 37.

22 Byrne, A., Laver, M., Forde, C., Cassidy, L., Keane, M. and O'Cinneide, M. (1991), *North-West Connemara: A Baseline Study of Poverty*, FORUM, Letterfrack, Galway.

23 ibid.

24 Fahy, K. (1991), 'Visitors' Survey of North-West Connemara', unpublished report which contributed to a local tourism development plan adopted by FORUM, Letterfrack, Galway.

25 This comment, taken from the 1991 Bord Fáilte campaign in France, is regularly mirrored in other Irish marketing campaigns on the Continent.

26 Urry, J. (1990), *The Tourist Gaze*, Sage, London, p. 14. See also Lash, S. and Urry, J. (1987), *The End of Organised Capitalism*, Polity Press, Cambridge.

27 This has been one of the most influential ideas in Turner, V. (1969), *The Ritual Process*, Aldine, Chicago. Nonetheless the questions of what liminality is, when it occurs, and what its effects may need much more exploration, to which we have tried to contribute here.

28 Edmondson, R. (1984), *Rhetoric in Sociology*, Macmillan, London.

29 Edmondson, R. (1992), 'Rhetoric and Truthfulness: Reporting in the Social Sciences', in R.H. Brown (ed.), *Writing the Social Text: Poetics and Politics in Social Science Discourse*, Aldine de Gruyter Press, Chicago.

30 MacCannell, D. (1973), 'Staged Authenticity: Arrangements of Social Space in Tourist Settings', *American Journal of Sociology*, **85**:1249-58.

31 Schudson, M. (1979), 'On Tourism and Modern Culture', *American Journal of Sociology*, **85**:1249-58. The articles mentioned in notes 30 and 31 are further exemplars of the debate about tourism and (in)authenticity mentioned in note 3 above.

12

The Irish on Holidays: Practice and Symbolism

Michel Peillon

Touring at home or abroad has become a current practice for many Irish families and individuals. The holiday experience is organised according to principles and orientations which offer a stark contrast to those of daily life. It creates a space for pleasure seeking and autonomy. But room is made only with difficulty for a practice which is organised according to principles not in harmony with the main cultural thrust. A culture which has retained a puritan streak in its traditionalism contrasts quite sharply with what constitutes the amoral character of holidays. The emphasis on breaking the routine and on liberation from constraints, the leaning towards self-indulgence, are only half-heartedly upheld by prevalent attitudes and norms in Ireland. At the same time, the importance of the holiday phenomenon nowadays rules out any possibility of its complete rejection. It has to be culturally acknowledged.

Holidaying manifests in that sense an underlying tension within Irish society. How does a culture which persists in defining itself in traditionalist terms assimilate a practice which is at the heart of modernity? The findings of a survey on holidaying conducted in 1986 (see annexe for details), point to the gap which exists between the practice and the imagery of the holidaying experience. Ideas, beliefs and rules have emerged to take in this practice, but they distort as well as reflect it. On the basis of the survey results, we argue that holidays in Ireland are made to inhabit an ambiguous cultural space, one in which the representation of holidaying cannot be reconciled with the behaviour and orientations associated with holidays.

Holidays as Inversion

As the opposite of routine, of everyday life, holidays represent an inversion, a turning on its head of what is mundane and habitual. Yet one should not perceive such an inversion simply as a reaction against the drudgery of daily life, for holidays are invested with a meaning of their own; they reactivate that which has been frustrated and eroded, they reassert values which have been denied. Moreover, they challenge the principles according to which ordinary life is organised. Holidays are concerned with the quality of life, when industrial living emphasises quantity; they aim at renewing affective relationships in an instrumental world; they restore individual autonomy in the face of manipulation. Sensitivity to nature, care for the body, sensory gratifications, creativity, spontaneity and autonomy, those are the values which are placed at the centre of the holidaying experience.[1]

The life of primitive societies, often poor in material wealth but rich in meaning was punctuated by festivities, in which the hardship and restraints of daily life were replaced by unbound generosity. Holidays form a kind of modern festivity, and they share the excess, wastage, indulgence of such occasions.

> Time and place: two of the constraints of everyday life from which the holiday offers relief. Another is self-restraint, replaced by self-indulgence. The pay-off for the saving of innumerable yesterdays is to spend as if there were no tomorrow. Food and drink are consumed to excess, known trivia purchased and treasured for their worthlessness. For a couple of weeks life is a funfair; being taken for a ride and not caring an essential part of the pleasure. Not only money can be wasted; so can time. Lying about, that primaeval Protestant sin, becomes on holiday a virtue. Time and money have been carefully hoarded to be carelessly squandered. [2]

Many holidaymakers make a point of eating and drinking more than usual. Not only do they lie about doing nothing, but also they practise an ostentatious and symbolic laziness. They hardly consider the expense and waste the money that they have often painstakingly saved during the year. The very idea of closely monitoring expenses remains largely alien to the spirit of holiday. 'Our contemporary, asked about his holiday expenditures, is reluctant to answer; he does not know, he does not want to know, he has not budgeted; if he had, it would not be a holiday any more.'[3]

The lifting of conventional restraints is also manifested by a more explicit show of affection by couples on holiday, by an uninhibited display of intimacy. Sasha Weitman has remarked upon this phenomenon: displays of intimacy seem more prevalent among tourists than among locals.[4] Tourists, she explains, do not have to heed the reactions or sensitivities of those around them, or to care about the possible disapproval of people with whom they have only a transient and superficial contact. In a similar way, the norms and conventions of wider society concerning sexual relations may not apply to the holiday situation. Reverse conventions about sexual availability often prevail among young holidaymakers. This occurence has been particularly observed in the context of holiday camps.[5,6]

Holidays are about enjoying oneself, and this involves play and fun. It also means an easy and uncomplicated sociability. Holidaymakers, who make themselves available to informal encounters, expect a sociable response when approaching other people. Meeting people and making friends belong to the holiday experience. 'Friendships are made instantly by children and adults alike, sealed by the recognition of a common interest — "We're all here to enjoy ourselves".'[7]

Irish holidaymakers are no exception: the message of the respondents' answers to our questionnaire was clear enough in this respect. They too seek to escape from daily constraints and drudgery, and live according to different principles. They do so, for instance, by eating out frequently. Financial concerns retain their relevance and the respondents had budgeted for their holidays, but very few would keep a regular record of their expenses. They engage in a great deal of self-indulgence: staying up later than usual and getting up later, drinking and eating more. Of the minority who normally follow some kind of diet, a great number simply stopped for the duration of the holiday. Respondents also became more sociable while on holidays, with two-thirds of them feeling that they talked more easily to people and were easier to talk to. Most would visit a pub or a nightclub while on holiday, and they would laze on the beach at some stage.

Behaviour is radically transformed while on holidays; it is organised according to principles or orientations which contrast with those of daily life: relaxation of the rules, a great deal of self-indulgence and easier social contacts. The entry into what constitutes such a different social world requires some signalling that boundaries are being crossed. The transition to holiday behaviour is facilitated by symbolic markers. The very act of travelling operates in this way, in that it introduces a kind of ritual no man's land, where old habits are shed and a new self is assumed. Travelling creates a distance between the old world of daily routine and the world of holidaying; like all indefinite times, it offers the possibility of renewal, of a renegotiation of the self. The break is even more clearly manifested by the buying and the wearing of holiday clothes: half the respondents bought new clothes for their holidays and, more significantly, half stated that they wore 'unusual clothes'. Holiday clothes are unusual, and labelled as such, because they are worn to signify all the values we have noted: excess, indulgence, playfulness, liberation of conventions, etc. The very labelling of such clothes as unusual sets them apart, in a category of their own.

Patterns of Holiday Behaviour

Tourist behaviour is mainly patterned according to age (closely associated with marital status, and for this reason we will treat them as one single factor). Younger/single respondents were more likely to go to nightclubs or pubs during their holiday, to eat out, to stay up, to buy new clothes, to drink more. They were less interested in visiting museums. These findings point to the existence of two distinctive holiday styles, each associated with age. One, more boisterous, is aimed at 'having a good time', while the other style is more settled and geared to touring and visiting. This difference is illustrated by the words which are associated with holidays in people's minds: the most frequent association for young respondents was 'fun', and 'rest' for the older respondents.

But these differences do not necessarily indicate two radically different modes of holidaying. Which principles organise the behaviour of respectively young and older people during holiday time? The liberation from daily routine and drudgery underlines holiday behaviour for young people. The constraints of daily life are gone altogether, as they eat out, stay up late, etc. Holidays become, in the words of one of our respondents, 'a licence to run wild'. It means in this case a liberation from inhibitions, but also the freedom of not being judged by others (or at least not by those whose judgement matters to them). They also indulge in drinking and exploit to the full opportunities for establishing new fleeting social relationships (often with a strong sexual orientation). The situation differs slightly for the more mature respondents. For them, self-indulgence takes a different form; that of eating more than usual rather than drinking more, for instance. Visiting new places and touring locations also forms a way of breaking away from daily routines. The option of a total destructuration of the normal is not always available for these more mature respondents, usually married and with family responsibilities. The liberation from daily routine will manifest itself in a less radical form. One respondent offered this comment in an in-depth interview: 'I like to see things. Places of interest. Interesting towns, interesting cities, museums, art galleries, historic sites. They all mean holiday to me. And that's my relaxation. They help me unwind as well.' The holidays of young and older people are organised according to similar principles. In both cases, one finds the same principle at work: that of a total change from daily life, of a break. But the way this principle is enacted differs considerably for these two categories of people. It cannot be applied in the same manner and to the same extent, as the constraints which weigh on these two categories of people greatly differ. The divergence is emphasised by the typical holiday behaviour of these age groups, one very boisterous and extreme, the other more controlled (even if geared to liberation and self-indulgence).

Tourists also engage in a range of typical and some would say, quasi-obligatory activities. They send postcards, they buy and offer souvenirs, they take photographs of the places they visit and of their activities during the holiday. These aspects of tourist behaviour have hardly been studied in any great detail, and few ideas are available to guide us in the interpretation of the results. However, one can put forward a few hypotheses. Tourists buy souvenirs, not so much for themselves as for relatives, friends and neighbours. The buying of gifts acts as a testimony that one has been on holiday and that one has had an interesting time. Holidaying possesses a symbolic value which, with the gift, outlasts its actual duration. 'The trip is prolonged in the photograph which is taken, in the postcard which is sent, in the souvenir which is bought.'[8] S. Weitman suggests that the gift-giving and the donation rituals on the occasion of holidays belong to the class of 'compensatory mechanisms of inclusion'.[9] One has left for a time the social world of family, friends and neighbours; one has cut one's self from the group. One comes back to it with a ritual offering, as a way of testifying that the relationship has not been impaired, that the group is reconstructed. Daily life may then start all over again. This typical activity would then be related, once more, to the crossing of boundaries between two worlds. It was found in our survey that only a third of the respondents sent a postcard during their holidays, mainly to relatives and friends. About half of the respondents bought souvenirs while on holiday, not for themselves but for relatives and friends. Principally it is women who purchase souvenirs, which emphasises the special place of women in friendship networks and their central role in the process of re-insertion.

The taking of photographs has been studied by Pierre Bourdieu in one of his earlier works, and he has come to some definite conclusions.[10] He made a distinction between popular use of the camera (concerned mainly with recording the important moments and rituals of family life), and a more aesthetic orientation (in which the camera becomes a means of acceding to an artistic experience). The taking of photos during holiday time would correspond to the popular use of the camera, far more centred on people than on landscapes or monuments. It would consist in recording moments of family history, for a future reappropriation of what constitutes a privileged experience. It could be seen mainly as a celebration of family life. Only a third of the respondents claimed to take photos while on holiday, mainly scenery and family photos. And they gave as reasons for taking photos: remembering the place (75 per cent), showing them to friends (44 per cent), and recording a moment of family history (31 per cent). Taking photos on holiday can hardly be interpreted as, primarily, a celebration of family life: it represents, rather, a celebration of the holiday experience itself back at home in which members of diverse networks ritually participate.

Only a minority of the individuals interviewed (about one-seventh) claimed to buy souvenirs, take photos and send postcards while on holiday. Such a result seems to undermine the stereotype of tourist activity. But while few holidaymakers undertook all these activities, less than a quarter of them did none of them, a third of them performed at least two of these tourist activities. Holidaymakers may not always, as individuals, take photos, send postcards and buy souvenirs, but they certainly do so as a group. As a collectivity, they practise typical tourist activities.

One observes then, at holiday time, several practices which are directed at those left behind. This behaviour, although by no means universal, is widespread and typical and is apparently intended to renew group affiliations. In that sense, such practices reveal the groups which matter for the individual: those in which full membership has to be reasserted by some activity of a ritual nature. The practices of sending postcards, buying souvenirs and taking photos are directed mainly at relatives and at friends, while neighbours and colleagues do not figure prominently. But this general statement must be qualified for younger people, whose friendship networks matter more; they also include colleagues as recipients of their activities to a far greater extent than other age categories. Women, more than men, tend to cultivate the friendship networks by offering souvenirs and displaying photos to friends. But for all, the crossing of boundaries is always a delicate matter. It has to be negotiated, and relies on rituals of transition and on symbolic markers.

Collective Representations

Holidays carry a meaning, they acquire a strong symbolic significance, mainly as a response to the lives people are made to live. This entails that they generate a set of 'collective representations', through which people represent to themselves the holidaying experience. One may talk of an ideology of holiday when people resort to a range of ideas and beliefs in order to explain, even to themselves, why they go on holiday, how they feel about not going on holiday, what they like to do during their holidays. In the process, the phenomenon of holiday is culturally acknowledged and defined. This cultural appropriation is accompanied by the development not only of shared ideas and norms about holidays, but also of feelings and expectations. We must address ourselves, even in a tentative and exploratory way, to the beliefs and rules according to which Irish people take stock of their holiday behaviour.

The feelings that people express at the thought of having no holiday give an indication of the salience of a holiday culture in the Republic of Ireland. While half of the respondents declared that they would feel sorry

Table 12.1   Frequency of Going on Holidays

	Frequency of holidays in general %	Frequency of holidays last year %
Rarely	38.4	18.9 (no holiday)
Once a year	48.0	58.6
More than once a year	13.5	22.5

if friends or acquaintances could not enjoy a holiday, two-thirds of them indicated unhappiness or upset at not taking a holiday themselves; only one third expressed indifference at such a possibility. Not having a holiday within a particular year would produce a feeling of deprivation for the great majority of the respondents, particularly among the young and unmarried. On the other hand, farmers and people in low-income categories would feel less unhappy about such a possibility; holidaymaking is not for them a high priority. These feelings are reflected in what people state about returning home at the end of the holiday; most find it difficult to go back, and more so for the younger and unmarried respondents. Such attitudes and feelings point to the cultural importance of holidays, to the strength of the holiday phenomenon.

The social significance of the holidaying experience is also measured by the extent to which this activity is culturally appropriated by the group. This implies that relevant feelings and ideas come to be shared, rules are developed about holidaymaking and there emerges a conception of the normal holiday. Two different questions were introduced in the questionnaire to investigate the frequency of holidays (see Table 12.1). One question asked the respondents to indicate how often they go on holidays each year; a second question asked them how often they went on holidays in the previous year. One question evinced an answer about a fairly general impression of the frequency of their holidays, while the other question was looking for a precise answer concerning a definite period. These two questions produced a very different pattern of responses as can be seen in Table 12.1.

When asked, in general terms, about the frequency of their holidays, half the respondents answered once a year, while more than a third asserted that they never or rarely went on holidays. But a different set of answers emerged from the specific question about the frequency of holidaymaking in the previous year. More people took holidays last year than they indicated in general terms; they generally understated the frequency of their holidaying. For instance, one-fifth of Dublin respondents claimed they took holidays rarely or never, but only one in seven had not actually enjoyed a holiday in the previous year. Half the rural respondents asserted that, in a general way, they never or rarely went on holiday; but less than a quarter

Table 12.2 Length of Holidays

	In general %	Last year %
One week or less	37.2	49.1
Two weeks	50.0	39.2
More than two weeks	12.7	11.7

of them had not actually gone on holiday in the previous year. And one notes that the groups which claim a particularly low level of holidaymaking are more inclined to under-rate their participation. The general under-rating of the extent of holidaymaking indicates that the norm, the view of what is normal, lags behind the practice of holidaying.

The length of holidays follows a rather similar pattern, and Table 12.2 gives the general results. Two weeks apparently represent the normal length of holidaying, as formulated by half the respondents. But one also observes a discrepancy between what people state as the length of their holidays in general terms and the length of their last holiday. Although half the respondents claimed to take holidays of two weeks, only slightly over one-third managed to have two-week holidays in the previous year. Dubliners were more likely to have had one-week holidays the previous year than one would have expected on the basis of their general answers. And a similar over-estimation of holiday length applies to working-class respondents. The discrepancy points to the gap which exists between a norm, a culturally shared belief concerning holidays, and the practice of holidaying. But while this gap expresses an under-rating of participation in holidaymaking, it produces an over-rating of the length of holidays.

The questionnaire also included a set of statements concerned with rules about holidays, with which the respondents were asked to agree or disagree. The respondents, or at least two-thirds of them, supported the view that a two-week holiday, once a year, was quite sufficient. Nearly all of them expressed a view about the necessity of holidays. That one should not care too much about money and that one should not go on holidays alone was widely accepted. On the other hand, the respondents did not uphold the idea that one could do as one liked, or be very lazy while on holidays. The sociable character of holidaymaking and the freedom from daily constraints were clearly supported by the respondents, but not to the point of uncontrolled or over-indulgent behaviour. These results signal the presence of a definite normative framework for holidays, they underline the existence of clear ideas about the *normal* holiday.

This normative framework does not quite correspond to the practice of holidays. The latter allows, as we have seen, for more self-indulgence, and many respondents expressed a desire for more than the conventional two-week holiday. Younger respondents were in any case less inclined to accept the normative framework of holiday, which is more strongly upheld by married people, rural residents and especially farmers. Those with a low income also tended to approve these normative restraints, although it is likely that they did so for different reasons; the same people were also more likely to disapprove of continental holidays. This upholding of a strong normative framework by low-income respondents probably corresponds to a strategy of containment of a type of activity in which they participate only with difficulty. This statement helps explain a final paradox, namely that although they favour a normative restraint on the extent of holidaying, this same category of people tend to agree with the norms of freedom and sociability during holidays.

The previous considerations reveal the existence of a gap between the cultural recognition of holidays and the practice and feelings associated with holidays. It could simply be that culture lags behind practice, as the cultural appropriation of this rather new phenomenon takes time. But one also observes the presence of some reluctance in Ireland to assume fully the holiday orientation. This reluctance reaches deep, to the point of refusing to acknowledge the strength of participation in the holiday phenomenon, or rather of the desire to participate in it. The intriguing and far-reaching discrepancy between general statements about holidaymaking and statements about holidaying in the previous year underlines the shaky basis of holidays in Irish culture, its possible lack of legitimacy. That people, even those one would least expect because of their central position in modern society (such as the middle class and urban respondents), understate their actual participation in holidaymaking suggests the weak cultural basis of modernity itself and of the modern life-style practised: they have not been able to appropriate fully, in cultural terms, their actual pattern of behaviour.

Such a gap probably results from an attempt to limit the cultural impact of holidays. Irish culture has to appropriate the practice of holidaying, however reluctantly, and endeavours to regulate and contain it. In the process, holidaying is recognised, constituted and sustained as a social phenomenon. Holiday norms, through which this appropriation is accomplished, create a space outside the control of everyday norms: they are enabling as well as restraining. Holidays occupy in Ireland an ambiguous cultural space.

The Holiday Orientation

Let us imagine that a society as a whole generates a basic drive which promotes and sustains holidaying as a form of social behaviour. Such a tendency, or thrust, manifests itself in the extent to which people practise holidays, organise them according to particular principles, collectively develop a range of ideas and rules about the holiday experience. We will call this the 'holiday orientation'. It constitutes a characteristic of the collectivity as a whole, a social phenomenon. It corresponds to the propensity, or rather the inclination, of the group to set aside time to leave home and visit other places.

Most of the information gathered in our survey is best interpreted as the many manifestations of a holiday orientation. The first result concerns the frequency of holidaying, and it was found that 80 per cent of the respondents took a holiday the previous year. Furthermore, the great majority of the respondents expressed the view that they would feel bad about not being able to go on holiday in a particular year. One can then conclude that there exists a strong commitment, in Ireland, to the idea and practice of holiday. But the latter is not simply characterised by a desire to visit other places for a few days or a few weeks. Holidays provide a break from the routine of daily life, a liberation from the constraints which shape our everyday life. Furthermore, they represent a time for taking care of one's self, for gratifying it. On all these counts, our respondents scored quite highly, indicating once more the strength of the holiday orientation.

Such an orientation does not manifest itself uniformly; cultures and societies differ in this respect. Some groups display a strong holiday orientation, while others manifest only a weak one. We have seen how the holiday phenomenon in Ireland is patterned according to particular factors. The results of our survey, as well as the analysis of the *Household Budget Survey* (1981),[11] shows that urban households take, on average, a greater number of holidays than rural households, and their holidays last longer. All these results correspond to the findings in other countries about the young, urban and affluent character of holidaymakers. They also spend more money on holidays, in both absolute and relative terms. But very little difference was observed in terms of the behaviour during holidays, although urban residents outside Dublin disclosed what one may call a 'touristic good will': that is to say a willingness to participate fully in the holiday phenomenon, to embrace those types of behaviour which mark out the holidaying experience. They displayed a greater and a more conspicuous eagerness to organise their holidaytime according to holiday principles.

As we have already seen, age constitutes a significant factor. Young (and unmarried) people are not only more positively orientated to the holiday phenomenon, and go on holiday more frequently, but their way of being on holiday differs drastically from other respondents. The results also show the relevance of the social class factor. Middle-class households enjoy holidays more frequently and spend more money on them. The *Household Budget Survey* reveals, however, that the higher-working-class exhibit quite a strong holiday orientation (measured in terms of frequency, length and spending), only slightly below the lower-middle-class respondents. The categories of non-manual workers, semi-skilled and un-skilled workers and farmers trail far behind.

An Explanation

But what is the source of the holiday orientation we have postulated? Fur-thermore, how can one explain the differences which exist in the strength of this phenomenon from one society to the other, from one group to the other?

The fact that the frequency of going on holidays is related to the degree of urban concentration is conventionally explained by the nature of the pressures that urban residents face in their daily lives. The pressure of the urban environment creates a need for escape. The desire to go on holiday derives from the difficulties that people encounter in work and city life.[12] It has also been observed that people residing in a collective habitat (e.g. flats) take more holidays than people living in individual habitats.[13] One wonders, however, if other types of pressure are not at work in the rural setting, such as the lack of diversity and opportunities for a wide range of leisure pursuits. Why should rural people feel less of a need for a change of horizon in their world which is in a sense more bound? In any case, the degree of participation in the holidaying phenomenon is directly deter-mined by the extent to which one wants to escape from the pressures of daily life. This interpretation in terms of escape hardly fits the findings of our survey. The frequency of holidaying is not related to attitudes towards work or the living environment. It bears no relation to the level of satis-faction with one's work or even with satisfaction with the area in which one lives. In a similar way, the extent to which one enjoys one's work, ex-periences pressures at work, assumes responsibilities, and finds work re-warding, has no bearing on the frequency of holidays.

A more realistic explanation of the variations in the level of partici-pation in holidaying is given by the structure of opportunities. The fact that urban residents go on holiday far more than rural residents is deter-mined by the greater facilities for holidaying enjoyed by urban residents. The work requirement in farming peaks during the summer, which also corresponds to the holiday season, and this militates against the taking of holidays by rural residents. Although relevant, this argument does not fully explain the dramatic gap which exists between urban and rural residents in terms of holiday practice. The constraining work requirements of agriculture only concern farmers, who nowadays constitute a minority group in the rural setting. Many rural residents, as wage and salary earners, enjoy as much time off for holidays and paid leave as do their urban counterparts. The frequency of holidaymaking is also said to be related to the number of weeks off one enjoys during the year, and chiefly whether holidays are paid or not. One would then expect the self-employed to take fewer holidays. Self-employed respondents did state a lower frequency of holidaymaking, although no significant difference emerged about the frequency of holidays in the previous year according to employment status. The structure of opportunities does not contribute, then, to the explanation of this pattern observed or, at least, our survey was not able to register such a relation unambiguously. However, on the basis of the Household Budget Survey, the self-employed are less likely to take holidays than employed individuals, and this may uphold the partial relevance of this factor of opportunity.

Opportunities also refer to the resources available for holidaying. Money constitutes a real constraint on holidaying, and the lower holidaying frequency of unskilled manual worker families, for instance, is clearly associated with their low income. Nevertheless, in general terms, participation in the practice of holidaying is poorly related, in statistical terms, to income or wealth: some low-income categories participate in it, while some high-income categories do not. Furthermore, social classes cannot be reduced to income categories, and class membership may have an effect on holidaying which remains independent of income considerations. Conspicuous consumption and industrial exemption formed, according to Theodor Veblen, the two major characteristics of the 'leisure class' and the basis of its claim for superior status and privilege.[14] This idea is easily applied to holidays, which are also based on an exemption from work and on conspicuous waste. Holidays would then function as markers of status, not only by their frequency but also by their length, destination and type.

A more sophisticated explanation is given by Dean McCannell when he writes that the growth of tourism represents an index of modernisation.[15] He emphasises how complex and differentiated modern society is, and how this fragmentation allows for the presence of alternative realities. The discontinuity of modernity produces a problem of meaning, that of bringing together its fragments into a unified experience, of reconstructing a cultural heritage or a social identity out of all the bits and pieces of modern culture. Tourism provides an answer to this problem of authenticity. Modernity, by offering the opportunity of choice, allows individuals a great deal of leeway in reconstructing their reality, in the way they choose and organise their experiences. Holidays constitute an essential moment in this reconstruction.

The idea that the frequency of holidaymaking is related to participation in modernity is tested only with difficulty. However, the difference between rural and urban residents, in relation to holidaymaking, manifests their unequal participation in modernity. This does not mean that rural residents are less influenced by the mass media which, through advertisements and programmes about faraway places, may well incite them to travel. The argument runs deeper. Rural people participate in a more traditional culture and they do not experience any fragmentation of their social world. At once more secure in it and more bound by it, they do not necessarily require the kind of experience of which McCannell is talking. They do not experience their tradition as tradition, that is to say as a choice between alternative ways of living. Holidays come with modernity, as representing the opposite of the traditional attitude which takes its own habitual world for granted and has little interest in, or is suspicious of, other places. The strength of the holiday orientation is then related to participation in, or exposure to, modernity. The higher participation of young people also manifests their greater participation in modernity, as does the class factor. The social classes which participate most in the 'holidaying' culture are those found at the centre of modern industrial society: non-propertied middle class and skilled working class. Even the discrepancy which exists between the practice of holidaying and the cultural orientations towards this phenomenon is explained in this light. The strong anti-modernist leaning which pervades Irish culture makes it difficult to acknowledge a practice deeply rooted in the modernity of Ireland. Holidays, in that sense, reveal one of the major tensions within Irish society.

ANNEXE: THE METHODOLOGY OF THE SURVEY

The present article is based on the responses to a standardised survey questionnaire, which covers general attitudes towards holidays and the actual (or rather the perceived) practice of the respondents while on holiday. The constitution of the sample relied on a mixed strategy. Different districts were selected in an effort to balance the rural–urban location of respondents, and to control the social class factor, mainly in Dublin. For instance, the Dublin sample included areas such as Palmerstown, Chapelizod, Castleknock and Finglas, to get a mix of old and new Dublin, of working-class and middle-class Dublin. For urban respondents outside Dublin several towns were chosen, mainly according to convenience. The respondents were selected randomly within each chosen electoral district, from the local electors' register. The same comment applies to the rural sample, diversely located in Counties Kilkenny, Louth, Mayo and Meath.

The mixed mode of sampling produced a kind of stratified sample, with a roughly equal number of Dublin residents, residents in towns outside Dublin (all medium-sized, midland towns) and rural residents. We were less successful in stratifying the social class composition of the sample, with 35 per cent middle class, 15 per cent for farmers and 55 per cent working class. Purely by chance, our four age groups in the sample are about equal. But clearly the sample cannot claim to be representative of the whole population.

Interviewing, which took place in the summer of 1986, was conducted by a group of honours sociology students from St Patrick's College, Maynooth. The interviewers reported a generally friendly attitude. The results are based on 292 questionnaires which were actually filled, while 72 respondents refused to answer or could not be located. This gives a response rate of 75.35 per cent. Some interviewers reported a certain amount of puzzlement among older respondents at being asked questions about holidays, a type of activity which was not considered particularly relevant to their way of life. A similar reluctance to answer a questionnaire on holidaying may also have come from people who did not perceive it as a serious topic for investigation. This could account for the slightly higher than expected rate of refusal.

NOTES AND REFERENCES

1 Lanquar, R. (1985), *Sociologie du tourisme et des voyages*, Presses Universitaires de France, Paris.
2 Clarke, J. and Critcher, C. (1985), *The Devil Makes Work; Leisure in Capitalist Britain*, Macmillan, London, p. 171.
3 'Notre contemporain, interrogé sur ses dépenses de vacances, est gêné de répondre: il ne sait pas, ne veut pas savoir, n'a pas compté; sinon, ce ne serait plus des vacances.' Boyer, M. (1982), *Le Tourisme,* Editions du Seuil, Paris, p. 220.
4 Weitman, S.R. (1970), 'Intimacies', *European Journal of Sociology*, 2:348-67, p. 352.
5 Bandyopadhyay, P. (1973), 'The Holiday Camp', in M. Smith et al. (eds.), *Leisure and Society in Britain*, Allen Lane, London.
6 Laurent, A. (1973), *Libérer les vacances,* Editions du Seuil, Paris.
7 Clarke and Critcher (1985), op. cit., p. 172.
8 'Le voyage est prolongé dans la photographie qui est prise, la carte postale qui est envoyée, le souvenir qui est acheté'. Boyer, M. (1982), op. cit.
9 S. Weitman, op. cit.
10 Bourdieu, P. (1965), *L'art moyen*, Editions de Minuit, Paris.
11 Central Statistics Office (1983), *Household Budget Survey*, 1981, vols. 1-4, Dublin, Stationery Office.
12 Laurent, op. cit.
13 Boyer, op. cit.
14 Veblen, T. (1970), *The Theory of the Leisure Class*, George Allen and Unwin, London.
15 McCannell, D. (1976), *The Tourist, a New Theory of the Leisure Class*, Schocken Books, New York, p. 182.

Index

accommodation, 76, 116, 142, 240-1, 246, 250
in Bray, 42
in Northern Ireland, 145, 151-3
see also bathing lodges, bed and breakfast guest-houses, camping, caravan sites, holiday camps, holiday homes, hotels
Achill, 88-9, 108
advertising and marketing, 53, 56, 163, 219, 233, 241, 250-1, 269
guidebooks and publications, 20, 163, 201, 241, 250-1; in Northern Ireland, 154-5, 157
imagery, 68-89, 222, 235, 258
in Northern Ireland, 148-9, 154-8
Aer Lingus, 142, 150, 219
agriculture, 105, 242, 245, 268
agri-tourism, 83, 241
air travel, 51, 128, 139, 142, 144-5
Anglo-Irish
agreement, 144, 146, 151
holidaymakers, 13, 17, 21, 22
Ireland, 59-60, 91
literature, 75, 90, 95
Annals of Tourism Research, 2
An Taisce, 203, 212, 216, 221
An Tóstal, 69, 81
Aran, 90, 105-8, 236
Arts Council, 204-5

Bangor, 15
bank holidays, 35
bathing
sea, 14-15, 18, 23-4, 30-8, 45
spa, 13-14, 18, 30
see also Purtill's seaweed baths, turkish baths
bathing lodges, nineteenth-century, 16, 19, 24, 30, 32
beaches, 45, 260
bed and breakfast guest-houses, 69, 240, 242, 244, 246-52
Belfast, 148, 156-7

Bettystown, 45
Blaskets, The, 89
Boland, Rosita, 55
Böll, Heinrich, 53, 57, 61
Bord Fáilte, 24, 72, 74-5, 78, 81, 148, 150, 154, 163, 169, 171-2, 218, 220, 222, 239-40, 249-51
Bray, 15, 29-48
services in, 39-41
Brennan, John, 33, 36
Breslin, Edward, 33, 36
British Travel Association, 148
Brontë, Charlotte, 17
Burren, Co. Clare, 132, 135

camping, 25
see also accommodation
caravan sites
in France, 25
at Kilkee, 24
see also accommodation
Carrick-on-Suir, Co. Tipperary, 54
Catholicism, 107
Catholics, rise to social dominance, 22-3
Celtic
as feminine, 87, 99, 106-8
character, 97-8
mythology, 54
ruins, 60, 156
CERT, 169-179
Chernobyl, 151
churches, 17, 24, 156
Clare Champion, 23
Clare, Co., 15, 25
West Clare, 13-28
climate, 55, 116
Bray, 45
ethno-climatology, 96-8, 103-4
Kilkee, 25
colonialism, 60-2, 71, 73-4, 77, 86-9, 91-102, 107-9
Congested Districts Board, 88
Connemara, 63, 90, 233-8, 240-3, 257

Conte, Giuseppe, 53-4, 57, 60, 64
continental holidays, 25, 266
Conyngham, Marquis of, 19-20
Cork city, 59, 215
Costello, John A., 63
croquet, 16, 39, 42
cultural and national identity, 68-85,
    86-112, 233-57, 258-71
    see also Celtic, cultural identity,
    feminisation, landscape, semiotics

Dargan, William, 29-30, 33, 36, 41, 45
Department of Economic Development,
    147, 152-3
discourse theory and travel literature,
    59
docks, 215
    Custom House Docks, 215, 217
domestic tourism, 121-14, 250, 258-71
    see also revenue
Donegal Bay, 75
donkey riding, 16
Douagh, *see* Kilkee
Dublin, 20-1, 30-3, 39, 43, 45, 54, 60,
    203-30, 270
    arts in, 204-5, 216
    housing schemes, 209-11
    see also railways, traffic congestion
Dublin Arts Report, The, 204-5

economy, Irish, 115, 118, 128
education, in Ireland, 243-4, 248
    foreign language policy, 162-180
    history, 186-7; in Britain and
    Northern Ireland, 186
    see also training
eighteenth-century estate towns, 29
eighteenth-century tourism, 13
emigration, 22, 63, 71, 73-4, 96-7, 101,
    189, 245
    migration, 241
    returned emigrants, 75, 79-81, 226
employment, 115-18, 122, 124-6, 128,
    130-2, 135, 143, 169, 173, 175, 183,
    218, 234, 240-2, 245-9, 269
    indirect, 116-17
    induced, 117
    in hotels, 170, 246-7, 251

in Northern Ireland, 152
Ennis Chronicle, 15
Enniskerry, Co. Wicklow, 31
environmental concern, 25, 116, 121,
    128, 132-5, 164, 213
    in Northern Ireland, 153
European Community,
    CAP, 83, 116, 216
    FORUM, 238, 240-1
    HOTREC, 170
    LEADER, 239
    membership, 68, 115, 208
    Structural Funds, 116-18, 128, 151,
    164, 216, 218, 220; for roads, 217
evangelists, in Kilkee, 17

famine of 1845-9, 20
feminisation
    of Ireland, 58
    of Irish character, 99
    of West of Ireland, 87, 99, 106-7
ferries, 72, 148-9
festivals, 69
Figgis, Darrell: *Children of Earth,*
    90-109
fishing, 38, 149, 237, 241, 250
food quality, 82, 142, 250
foreign exchange, 132
    fluctuation of dollar, 121
Fussell, Paul, 51-2, 55, 61, 65

Gaelic, as masculine, 87, 99, 108
Gaeltacht regions, 9, 88, 108
Galway city, 54, 57, 63-4, 215
    county, 236
Gauthier, Louis, 53, 55, 57-8, 60, 64
gender issues, 58-9, 62-3, 90-1, 95, 97-8,
    100, 104-5, 108, 262-3
    in foreign language study, 165
    in tourism development, 234-5, 238,
    240-1, 244-5, 248-9, 255
    see also Celtic, Gaelic, feminisation
Georgian Society, 212
Georgian Society Records, 212
golf links
    Bray, 42, 55
    Kilkee, 20-1
    Killarney, 81-2

Portmarnock, 63
grand tour, 13
Graves, Charles, 53-4, 56, 58, 60-1, 63
'green' image, 74-5, 164
    of Northern Ireland, 153
    see also environmental concern, pollution
Gregory, Lady: *Visions and Beliefs in the West of Ireland,* 105, 205
Greystones, 45
Guillebaud, Jean-Claude, 53
Guinness, 78

Herbert, Dorothea, 14
heritage
    architectural, 204, 220
    Big House of nineteenth century, 59, 76
    cultural, 25, 184, 218
    heritage industry, 183-230, 250
    'listing' of buildings, 220-2
    monuments, museums, etc., 76, 132, 164, 187, 220, 234, 250, 261; in Northern Ireland, 152, 156
    urban, 203-30
    see also Anglo-Irish, churches
historical emergence of tourism, 13-48
hitch-hiking, 53, 250
Hogan, Mr., 18-19
Hogg, Garry, 53-4, 56, 60-1, 63
holiday camps, 260
holiday homes, 25, 45
hospitality, 71, 74, 78-9, 82-3, 134, 164, 171, 249-50
    in Finland, 116
    in Northern Ireland, 145
hotels, 23, 42, 76
    Atlantic Hotel, Kilkee, 23
    Hunter's Hotel, Rathnew, 32
    International Hotel, Bray, 36, 43
    Lacy's Bray Head Hotel, 36
    Marine Station Hotel, Bray, 36, 40, 43
    Moore's Hotel, Kilkee, 23
    Royal Hotel, Bray, 31-3, 36-8
    see also employment, European Community
Household Budget Survey, 267-71

Industrial Exhibition of 1853, 33
industrialistion, 87, 96, 115, 207-8, 244
    of England, 91, 99, 102
industrial revolution in Britain, 13
International Exhibition, London, 36
International Fund for Ireland, 151
International Union for the Conservation of Nature, 132
investment, 69, 115, 164, 183, 216-17, 219-20
    commercial loans, 130
    government, 128-31, 164
    Irish Business Expansion Scheme, 130
    in Kilkee, 18-9
    in Northern Ireland, 145, 150-2
    see also European Community
Irish-English, 56-61
Irish language, 96, 108
Irish Review, The, 96
Irish Tourist, The, 69
islands, 88, 90-2
    in literature, 95-109

James, Henry, 56
Japan, tourists from, 178
Joyce, James, 54, 59

Kerry, North, 15
Kilkee, Co. Clare, 13-28
Killala, Co. Mayo, 55
Killarney, 20, 135
Kingstown, Dún Laoghaire, 35, 46

Land Commission, 59
landscape, 74-5, 132-3, 164, 219
    literary response to, 55-6, 61, 90-1
    Northern Ireland, 155-8
    West of Ireland, 86-112, 233, 235, 237, 250
Lawless, Emily: *Grania-The Story of an Island,* 90-109
Laytown, 45
leisure-recreation, activities, 23, 25, 32, 36-9, 42-3, 116, 164, 218, 240, 244, 249-51
    activity holidays, 82
    in Northern Ireland, 149, 151-2, 155-6
    piers, 42

wet weather facilities, 25, 249, 251; in Northern Ireland, 153
see also croquet, fishing, golf, music, sailing, theme parks
Limerick, 14-5, 17, 19, 20, 24-5, 56, 215
Limerick Chronicle, 16
Limerick Leader, 22
Lingua, 178
'listing' of buildings, *see* heritage
literary tradition, 69, 87, 211, 215, 219, 225-6, 236
　islands in literature, 88-109
　national identity in literature, 90-109
　post-colonial, 89
lower-income holidaymakers, 13-14, 21, 23-4, 35, 265-6, 268-71
Lucan, 14

McDonald, Frank, 204
MacDonnell, Major, 19
Malahide, 14
Mallow, 14
Malone, Father Sylvester, 16
mariculture, 132
marinas, 153
mass tourism, 6, 10, 13, 121, 134-5, 154, 234, 252
Meath, Lord, 38, 41
media
　and Dublin, 204, 206
　and Northern Ireland troubles, 144, 147-50, 155, 157-8
　travel programmes, 269
Michelin Guide, 1992, 156
Mills, Sara, 53, 58-9, 62
morality and holidaymaking, 18, 23-4, 259-61
Morony, Henry, 15
Murphy, Dervla, 56-7, 60-3
music
　cultural heritage, 97, 226
　leisure activity, 72, 250-1

Napoleonic Wars, effect on tourism, 15
National Development Plan, 118
national identity, *see* cultural and national identity

Newby, Eric and Wanda, 52, 54-8, 60-1, 63
NITB, *see* Northern Ireland Tourist Board
Northern Ireland, 22, 52, 57, 60, 62-4, 138-61
　the Troubles, effect on tourism, 60, 121, 138-61
　see also accommodation, advertising and marketing, education, employment, environmental concern, 'green' image, heritage, hospitality, investment, landscape, leisure-recreation, media, railways, restaurants, revenue, scenic tourism, signposting, statistics, theme parks, training, transport, youth market
Northern Ireland Folk Park, 190, 199
Northern Ireland Tourist Board, 138-61

O'Brien, William Smith, 17
Offaly, 15
Office of Public Works, 81, 239
OPW, *see* Office of Public Works
ozone depletion, 25

package holidays, 14, 24-5
plantation towns, 29
pollution, 32, 54, 74, 129, 132-4, 148, 241
population census 1986, 242-3
Portmarnock, 45
Portrush, 22
postcards, 56, 72, 262-3
　see also semiotics
post-modern tourism, 9-10, 56, 82
Poulnaclough Bay, Co. Clare, 55
poverty, 88, 209, 210, 212-3, 223, 234-5, 238-57, 264
Powerscourt
　House, 30
　Waterfall, 29-30
Programme for National Recovery, 118, 123
Purtill's seaweed baths, 22

quays, in Dublin, 215, 223, 225-6
Quin, Co. Clare, 54
Quin, John junior, 33, 36

railways, 15, 19, 20-22, 29, 32-9, 43, 45
  Bray-Enniskerry light railway, 42
  Chester and Holyhead Railway, 35
  in Connemara, 20
  Dublin to Belfast, 147
  Dublin and Kingstown, 20, 35
  Dublin and Wicklow, 33, 36
  in Second World War, 24
  South Clare, 20
  West Clare, 20
Regional Tourist Offices, 154
resorts
  in England and Wales, 35
  Irish Sea resorts, 45
  Victorian seaside resorts, 13-48
  see also Kilkee, Bray
restaurants, 170, 216, 240, 251
  in Northern Ireland, 148, 154
revenue, from tourism, 116-28, 131, 135,
    233-5, 240-51
  business visitors, 120
  domestic tourism, 121-4
  European visitors, 120
  indirect spending, 122
  induced spending, 122
  in Northern Ireland, 143, 145-7, 150,
    154
roads
  in Bray, 38, 41
  in Dublin, 212-3
  Dublin-Belfast road, 147
  potholes, 251
Rosscarbery Bay, 60
Rough Guide to Ireland, 157
rural Ireland, 72, 81, 83, 102, 205-6,
    233-5, 238, 240-57
  see also European Community, CAP
rural tourism, 233-57

sailing, 53
Salthill, 15
Scalp, The, Co. Wicklow, 30-1
scenic tourism, 14, 30, 32, 39, 53, 55, 69,
    74, 82, 133
  in Northern Ireland, 155
  see also landscape
semiotics of tourism, 58-9, 88-90,
    96-109, 254, 258-67

sewerage, 134, 241
Shannon Airport, 24, 142
Shannon Development, 24, 208
Shannon River, 15
signposting, 59
  in Northern Ireland, 148, 153, 251
Skerries, 14
Somerville-Large, Peter, 52, 54, 55, 57,
    59, 60
souvenirs, 262-3
  see also semiotics
statistics for tourism
  international, 1
  in Ireland, 118-28, 131, 134, 168-9,
    234; overseas visitors, 118-20, 162;
    European visitors, 118-21, 162-3,
    169, 171
  in Northern Ireland, 139-44, 148-9,
    154
stone monuments, 55
  see also heritage
storyline themes, 219-20
sun holidays, 25, 134, 164
  see also ozone depletion
sustainable tourism, 83, 132, 233-4
Sutherland, Halliday, 51, 53, 59
Synge, J.M., 236-7
  Aran Islands, 90, 105-6, 108

Tansey Webster report, 118, 123-5
Tax incentives, 215-17, 223
tax recycling, 124-5
Teagasc, 239-40
Temple Bar, 216-7, 222-4
Tennyson, Alfred Lord, 17
Thackeray, W.M., 16, 52
theme parks, 10, 183-7, 189-202, 219,
    222
  see also Northern Ireland Folk Park,
    Ulster-American Folk Park
Third World nation, Ireland as a, 10,
    77
Third World tourism, 71, 77-8
Tidy Towns competition, 69, 81, 241
Tipperary, 15, 56-7
Tóibín, Colm, 52-3, 62
tourism policy, 115-180
  in Cyprus, 134

Irish government policy, 8, 117, 124; *see also* Programme for National Recovery
in The Netherlands, 131
traffic congestion, 132, 134-5
in Dublin, 212-13
training, for tourism, 164, 168-72, 174-5, 240, 244, 248
in languages, 168-78
in Northern Ireland, 154, 156
Tramore, 14-15
transport links, 90, 243, 245
bus, 22-4
in Northern Ireland, 151-2
public transport, 217, 243, 248
steamer boat to Kilrush, 15, 20
see also Aer Lingus, ferries, railways, roads, Shannon Airport, traffic congestion
travel agents, 148-50, 250
'Travellers', 52
travel literature, 51-67, 86-90, 92-3, 99-100, 237-8
Troubles, The, *see* Northern Ireland
turf cutting, 72-3
turkish baths, 36, 39, 41

UN Conference on International Travel and Tourism, 77

Ulster-American Folk Park, 184-5, 189-99
unemployment, 115-16, 183, 205, 207, 234, 239, 242-5, 248
Urry, John: *The Tourist Gaze,* 2, 53, 82

Vartry reservoir, 39
visual representations of Ireland
art, 90, 92, 108, 156
film, 69-70, 93, 266
photography, 53, 92; as holiday activity, 262-3; in Northern Ireland, 155-6, 204, 211
see also advertising and marketing, theme parks

Waterford city, 215
Waugh, Evelyn, 55, 59
West of Ireland, 5, 74, 86-112, 233-57
see also landscape
Wexford, 31, 45, 61
working-class holidaymakers, *see* lower-income
world recession, 144-5

Youghal, 15
youth market, in Northern Ireland, 153